Chicano Speech in the Bilingual Classroom

American University Studies

Series VI
Foreign Language Instruction

Vol. 6

PETER LANG
New York · Bern · Frankfurt am Main · Paris

Chicano Speech in the Bilingual Classroom

edited by
Dennis J. Bixler-Márquez
and
Jacob Ornstein-Galicia

with a preface by
Robert L. Politzer

PETER LANG
New York · Bern · Frankfurt am Main · Paris

Library of Congress Cataloging-in-Publication Data

Bixler-Márquez, Dennis J.,
   Chicano speech in the bilingual classroom/Dennis J. Bixler-
Márquez and Jacob Ornstein-Galicia.

   p. cm.—(American university studies. Series VI, Foreign
language instruction ; vol. 6)
   Bibliography: p.
   1. Mexican American children—Language. 2. Mexican Americans—
Education—Language arts. 3. English language—Spoken English—
United States. 4. Spanish language—Spoken Spanish—United States.
5. Education, Bilingual—United States. 6. Bilingualism—United
States. I. Ornstein-Galicia, Jacob II. Title.
III. Series: American university studies. Series VI, Foreign
language instruction ; v. 6.
PE3102.M4B58   1988
420′.4261′0973—dc19
ISBN 0-8204-0475-6   87-21473
ISSN 0739-6406   CIP

CIP-Titelaufnahme der Deutschen Bibliothek

Chicano speech in the bilingual classroom / ed.
by Dennis J. Bixler-Márquez and Jacob Ornstein-
Galicia. With a pref. by Robert L. Politzer. –
New York; Bern; Frankfurt am Main; Paris:
Lang, 1988.
   (American University Studies: Ser. 6, Foreign
   Language Instruction; Vol. 6)
   ISBN 0-8204-0475-6

NE: Bixler-Márquez, Dennis J. [Hrsg.] ; American
University Studies / 06

© Peter Lang Publishing, Inc., New York 1988

Printed by Weihert-Druck GmbH, Darmstadt, West Germany

Acknowledgments

The editors gratefully acknowledge the financial assistance provided by the Chicano Studies Center, the Center for Inter-American and Border Studies, the College of Education, the College of Liberal Arts, and The Graduate College at the University of Texas at El Paso.

The excellent editing by Rosalind Federman and Ann Holder is very much appreciated, as is the clerical support lent by the staff of the Department of Teacher Education at the University of Texas at El Paso.

The editors also express their appreciation to Longman Publications, Inc. of London, the Center for Applied Linguistics, and the Chicano Studies Research Center at the University of California at Los Angeles, publisher of AZTLAN, for granting permission to reprint their publications.

Contributors

Adalberto Aguirre, Jr.
Department of Sociology
University of California at Riverside

Kathleen M. Bailey
TESOL Department
Monterey Institute of International
Studies

Marie E. Barker
Department of Teacher Education
University of Texas at El Paso

Dennis J. Bixler-Márquez
Department of Teacher Education and
Chicano Studies Research Center
University of Texas at El Paso

Donna Christian
Center for Applied Linguistics

John Edwards
Department of Psychology
St. Francis Xavier University

José Galván
Office of the Vice Chancellor
University of California at Los
Angeles

Willard Gingerich
Department of English
University of Texas at El Paso

Gustavo González
Bilingual Education Center
Texas A & I University

Rodolfo Jacobson
Division of Bicultural-Bilingual Studies
University of Texas at San Antonio

Mary McGroarty
Department of TESL/Applied Linguistics
University of California at Los Angeles

Robert Milk
Division of Bicultural-Bilingual Studies
University of Texas at San Antonio

John Oller
Department of Linguistics
University of New Mexico

Maureen A. Potts
Department of English
University of Texas at El Paso

Rosaura Sánchez
Department of Literature
University of California at San Diego

Walt Wolfram
Department of Linguistics
University of the District of Columbia
and the Center for Applied Linguistics

Preface

The table of contents as well as the editors' introduction make it clear that the subject matter covered by this anthology involves essentially three topics: 1. the nature of concepts like "standard" or "dialect"; 2. the specific features of the nonstandard English and nonstandard Spanish spoken in the United States; 3. the educational problems and possible educational interventions in pedagogical situations involving speakers of nonstandard English/Spanish varieties.

The editors are to be congratulated for having chosen a series of articles which give excellent coverage to the problems of bilingual/bidialectal education and which present solutions in a nonprejudiced, positive manner. When suggesting possible solutions to such problems as teaching Standard English or Standard Spanish for either oral communication or literacy or guarding against test bias created by language variation, the authors of the various articles do identify their own preferences and points of view. Their own point of view is always clearly identified as such and alternatives are never omitted without thoughtful and fair discussion.

The reader of this anthology will be left with several general messages about which there is almost a consensus among the contributors to this work. Some - not necessarily all - of these messages are:

1. No language variety - standard or dialect -- is inherently superior to any other (i.e. more "logical", more esthetic, etc.).

2. The status assigned to any language variety is largely determined by the social role and status of its speakers.

3. The pedagogical problems related to language variation cannot be separated from those created by differences in social class and culture.

4. All those involved in pedagogical intervention concerning bilingual and/or nonstandard speakers must be informed of the essential facts concerning the nature of nonstandard dialect.

5. Negative attitudes toward nonstandard dialects (and their speakers) must never spill over into the classroom or into any feature (e.g. the curriculum materials) of the educational program.

6. The goal of any educational intervention concerning nonstandard speakers should be adding the standard to the students repertoire and not the extinction of the nonstandard.

I hope that the messages contained in this book will find a large audience and that this book will be read by educators, especially teachers or prospective teachers of Spanish/English bilinguals in the United States.

Robert L. Politzer
Stanford University

CONTENTS

Introduction

Educators have contended with the dilemma of what role to assign nonstandard varieties of Spanish and English since the inception of bilingual education in the Southwest. Before bilingual education teachers of Spanish and English generally did not permit the use of Chicano Spanish or English in their classes. Texts, materials, and ability grouping practices did not account for dialects or differences between native and non-native speakers of Spanish or English. The first curricular responses were apparently designed to "correct" systematically the nonstandard varieties of these languages. While there was some pedagogical recognition of Chicano Spanish and English in the sixties and early seventies, the primary goal of the educational system remained unchanged: to eradicate these varieties, rather than accept and use them for instructional purpose.

The advent of the civil rights movement brought about a resurgence of ethnolinguistic pride, as well as Hispanic dissatisfaction with their education. Hispanics clamored for a more substantial and meaningful role for Spanish, in the form of bilingual education in schools. They also argued that dialectal forms should be respected and even incorporated into the curriculum. However, the notion of accepting and employing Chicano Spanish or English in education was not particularly well received in some educational circles.

Fortunately, since the mid-seventies wider recognition and better understanding of the educational potential of Chicano Spanish and English is increasingly reflected in public schools' teacher guides and supplementary materials. In higher education, second language education and teacher training programs also reflect this trend, particularly in bilingual education.

It should be noted that a strong sentiment in some quarters still militates against the use of dialects in schools. Proposed legislation opposing such use in some states, such as California, clearly indicates the persistence of a bias against nonstandard speech. Furthermore, mass media portrayals of ethnic minorities, their culture, and language as threats to the nation has had a negative impact on bilingual education and, by extension, on dialects. Legislation partially offseting this trend has appeared in some states, notably Michigan, which requires teachers to be familiar with, though not teach, black English. Therefore, in spite of some enlightened efforts on behalf of dialect speakers, nonstandard varieties of Spanish and English continue to face opposition in educational settings.

Educators, however, cannot ignore the linguistic and cultural reality of their schools. Students who speak nonstandard varieties of Spanish or English continue to enroll in American schools in record numbers, making them a significant educational challenge in the Southwest and other parts of the nation. A pragmatic approach to the education of ethnolinguistic groups in the United States calls for greater recognition, understanding, and acceptance of speech diversity on the part of educators.

This collection of articles constitutes an attempt to convey information to teachers and teacher trainers about Chicano Spanish and English in bilingual education. The editors promote a pluralistic posture, one that is also pragmatic. As several contributing authors point out, educators cannot ignore their linguistic and cultural environment, as well as the communication requirements of our society. Bilingual education must produce students capable of effective communication in Spanish and English in a variety of societal domains. The nonstandard speech of students can serve as a foundation

2

on which to build the communicative competence in the standard speech required to become economically mainstreamed in this country. This volume exhorts educators to explore avenues for language development that respect the linguistic and cultural background of all students.

Three major sections comprise this book. The first addresses the nature of dialects in society and particularly in education. The second covers the characteristics of Chicano Spanish and English, as well as linguistic phenomena associated with them. The concluding section concentrates on educational issues and practices, including the topic of language assessment and testing, a key component of bilingual education. A bibliography of suggested readings can be found at the end of the book.

In the first section the research examines in depth social attitudes and perceptions in the United States about Spanish and English dialects. In the comprehensive article by Walt Wolfram and Donna Christian, the authors present Chicano Spanish and English in a broad context of linguistic variation, the nature of an accent, and the regional distribution of the two dialects in the United States.

José Galván and Kathleen M. Bailey analyze attitudes about the intellectual ability and academic potential of speakers of different speech varieties. This work should enable teachers to ascertain the importance of communication across sociocultural levels and settings and to appreciate the impact these attitudes have on the education of language minority children. It also addresses the important topic of teacher attitudinal behavior modification and includes specific recommendations for the preparatory and inservice education of teachers.

John Edwards discusses the controversies that surround any effort to assign an educational role to a nonstandard dialect. In his international approach, Edwards examines the problems of educational treatments in three language situations: a) nonstandard dialects of a foreign language; b) nonstandard dialects within the same language; and c) nonstandard dialects in bilingual education. He recommends that for the future educators examine objectively bilingual education in its full context in order to clarify the role of the nonstandard dialect.

The second section presents information about the features of Chicano Spanish and English that create the essential basis for understanding the dynamics of the two dialects in a socioeducational context. Code switching, or the presence of both Spanish and English in a dialogue, is one such practice discussed as an important dimension of language learning. Authors also note the theoretical and practical educational implications of their research.

Rosaura Sánchez leads section two with a full description of Chicano Spanish. She analyzes the many variations of Chicano Spanish in a sociolinguistic context, including the interesting Caló. She also adds a set of caveats and recommendations for teachers regarding the presence of Chicano Spanish in the classroom.

In his chapter on Chicano English, Gustavo González presents the differing schools of thought associated with the origin, nature, and sociolinguistic definitions of Chicano English. He then concentrates on the features of two major types of Chicano English: those directly attributable to Spanish and those not linked directly to Spanish but also not typical of "standard" English. He concludes with a list of recommendations on the subject of Chicano English for teachers.

Code switching, a linguistic phenomenon that is often misunderstood and consequently perceived negatively as a "mixture" between Spanish and English, is analyzed in depth by Adalberto Aguirre, Jr. He initially describes the factors associated with code switching, which he follows with an exploration of what it means, why it happens, and how can teachers capitalize on the communicative competence of bilinguals. Teachers can accomplish this last goal by analyzing pros and cons of the controversial use of code switching in the classroom. Lastly, Aguirre recommends a meta-theoretical approach to the examination of code switching, one that may enable bilingual teachers to begin to make communication and instructional interventions, based on their intuitive knowledge of code switching, in the classroom.

Section three addresses some of the implications of bilingualism for cognitive development and offers some specific strategies for helping students exploit standard and nonstandard language use. From the range of methods, classroom teachers can determine the viability of the proposed strategies for their individual situations. The strategies encompass three facets of the language curriculum: reading, oral language, and writing development. In addition to providing material to assist educators in making better informed, instructional decisions, the section reviews some assessment options and the dialectal implications for the evaluation of language proficiency, dominance, and achievement.

Robert Milk in the first chapter of this section stresses that the key pedagogical concern in bilingual education should not be code selection but rather cognitive development through the linguistic medium that produces the best results. He goes on to differentiate between the major philosophical approaches behind proposed strategies for a nonstandard dialect role in education and the available models of language instruction, as well as the social significance of factors that affect them.

Marie Barker delineates the relationship between oral language development, cognitive development, and the acquisition of a second language in the context of bilingual education. She emphasizes the need to accept and respect the home dialect in the process of teaching standard Spanish and English. She presents the read-aloud technique as a tool that teachers can use with speakers of dialects in the development and enhancement of communication skills in bilingual education.

Maureen A. Potts and Willard P. Gingerich examine the acquisition of written literacy by Hispanics. They discuss specific factors that contribute to low achievement in written English and strategies to combat the resulting deficiencies. The authors indicate there is a need to convince Hispanics that dialectal speech is an acceptable form of communication for selected situations and that the acquisition of English is merely the learning of another very useful dialect.

Rodolfo Jacobson complements the work of Adalberto Aguirre, Jr. by proposing a specific classroom application for a particular feature of Chicano speech. He first reviews available language strategies for the bilingual education classroom. Then he analyzes the discourse of selected classroom interactions from schools in San Antonio, Texas. He projects intersentential code switching as a viable form of communication for classrooms with bilingual students. He emphasizes that intersentential code switching has no demonstrable negative effects on language acquisition and development in either language. Rather, it facilitates language development in two languages. Furthermore, it promotes learning generally by increasing the effectiveness of classroom communication.

Dennis J. Bixler-Márquez first reviews the assumptions about the relationship between orality and literacy. He then examines instructional approaches for initial reading in transitional bilingual education and the variety of roles the use of Chicano Spanish might play in each one. He suggests that teachers should not be overly preoccupied with the dialect of the student but with the acquisition of initial literacy and subsequent development of language skills. He further proposes an increased but judicious role for Chicano speech in reading beyond the initial literacy stage.

Mary MacGroarty explores the potential of classroom discourse analysis in reading to yield critical linguistic information that teachers may use to understand and improve instruction. Research on Spanish reading in two bilingual education classrooms, carried out under the auspices of the Stanford Program on Teaching and Linguistic Pluralism, is the source of information for the content of this chapter. The author concludes that discourse analysis techniques are valuable diagnostic skills in understanding why instructional scenarios in bilingual education settings occur or, just as important, do not occur as planned.

John Oller provides the finishing touch to this volume with his unit on multilingual assessment. He discusses the dialectal implications of language testing in light of problem areas like test bias, translation difficulties, and, of course, multilingualism versus multidialectalism. John Oller summarizes the key factors that educators should keep in mind when developing, administering, or interpreting language tests.

It is the intent of the editors to enable the reader in acquiring an understanding of the social and educational issues involved in establishing a role for any given variety of Chicano speech in the first section. Section two then presents research about Chicano Spanish and English, their distribution, characteristics, and pertinent potentials for educational applications. The reader can then proceed to analyze practical classroom issues, suggested applications, and options for Chicano speech appearing in section three. This volume presents pedagogical issues on a case specific basis in deductive order. The general issues in bilingual education appear at the outset, supporting research about those issues constitutes the second section, and practical applications and options comprise the concluding section. The order of the articles and their substance should provide easy access and valuable information to those interested in the bilingual education classroom.

Language, Society and Education

Dialects, Society, and Education
by Walt Wolfram and Donna Christian

The article is a revised version of the booklet entitled *Dialogue on Dialects*, originally published as part of a series entitled *Dialects and Educational Equity* by the Center for Applied Linguistics. Some additional questions have been addressed in this version, and references have been updated.

Dialects

The topic of dialects has received considerable attention recently in newspapers,on television, and in schools. It's not always clear, however, what is meant by "Dialects." What does the term DIALECT refer to?

The term "dialect" is actually used in several different ways. One is a technical meaning used by students of language and, within this group there is general agreement on what this term means.

In the technical meaning *dialect* refers to any given variety of a language shared by a group of speakers. These varieties usually correspond to differences of other types between the groups, such as geographical location, social class, ethnicity, or age. People who share important social and regional charactertistics will typically speak quite similarly, and those who do not will often differ in certain aspects of their language usage. The definition is not a rigorous one, but it carries an important implication. In this technical use of the term, the relative status of a dialect with respect to other dialects of the language (its "social position") is irrelevant. The term used this way is completely neutral-there is no evaluation implied, either positive or negative.

For example, a difference between English dialects has been found in the use of *anymore*. Some dialects require that *anymore* be used only in negative sentences like *Houses in this neighborhood aren't cheap anymore*. In other dialects, it can also occur in positive sentences like *Houses in this neighborhood are expensive anymore*. This difference usually corresponds to regional characteristics. Similarly, some Spanish dialects in the Southwest may use -nos for the first person plural form where other dialects use -mos under certain conditions. The important point here is that neither use is right or wrong although some dialects contain a restriction that others do not have. According to the technical meaning of dialect, one pattern is not "better" than another.

A second significant consequence of the technical meaning of dialect is that *you cannot speak a language without speaking a dialect of that language.* Everyone is part of some group which can be distinguished from other groups, and one of these groupings depends on how you talk. In other words, *if you speak the English* or *Spanish* language, *you necessarily speak some dialect of* that language.

How does the non-technical use of "dialect" differ from the technical meaning?

There are several popular ways in which the term dialect is used, each differing to some degree from the the technical meaning. One of the most common uses of the term carries a negative connotation, unlike the neutral, technical meaning "Dialect" is sometimes used to refer to a particular social or geographical variety, which is not the "standard" one. For example, a native midwesterner might say "That person speaks a dialect" after hearing the speech of a Black from the deep South or a rural Appalachian White, or, a Spanish speaker from California may say that a New Mexican speaks a Spanish dialect. This use of the term also assumes that only certain groups of people speak a dialect. These implications are unwarranted since everyone speaks some variety -or dialect- of their language, and any evaluation of relative merit is based on social, not linguistic grounds.

The label is also sometimes used as a synonym of "language." For example, you might hear someone say "There are many African dialects" or "American Indians speak a large number of different dialects." In reality, a distinction between separate languages can be made, and this use of "dialect" usually occurs only when the speaker is unfamiliar with the situation and languages being talked about. For example, someone who might make the above statements would probably not say "There are many dialects spoken in Europe," in reference to the different languages in Europe.

Students of a language often object to the popular usage of "dialect" because of this negative sense it carries and the different interpretations that are possible. Sometimes, terms like *language variety, language difference,* or *linguistic diversity* are used to convey the technical sense so that misinterpretations from the different uses of the term "dialect" can be avoided.

What about the term *ACCENT?* Is there a special meaning for that, too?

When it comes to language differences, the term *accent* is usually used to refer to how people pronounce words. So, if a person pronounces *car* without the final *r*, as in *cah,* or *sheep* the same as *cheap,* someone might refer to this as characteristic of a particular accent. The reference to accent may include differences other than pronunciation, but the focus is usually on pronunciation.

Several situations in which the term "accent" might occur can illustrate more clearly how it is used. These occurrences also give a basis for comparing what is meant by "accent" with the uses of "dialect."

(a) A Spanish waiter asks some diners what they would like to order. His question is in English, but the pronunciation sounds as if he were using Spanish rather than English sounds. The patron might remark, "That waiter has a very heavy accent."

(b) Someone who grew up in northeastern New England visits Chicago. The native Chicagoan might observe "That person has a real New England accent."

(c) Somone originally from Cuba visits Puerto Rico. The Cuban might observe "People from Puerto Rico say some words with a real strong accent."

The first situation involves someone who presumably learned English as a second language and still shows influence from the native language. This is the classic "foreign accent," etc. The other situations- (b) and (c)- contain references to differences within a language. In this respect, "accent" is closer to the term "dialect" we just discussed. Of course, it is more restricted in that "accent" refers primarily to pronunciation and there are differences other than pronunciation among dialects.

The term "accent" carries some implications like those for the popular use of dialect, but they are typically less severe. Although each variety includes its own peculiar pronunciation pattern, the assumption is often made that only "other people" have accents. Thus, the native Chicagoan meeting someone from New England may think it is only the New Englander who speaks with an accent, while a native New Englander meeting a Chicagoan may think that it is only the Chicagoan who speaks with an accent. In reality, of course, both of them "have an accent" just as everyone speaks a dialect. Although there are sometimes negative connotations associated with "having an accent" there can be postitive evaluations as well. For instance, many North Americans hold a "British accent" in high regard, and some North American Spanish speakers place a high value on Castilian Spanish pronunciation patterns.

So, differences between dialects can be found in the way things are pronounced. What other kinds of language differences are there?

Dialects or language varieties may differ from each other at several levels in addition to pronunciation. One fairly obvious difference is in vocabulary items. The use of a term *tonic* in some regions of New England to refer to what in other regions is called *pop, soda pop,* or simply *soda* is basic vocabulary variation. The retention of the term *icebox* by older generations where the younger generation may use *refrigerator* also reflects this level of difference. Similarly, some dialects of Spanish use the word *encino* to refer to an 'oak tree' whereas others use *bellotero.*

Dialects also vary from each other in the grammatical patterns of the language system-the way items combine to form sentences. For example, different ways of forming an indirect question such as *He asked could he go to the movies* versus *He asked if he could go to the movies* or different negative patterns such as, *He didn't do anything* versus *He didn't do nothing,* reflect basic grammatical alternatives. In the same way, a Spanish dialectal difference, the use of *comencé trabajar* as opposed to *comencé a trabajar,* reflects grammatical alternatives. In some dialects, both alternatives are used in others, only one is found.

The extent of variation in language is not limited to the form of particular items. It is also possible for varieties to differ in how particular forms are used in the context of speech interaction. Thus, a northerner and a southerner may both be familiar with the respect terms *sir* and *ma'am* but use them in varying situations. In Spanish, the use of the familiar form *tú* may have a much wider range of acceptability in some Chicano Spanish dialects compared to others. The different social rules governing respect familiarity may be reflected in language rules for the use of these forms. Such differences in language use, often related to social and cultural differences, are sometimes hard to pinpoint, but they can be highly sensitive areas of difference between groups.

Where do language differences come from?

Language differences ultimately reflect basic behavior differences between groups of people. There may be diverse reasons underlying differences in language, but they all lead to this basic principle. Given physical or social separation of one type or another, language differences can be expected to follow. Also, as language changes (and it is always changing), differences between groups emerge as they follow different paths.

In the United States, both physical and social facts are responsible for the variation in English and Spanish. Many of the regional differences in both languages can be traced to combinations of physical factors in the country's history and geography. Some characteristics can be explained by looking at settlement history, which reveals the patterns of the early settlers and later immigrant groups. The movement of the population, historically and currently, also has a bearing on the language of regions, since differences can be expected to coincide with the major drifts of the population. Finally, characteristics of physical geography must be considered. Natural barriers such as mountains and rivers have historically cut off people from each other, creating a natural basis for differences to emerge and be maintained.

Many social factors are also responsible for much of the diversity in ways of speaking Class and status distinctions found in our society are often reflected in language differences as well. We would certainly expect that the greater the social distance between groups, the greater the language differences. This principle doesn't always work exactly, but it is a reasonably accurate reflection of how language differences can be expected to reflect group behavior differences.

When we consider the general principle that differences between groups correlate with language differences, it seems reasonable enough to expect that a lawyer from the deep South will speak considerably differently from a northern working-class person, or a Spanish-speaking rural farmworker in Texas will speak differently from a Spanish-speaking California executive. Notice that the characterization includes historical, geographical, social, and ethnic factors, all of which have been prominent in distinguishing groups of individuals from each other in American society. The same distinctions are important in understanding language differences.

If we eliminated some of the social differences between groups of Americans, would it follow that language differences would be eliminated?

Based on the understanding of how dialects came about to begin with, we would certainly expect that language differences would be minimized if differences between groups of Americans were minimized. To a certain extent, however, this question is purely academic. Geographic dispersion is unavoidable, given a population of over 200 million. And, although we certainly strive to eliminate social inequalities, social and ethnic differences are a part of the history that makes up this country's heritage. We can safely predict that none of us will be here to witness the day when differences in American English or Spanish no longer exist.

What are the main differences between dialects of English?

Dialects vary at all the levels of language difference discussed earlier. Studies of various dialect groups indicate that regional dialects tend to be distinguished by pronunciation and vocabulary features, while social dialects show variation in these areas as well as in grammatical usage. We might guess that someone was from Massachusetts if they pronounced the word spelled *idea* with an *r* sound at the end (idear) and "dropped" the r on a word like *car* (cah). Many of these pronunciation differences concern the vowel sounds in words. For instance, southern regional dialects often vary from others in the way they pronounce words with vowel glides, like *line* or *ride*. People from these areas would most likely say something like *lahn* or *rahd*. Where people from, say northern areas would pronounce them with the glide. Other pronunciation variants involve particular words, rather than sets of words. *Route* for some people rhymes with boot; for others, with bout. These pronunciation differences are typically what is referred to as "accent," as we saw above. Regional dialects also differ in the words they use to refer to certain things. Depending on what part of the country you were in, for instance, you would need to order a *submarine*, a *hoagie*, or a *grinder* to get a particular kind of sandwich. Water might be obtained through a *faucet*, a *tap*, or a *spigot*.

Children would *favor* or *resemble* one of their parents. These alternative vocabulary items are readily noticed and commented on when speakers from different regions meet.

Social dialects not only show variation in vocabualry items and pronunciation features, they also often have differences in areas of grammar. A member of a poor rural farming community might say *You was right and I done it* while a middle-class office worker might use *You were right and I did it*, meaning the same thing. These variations around the verb are typical of some of the more frequent grammatical differences between dialects. These affect the systems for relating subjects to verbs (i.e. agreement patterns) and for choosing a form of the verb for a particular tense in English.

What are the main differences in the dialects of Spanish spoken in the United States?

As we observed for English dialects, Spanish dialects may differ on all levels of language. Pronunciation differences are particularly important in distinguishing dialects of Spanish. Unlike English, however, where the major differences are found in the vowel sounds, the majority of the Spanish dialect differences are in the consonants. At the end of a word, consonants such as s (pronounced as s, h, or no sound at all, as in the word dos), the nasal sounds (pronounced m, n, ng or as a nasalized vowel, as in bien), and d (pronounced d or no sound at all, as in verdad) are particularly susceptible to dialect differences. Dialect sensitivity can also be found for the consonants b, d, and g when they occur in the middle of a word, and for the sounds ll and j.

In the formation of words, the differentiation of dialects often involves the "regularizing" of certain irregular forms, so that particular verb conjugation (e.g. podamos versus puedamos or hablaste versus hablastes) and agreement forms (e.g. l'agua and l'amiga for el agua and la amiga) that may differ from the regular, or productive, pattern are quite sensitive to dialect differences. These kinds of dialect characteristics seem to be typical regardless of the language, so that regularization of patterns is found in both English and Spanish. Such alternations of language forms often participate in social dialect differentiation.

In the Spanish dialects in the United States, vocabulary differences are accentuated, not only because of the varying origins of the Spanish variety in use in a particular area, but also because of the role of "loan" words from English. It turns out that it is critical to the definition of Spanish dialects in the United States to consider the kinds of works that are borrowed and the way in which they are integrated into the Spanish system, both in terms of pronunciation and grammatical conjugation (i.e., lonchar 'to lunch'; rentar 'to rent'). No realistic examination of the Spanish language can afford to neglect this important feature, since vocabualry differences play a much more significant role in the social dimension of dialects of Spanish than they do for English.

How many different dialects of American English are there?

There is no widely agreed upon answer to this question, even after decades of research on differences in American English. We can talk, as we have, about the many differences in the speech patterns of different groups of people, but deciding where one dialect ends and another begins and how many there are is a different matter. Dialects simply do not come in neat little self-contained packages, and many factors, of varying degrees of importance, must be considered.

There have been some attempts to delineate dialect groups by region. Students of regional dialects generally recognize several major dialect areas in the U.S. and a number of sub-areas within them. Although many cautions are given about the lines of demarcation and the importance of different lines, the map of dialects given below is representative of a fairly common perspective on the varieties of American English. This map just gives a regional distribution, however, including some Hispanicized English dialects. Within and across areas, there are social, ethnic, age, and sex considerations as well, which will, of course, complicate the picture immensely.

How many dialects of Spanish are there in the United States?

As in the case of varieties of English, there is no agreed upon answer to this question, since it depends on how finely the distinctions are made. Generally, however, there are four major Spanish dialects identified and then some minor ones. First, there is the Spanish of the Southwest U.S., which has its roots largely in the dialects of Mexico. In the Southwest, distinctions are often made between the dialects of California, New Mexico and southern Colorado, Arizona, and Texas. The Southwest variety also extends to some northern urban areas with Hispanic communities, such as Detroit and Chicago. The second major region, derived from Cuban Spanish, is located in southern Florida and those places where large concentrations of Cubans have settled. The third area is derived from Puerto Rican Spanish, and communities of speakers of this dialect are located for the most part in urban areas of the Northeast, such as the Hispanic settlements in New York City, Hartford, Boston, Philadelphia and so forth. Finally, there are dialects reflecting Central American and South American origins, found especially in cities like Washington, D.C. and New York City. Although none of the major or minor dialect areas being mentioned is homogeneous, these latter communities are probably even less so because of the diversity of Central and South American countries represented (e.g. Nicaragua, El Salvador, Venezuela) which make up the historical source and the fact that such a large proportion of the community's members are fairly recent arrivals. The map below gives some of the major regional areas, with the subdivisions of dialects in the Southwest delineated as well. Natually, we have to recognize social class distinctions and age distinctions within each area, as well as differing levels of English borrowing found for various subgroups with the regions.

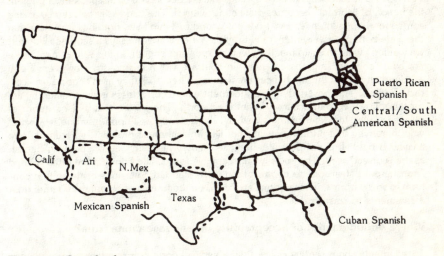

Language Standards

Even though there are many dialects of English, isn't there just one way of speaking English that is generally recognized as correct?

There are numerous dialects within the English language. (In the last section, we talked only abut U.S. English--imagine if we tried to include England, Australia, and other countries where English is spoken.) However, there is no one correct way to speak English, in the sense that one set of language patterns is somehow inherently better than all the others in terms of what is generally recognized. There are certain language patterns that are preferred over others, according to social norms. These are often talked about as the "correct" use of English, but this is actually a decision based on social not linguistic, acceptability.

"Correct" is a judgement that we make, usually based on some objective set of information. For example, the result of an addition problem, like 7 plus 3, has one correct solution (10) and all others are incorrect (11, 9, etc.). In arithmetic, we can assume that there will be one, and only one, correct answer. To compare this with language use, we must look for a set of objective facts against which we might judge whether something in language is correct or incorrect.

One set of facts we might be able to depend on is our ability to decide what can and cannot count as English. So, for example, when we hear a sentence like *They will arrive tomorrow* we can observe that it is English and therefore in that sense "correct." On the other hand, we would know that *Arrive will tomorrow they* or *Ils arriveront demain* are both "incorrect" as English sentences in that sense, although the latter would qualify for another language. Similarly, we would judge *pencil* to be a correct form of English, but *tloshg* would not be accepted. In each case, we seem to be identifying things that speakers of English might say as opposed to everything else. This is based on our knowledge of the English language. This is one set of objective facts that we share as speakers of English.

When it comes to ways of saying things that are not shared by all speakers of English, the notion of "correct" becomes quite controversial. This can easily be seen by asking someone about sentences like I done it wrong or I can't see nothing. It is clear that these are both possible sentences in English. When someone says a sentence like this, we wouldn't want to claim that they weren't speaking English. In this sense, then, these are both "correct" English sentences, in contrast with non-English. However, if you ask someone about them, chances are that you'll hear that they aren't "good" or "correct" English. This observation is a judgment where correctness is determined by acceptability, rather than accuracy or intrinsic worth. There is no real basis, in terms of objective facts, for determining whether I did it wrong or I done it wrong is a better way to convey that information. It's not like an arithmetic problem, where only one answer is right. It is not possible, then, to identify just one way of speaking English as the "correct" way. The socially unacceptable forms, like I done it are often termed "nonstandard" features, to contrast then with "standard" versions or those that conform to social norms. These norms are based on judgments of acceptablity rather than assessments of correctness.

Where do judgments of acceptability in language come from?

Judgments about sentences like I did it versus I done it or puedamos for podamos are based on our attitudes about our language and the different groups of people who speak it. The value placed on a certain way of saying something is very closely associated with the social status of the people who say it that way. This is not an individual decision made by each person, it is the society's evaluation of different groups that includes their ways of speaking. We are socialized when we learn these attitudes just as we learn what constitutes polite behavior, like not talking with your mouth full of food. This common set of beliefs about our language is shared by most members of our society. Speakers from groups whose dialects are not highly considered by society are usually aware of this evaluation and feel that their language is not as good as other people's. The use of "correct" in terms of this social evaluation, then, does not involve real value or assessment by any objective standard. What is acceptable according to the standards of society at large is considered "correct", what is not acceptable will be looked on as "incorrect."

Are some dialects more logical than others?

No. Very often we hear that a particular English or Spanish dialect is preferred because it is "more logical" than some other dialect that has nonstandard features. The quality of being "logical," we assume, relates to being able to express various logical concepts using the means available in a dialect. These concepts include relationships like negation or conditionality (i.e. if...then), as well as the process of linking expressions in sequence in a so-called "logical" manner. The idea that some dialects are more logical than others results from the influence of language attitudes, like the concept of "correct" language. Believing that standard forms of English or Spanish are somehow inherently better than others, many people will go on to maintain that certain linguistic structures are more logical than others, more systematic, even more advantageous for cognitive development. There is no evidence, however, to support the contention that any language variety will interfere with the development of the ability to express logical concepts. All languages—and dialects of languages— adequately provide for the conceptualizations and expression of logical propositions, but the particular manner of this expression may differ among language systems.

What about the use of double negatives? Isn't that illogical?

The use of so-called "double negatives," or two negative forms in a single sentence, is often cited as evidence that a particular variety of English is illogical. According to this argument, the two negatives in a sentence like *They can't go nowhere* should cancel each other so that the meaning should be a positive statement (They can go somewhere). Since sentences like this are used with a negative interpretation, the claim is made that the structure is illogical. (According to this position, *Nobody can't go nowhere*, with three negatives, would have to be accepted as a negative sentence.) However, the natural logic of language users is not identical to formal mathematic logic, where two negatives do yield a positive. Natural logic allows both sentences, *They can't go anywhere* and *They can't go nowhere*, to have a negative interpretation, depending on the conventions of the particular dialect. Both are expressions of the logical concept of negation; the singly negated form is socially acceptable, the doubly negated form is not. It is interesting to note that multiple negation has been an acceptable structure in English in the past, during the Old English and Middle English periods. The change to favoring the use of a single negative in a sentence like *They can't do anything* is a relatively recent development. In Spanish, of course, the use of two negative words (no...nada) is the current standard for making a negative utterance, as in *no hace nada* 'he/she doesn't do anything'.

But aren't some dialects simpler versions of others?

No again. Dialects of a language are related to one another in patterned ways. When these patterns are examined, we can see how intricate and complex the features of any dialect are. The comparison of varieties of a language will show each having areas of greater and lesser complexity in relation to the others.

A closely related idea is that people who use dialects with nonstandard features are reflecting incomplete learning of the standard dialect. This is also untrue. Common phrases used to describe certain features reinforce this notion, such as "leaving off the ending of words," or "not using complete sentences." The English or Spanish speakers who are said to "leave off the endings of words" are really using a pronunciation rule that many speakers may actually use. For example, all speakers of English will, in casual speech, sometimes pronounce a word like *fast as fas*, "leaving off" the final t, as in *fas'break*. If you listen carefully to the speech of those around you, you'll probably notice this rule in use to varying degrees. It's not sloppy speech at all, it's just one of the pronunciation rules of English that happens more often in casual speech.

This rule of English is used somewhat differently in certain dialects, and so it is often noticed and commented on by speakers of other dialects. One difference is that it is used more often in general, so the higher frequency makes it noticeable. Also, fast can be pronounced *fas* in a situation like *fas or slow* where the absence of the t sound is noticeable because of the vowel at the beginning of the next word. The quality of "leaving off endings of words" is really a case of a rule of English that is used with minor, but noticeable differences by different groups, but it is not at all a question of "simpler versions."

Certain groups of children have been referred to as "disadvantaged." Often, people talk about "cultural disadvantage" and "linguistic disadvantage," which would seem to mean that these children need help with their language. If the dialects aren't less logical, or simpler, what's the problem?

The term "linguistically disadvantaged" is a misnomer in the way it is typically used. As we have seen, no variety of a language is inherently better than another, none is less logical or less complex than others. Therefore, no speakers have a disadvantage in their ability to function as a result of the variety of the language that they acquire.

The reality of the social situation in this country cannot be denied, however. In many ways, culturally and linguistically different groups are at a disadvantage because of their less favored status within society. The social disadvantage is a product of the fact that these groups are viewed as lacking in certain areas (the so-called "cognitive" or "enviromental handicap"). Therefore, they xx
must change in order to be accepted. Success in school, for example, may depend on their being able to change their language and cultural and cultural behavior and adapt to school norms. For the member of a mainstream group, no change or adaptation is necessary. In this sense, culturally different groups may be considered "at a disadvantage" although they are not intrinsically "disadvantaged.

This view seems very different from what most people have said. Is this now the generally accepted position about these different groups?

There are two major schools of thought on questions relating to groups that differ linguistically and culturally from mainstream society. Briefly, they can be referred to as the *deficit* position and the *difference* position. In terms of language proponents of the "deficit" position believe that speakers of dialects with nonstandard forms have a handicap,not only socially, but cognitively, because the dialects are "illogical," or sloppy, or possess various other negative qualities. Intelligence test scores and results of other standardized measures are often cited as evidence for this position (Problems of bias in testing are typically not addressed). Based on these test scores, recommendations are often made for remedial language training and other treatments. The concept of "compensatory education" evolved from this position, where education programs were designed to fill in the gaps in language and other skills caused by the students linguistic and environmental handicaps. According to this position, the speakers of nonmainstream dialects have a language deficit that can impede their cognitive and social development.

The other position, and the one advocated here, views various groups of speakers in terms of the differences in their language systems. Since no one system can be shown to be inherently better, there is no reason to assume that using a particular dialect can be associated with having any kind of deficit or advantage. The evidence from test scores and school performance that is called on to support the need for remediation should and encourage only that dialect during the ducation process, and ifyou also test ability and achievement through the medium of that dialect, then it should not be surprising that students who enter school already speaking it tend to fare better than those who use a different dialect. According to the "difference" position, the equality and inherent adequacy of the functioning dialects should be accepted, and an understanding of the attitudes and values of society toward the dialects and their speakers is needed in order to deal with them. The U.S. situation is in no way unique, by the way. The acceptance of a standard language accompanied by negative attitudes toward the other language varieties is an unavoidable product of the interaction of language and society.

The topic of standard English seems to be quite controversial, especially in education, but it's often not clear what is meant by the term. What does the term *STANDARD ENGLISH* refer to?

There is really no single dialect of English that corresponds to a "standard" English, although the popular belief is that there is a uniform reference dialect that exists in the speech of those who speak so-called "good" English. In fact, the speech of a certain group of people does define what is considered standard in English. However, the norms are not identical in all communities, they are not unchanging and there are two sets of norms that can be recognized-the *informal* standard and the *formal* standard.

The norms of language usage that members of a community consider to be acceptable constitute the "informal standard American English." This set of norms relates to the way certain people actually speak and allows variation between communities. "Formal standard English," on the other hand, includes the norms prescribed in grammar books and finds its reflection, if anywhere, in the written language. For example, the formal standard dictates that certain distinctions should be made in the use of *shall* and *will*, that one should avoid ending a sentence with a preposition, and so on. However, acceptable usage does not necessarily conform to these norms and informal standard English would admit sentences like *They're the ones you should depend on*, with no stigma attached, despite the final preposition. In fact, an utterance like *They are the ones on whom you should depend* is probably less acceptable in many circumstances because of its formality.

Does anyone speak standard English?

It is unlikely that anyone speaks the standard language if the formal standard is used as a reference point. The formal standard is generally limited to the written language of certain people, so that it appears only in the most formal style of the highly educated, and probably older members of society. The informal standard is spoken, however, by those whose language usage sets the guidelines for what is acceptable in each community.

Two observations need to be made about the informal standard. First, since all speakers control a range of styles, someone who is considered a standard English speaker may use particular language patterns that are clearly nonstandard. For example, in an appropriate situation, a standard speaker might use *ain't*, or *Fred and him went...* This would not indicate that the speaker had become a speaker of a nonstandard dialect of English. Rather, it is a manifestation of a basic feature of language, the variability of its forms. Second, there is no one standard English according to this set of norms, but many different varieties that qualify as standard. For example, a standard speaker from Maine and a standard speaker from Tennessee would have quite different pronunciation patterns, and probably certain other differences as well. They would both be accepted as English speakers in their own communities, though, and in most others as well despite the fact that their "accent" might be noticed outside their home region. Thus, there is a range of language patterns, particularly in the area of pronunciation, that is acceptable according to the informal norms, but there is also a unified notion of what is *not* acceptable that constitutes part of the informal standard for American English.

How about Spanish? Can't we say that there is a generally recognized standard variety?

Looking at the question of defining a standard for the Spanish language, in comparison with the situation for English, we find both similarities and differences. Unlike English, there exists for Spanish a recognized reference dictionary for standard vocabulary, produced by the Spanish Language Academy in Madrid, Spain. However, no one really speaks the prescribed way, even in Spain, and the dictionary tends to be conservative in setting its standards, with an inevitable time lag in reporting usage accounting for some of the discrepancies. This is emphasized for Spanish in the Americas.

In the United States, where Spanish has no official status as a national language, the definition of standard may be quite informal, very local, and largely a function of social class differences within the community. Certainly, the working notion of a standard for Spanish in Los Angeles is quite different from what we would put forth for New York City, but it is also different form that of Albuquerque, or even San Diego. Because of the contact situation involving English in the United States, the role of anglicized" or loan words has become much more prominent in the definition of standard language than it is in other countries where Spanish is a national language. According to the norms that would be prescribed for dialects of Spanish in the United States, fewer items borrowed from English would correlate with greater standardness. In reality, however, the informal standards usually contain many such loan words.

Who decides which dialects are standard and which are nonstandard?

In every society, there are people whose position or status makes their judgments about language use more powerful than those of other people. This group includes those who make decisions that can significantly affect the lives of others, including, for example, teachers and employers in our society. These are the people who decide who will be hired or who will progress in school; their judgments about what is good and bad in language enter into their evaluations of people, giving those judgments added weight. These are also the people who are looked up to by members of their community, whose opinions about matters like language would typically be respected. Their speech habits are admired and serve as a model of acceptable behavior.

Standard English or Spanish, then, is a composite of the real spoken language of this group of professionals, the educated middle-class. Since members of this group in Chicago might sound quite different from their counterparts in Miami, we need to recognize the existence of a number of standard dialects. This informal set of norms is the one that really counts in terms of social acceptance. It is important, for this reason, to discriminate carefully between those artificial norms that make up the formal standard and the informal, influential norms of social acceptability.

Dialect Diferences & Education

What are the consequences of dialects in education? Do they pose any problems?

Complex and controversial issues concerning dialects and education have been debated for quite a while, most intensely since the late 1960s. Because of the close relationship betwen minority and dialect groups, questions about the civil rights of the people involved have also come up in this regard. One central issue has been whether or not to require the use of a standard dialect in the course of education. Such a requirement is considered to be discriminatory by some, since it places an extra burden on certain groups and may mean they will not receive the same educational opportunity as other groups. An insistence on standard language forms may hinder the acquistion of other educational skills and make it more difficult for these students to succeed in school. Others argue that it is a responsibility of the education system to teach a standard dialect so that all groups will have a better chance for equal opportunity in later life. For instance, a lack of facility with standard English or Spanish may cause problems for the adult in obtaining employment. Prospects for success in school and in later life, then, may be related to some of the attitudes society holds toward different dialects.

But doesn't everybody have to learn to speak better in school? Why is it so hard for some groups?

There are aspects of schooling that deal with language skills, such as composition and in that sense everyone studies language. Students also may develop a wider range of language styles in school. They may learn, for example, that ways of speaking used at home are not always appropriate for the classroom, when meeting people for the first time, etc. They may also increase the size of their vocabulary as they work through content area as well as language skill instruction. While this is not actually a question of learning to speak "better" English, there is certainly some development of language skills for educational and social purposes.

The reason it is "so hard" for some groups is that they don't necessarily start from the same base that others do in terms of the language and social habits that have been developed in the home community. Before they can progress through a school curriculum in this area, members of these groups must often develop a facility with certain standard dialect forms. Thus, these students have extra work to do simply because they don't have the same background as others.

Are there other ways in which dialect differences can affect education?

Yes. Dialect differences between groups of students can affect the quality of education received by the students in at least two ways. One area that has been widely discussed is the possibility that a child's dialect may interfere with the acquisition of various skills (such as reading) and information on which later success might depend. More subtle, and perhaps more crucial are the social consequences of being a member of a different dialect group. The attitudes of teachers, school personnel, and other students can have a tremendous impact on the education process. Often, people who hear a nonstandard dialect make erroneous assumptions about the speaker's intelligence. When a teacher or other school official reacts in this way, the result can be very serious. Studies have shown that there can be a self-fulfilling prophecy in teacher's beliefs about their student's abilities. It is possible that, if a teacher underestimates a child's ability because of dialect differences, perhaps as a direct result, the child will do less well in that class. In some cases, students are "tracked" with the so-called slower groups or even placed in special classes for the mentally handicapped because of their speech patterns. The child's self-concept may also be injured if negative opinions are encountered frequently. So, matters of educational and social equity are related to dialect differences.

Are all these problems caused by dialect alone? There seem to be other factors contributing to difficulties in the classroom beyond the way some students speak.

Linguistic differences between groups are just one factor in the larger context of cultural differences. Members of society's various groups tend to share a set of linguistic and cultural characteristics(Culture is used here in the sense of patterns of behavior shared by members of a social group). Not only ways of speaking, but values, attitudes toward education, conceptions of politeness, and virtually all socially determined features can vary from one group to the next. Mainstream groups are considered to exhibit socially acceptable behavior, both linguistically and culturally. Nonmainstream group members tend to diverge to some extent from the norms on both counts.

The classroom consequences of cultural attitudes affect the interactions of students with teachers and fellow students. There are numerous instances recorded where behaviors have been misinterpreted because of a cultural difference between teacher and student. For example, Native American children in the Southwest have been labeled as passive or nonverbal and have had their level of intelligence misjudged because they seem unresponsive in the classroom. According to the rules of their culture, however, they are behaving appropriately in that situation and a response or any real active participation would be impertinent or disrespectful. Others report instances of culture clashes in newly integrated classrooms. Black children sometimes get reprimanded for "blurting out" an answer before being called on, or humming and making other noises while working independently. Although these actions may reflect cultural patterns that are accepted and expected in the community, the teacher may see them as disrespectful and disobedient. Such cultural differences, like linguistic differences, present complex issues for classroom practice, and failure to recognize them can lead to educational inequity.

Shouldn't we be realistic about how the student needs to speak and behave in order to succeed in life? Aren't we doing more of a disservice if we ignore the differences and pretend that they don't matter?

Being realistic about the social situation in terms of being aware of the social factors at work is important. Certainly ignoring the differences and pretending they don't matter is not advisable. The specific course of action taken in response to the differences, though, depends on the beliefs and goals of the individual teacher, the school, and the community. There is really only one recommendation that can be made at a general level. Whatever decision is reached, the people involved should have enough information to make a choice and understand its consequences. This includes our own and other's attitudes toward different varieties of English and Spanish.

What are some of the alternatives?

There are three basic alternatives that can be identified in terms of how a school program can deal with dialect differences: (a) *accommodate all dialects* (b) *require that a standard dialect be learned and used*, or (c) *identify a position somewhere between (a) and (b)*.

The first alternative accommodating all dialects, is based on the belief that all dialects are equal and no one should be penalized because of their acquired dialect. This could mean that a conscious effort would be made to allow full use of a student's native dialect of English or Spanish and it would form the base on which education could build. Special programs might be adopted and tested to lessen any interference from the native dialect in the acquisition of certain skills and information in the school setting. The other extreme position that can be taken is to insist that a standard dialect be acquired and used in the school context. Support for this position comes from the belief that such a variety is needed for success in later life. Following this philosophy, special programs might be allowed to teach standard forms, but other programs would not need to be changed. The native dialect is accepted for certain outside school contexts or discouraged entirely (although presumably someone who is familiar with the social factors in the situation would not advocate the latter course). If a standard is required, but the native dialect is also accepted, then the goal being worked toward can be termed "bidialectalism" (like "bilingual"), referring to near equal facility with two dialects of a language.

The third alternative falls between these two extremes, and is undoubtedly the direction most often followed. The native dialect is accepted for certain uses and a standard dialect is encouraged or demanded for other uses. For example, in terms of mastering certain skills in school, a plan like the following might be developed. In recognition of the fact that most written language that will be encountered in life will be a standard variety, a student will be expected to develop the capability to read and write a standard dialect. A student would not be required to eliminate the dealing with the standard written forms of the language, both in reading them and in producing them in writing. In this way, the two (or more) dialects would be used by the student for different purposes, much in the same way that people use different styles of speaking for different situations. This is just one example of the type of compromise that can be reached between the first two positions.

Dialect Differences & The Broader Context

Is information about dialect differences useful for people in areas outside education?

The issues arising over dialect differences in education are actually just a reflection of these issues in the broader social context. There are many different practical consequences of dialect differences, but the most pervasive issue is related to attitudes about language. A number of research studies focusing on language attitudes show that speakers of nonstandard dialects are generally held in low esteem. Furthermore, this low esteem is typically extended to other personal attributes, including morality, integrity, and intelligence. In other words, attitudes about language trigger a whole set of stereotypes and prejudices based on underlying social and ethnic differences. Since people readily recognize social and ethnic differences in language, it is crucial to promote accurate knowledge about the nature of dialect differences in language in all segments of our society.

One of the interesting aspects of recent studies of language attitudes is the young age at which such attitudes may be acquired. In fact, one study showed that children as young as three to five years of age were quite accurate in recognizing differences in language and made associations with other types of behavior on the basis of language differences. These findings are in line with research findings about the socialization of prejudice, which takes place very early in life and manifests itself in many different details of behavior.

Regardless of what linguists say, don't people have a right to have an opinion about what is good and bad in language? After all, there are standards for good and bad manners, and people don't view them in terms of prejudice. Why can't good English or good Spanish be considered the same way?

No one can really argue with a person's preference for one dialect over another, and such preferences do not in themselves create problems. The problems arise from the interpretation of the significance of dialect differences. If the preference of one dialect is accompanied by an understanding that this choice does not imply inherent individual or social superiority, and that dialect differences are unrelated to matters of morality and intelligence, then no argument can be made with such a choice. What linguists object to is the unwarranted interpretation of differences in terms of negative stereotypes and prejudices.

Judgments concerning language preference are similar to judgments about other kinds of preferred manners, but they are also different in some important ways. A fork may be preferred to a spoon in eating peas, just as the form *isn't* may be preferred over *ain't*, but in the former case, no one would argue that there is greater nutritional value, or even that it is more efficient to eat peas with a fork. In the case of language, however, traditional values about language usage often involve judgments about adequacy and efficiency in communication, they are not limited to simple preferences. In a sense, this is akin to saying that there is greater nutritional value in eating peas with a fork.

Linguistics seem to give the impression that anything people say is okay. Is this really true?

There are several dimensions to the question of "being okay" from a linguistic viewpoint that need to be clarified. Linguists typically maintain that all dialects have rules which govern the patterns of speech, and , as long as people follow the rules of their dialect they are "talking okay." From a technical linguistic perspective, then, acceptable speech is defined as that which follows the linguistic rules of the dialect.

To say that something is linguistically okay does not necessarily mean that it is socially acceptable. A form like *We was here* or *no son igual*, might be governed by a linguistic rule in a particular dialect, but it is not preferred as a standard form. Linguists are aware of this fact and often have their own social preferences about speech. But the social preference is clearly distinguished from a linguistic assessment of acceptability made in terms of language rules.

The dimensions of linguistic and social acceptability also relate to how the label "ungrammatical" is used. As linguists use the term, it is reserved for those cases in which structures do not follow the rules of a particular dialect. So, the sentences *We was here* or *no son igual*, would be considered grammatical in this definition, since they follow the rules of a particular dialect, even if they do not follow the rules of the standard variety. Sentences such as *boy the is here* or *muchacho el aqui*, would be considered ungrammatical, however, since they do not follow the rules in any particular dialect of English or Spanish, respectively. This technical definition of grammatical and ungrammatical structures should be distinguished from the popular use of the terms in which ungrammatical usually refers to socially unacceptable sentences, such as *We was here* or *no son igual*. From the standpoint of describing language, it seems essential to separate linguistic and social acceptability.

After all is said and done, we will have dialect differences, and they are associated with various social differences. Wouldn't it be simpler if the dialect differences were just leveled, and everyone spoke the same way?. At least we would eliminate some of the prejudices associated with dialect differences, couldn't we?

Dialect differences are a fact of life in our own diverse society. As long as there are socially and regionally differentiated groups, these differences will be maintained. So any expectation that dialect differences might be eliminated is unrealistc given the facts of social structure. Furthermore, the expectation of uniformity is contrary to the varied traditions which have contributed to this country's make up. The possibility of leveling of dialect differences would also depend on a desire on the part of speakers of different dialects for this form to take place. As it turns out, this is certainly not the case. Despite the high esteem associated with standard English and Spanish on a superficial level, there is research supporting the conclusion that dialect differences are viewed positively on a deeper level. For example, positive values of forthrightness, physical prowess (i.e "toughness") and ethnic and social identity may be tied up with different nonstandard dialects.

What about the effect of mass media on dialects? Don't these really have a leveling effect on them, so that they reduce the differences between the varieties?

The effect of the mass media on dialect differences is difficult to determine. For the most part, however, individuals are not prone to use "media language," such as that of national newscasters or journalists, as a model for their own speech. They may recognize it as different but not as a model to emulate. This is partly due to the fact that they are not in direct social contact with the writers for the print media and the speakers in the broadcast media (radio and television). There is little point in adjusting your speech to match that of a television newscaster if they will never know you did it. This lack of direct social contact makes the mass media much less influential than other peer group members that an individual speaker interacts with frequently.

There are also aspects of media language usage which may actually reinforce the usefulness of dialect differences. Some personalities may project a regional and/or ethnic dialect as a positive attribute through the media. When they appear or are reported on in print or in the broadcast media, the dialect they use receives favorable attention. And, on a local level, the use of regional and ethnic dialects may be directly programmed to appeal to a local population. Local radio "soul stations" are an example of this programming. So, the effect of the media with respect to dialect differences is certainly not uniform.

**Haven't some of the major dialects leveled to some extent in the past genera-
tion? Don't people in America actually talk more alike now than they did,
say 50 years ago?**

The examination of dialect differences across different generations does show some
leveling between dialects. Older representatives of different social, regional, and ethnic
varieties tend to differ more in their speech than the younger generation. The exact
cause of this is hard to determine, although increased education, greater accessibility
to regionally isolated areas, and expanded occupational opportunities have all played
some role. It is probably a combination of factors rather than one primary reason which
accounts for this leveling.

While some dialect differences have lessened, this should not be taken to mean that
we can predict the extinction of dialects. There is every reason to believe that different
dialects will continue to be maintained. In the long run, these differences are a tribute
to the various traditions and heritages which have combined to make up the dialects
of English.

References

Christian, D. *Language arts and dialect differences*. Washington, D.C.: Center for Applied Linguistics, 1979.

Christian, D. & Wolfram, C. *Exploring dialects*. Washington, D.C.: Center for Applied Linguistics, 1979.

Ferguson, C.A. & Heath, S.B., Eds. *Language in the USA*. Cambridge: Cambridge University Press, 1981.

Hernández-Chávez, E., Cohen, D. & Beltramo, A.F., Eds. *El lenguaje do los chicanos*. Washington, D.C.: Center for Applied Linguistics, 1975.

Labov, W. The logic of nonstandard English. In J. Alatis (Ed.), *Linguistics and the teaching of standard English to speakers of other languages or dialects*. Washington D.C.: Georgetown University Press, 1969.

Ornstein-Galicia, J., Ed. *Form and function in Chicano English*. Rowley, Mass.: Newbury House Publishers, Inc., 1984.

Peñalosa, F. *Chicano sociolinguistics: A brief introduction*. Rowley, Mass. Newbury House Publishers, Inc., 1980.

Shuy, R.W. *Discovering American dialects*. Champaign, Ill.: National Council of Teachers of English, 1967.

Wolfram, W. *Speech pathology and dialect differences*. Washington, D.C.: Center for Applied Linguistics, 1979.

Wolfram, W. & Fasold, R.W. *The study of social dialects in American English*. Englewood Cliffs, New Jersey: Prentice-Hall, 1974.

Wolfram, W., Yanofsky, N.M. & Shuy, R.W. *Reading and dialect differences*. Washington, D.C.: Center for Applied Linguistics, 1979.

Accentedness in the Classroom
by Kathleen M. Bailey and José L. Galván

Introduction

While we cannot deny the historical validity of the melting-pot concept (in spite of the fact that not all groups fully melted) nor indeed the necessity of developing common cultural institutions in the process of building a nation, we must recognize that we have entered a new period in American history, for which a new metaphor is appropriate—that of the salad bowl. This metaphor is particularly apt, for a salad is not just a mere mechanical mixture of elements: it is rather an emergent entity which is more than the sum of its parts, in which the parts remain distinguishable and we can still recognize their separate contribution to the whole. It is this integrity of our cultural component, then, and their identifiability, which form the basis of the new metaphor (Saville-Troike, 1976).1

The metaphor of the salad bowl has interesting implications for teacher training with regard to cultural and linguistic differences among students. For example, there are many recent immigrants and linguistic minority children in our schools today whose English may be accented to some degree. We need to ask ourselves what our educational system can or should do to accommodate these differences. How do we as teachers respond to language variation or accentedness? What is known about the influence of such attitudes on teacher behavior? What provisions should teacher training programs include for educating teachers about these cultural and linguistic differences? What can local school districts do to better equip their teachers to deal with cultural diversity in the classroom?

In recent years, research has been directed toward these questions. Investigators have identified accentedness as a factor in hiring practices (Baird, 1969; Thompson, 1973). More recently, studies of accentedness have been conducted in the school setting. Preliminary findings indicate that accent variations in the English of Chicanos are reflected in teachers' behavior in two ways (Galván, Pierce and Underwood, 1975). First, teachers perceive accented speakers differentially. Second, their subsequent attitudes toward those speakers vary according to the degree of the students' accentedness.

This essay will attempt to formulate a framework within which these issues may be examined with respect to teacher training. We start by reviewing some of the pertinent literature on teacher expectations and accentedness. In each case, we make specific recommendations for future research. Then we address the issue of teacher training as it relates to attitudes toward accentedness. Finally, we consider the implications of this review and make recommendations for the future regarding teacher training.

This article first appeard in *AZTLAN: International Journal of Chicano Studies Research, V.8*, 1977.

Teachers' Attitudes in the Classroom

In an extensive review of the research on teacher expectations, Brophy and Good (1974) found that teachers' attitudes directly influence their classroom behavior. They also found that teachers were frequently unaware of those attitudes and the resulting "inappropriate" behavior. They report that differential treatment of students within classes is usually done unconsciously by teachers and that the teachers usually change their behavior once they are aware of it. Furthermore, changes in teacher behavior are usually followed by complementary changes in student behavior.

The authors found that teachers make early and lasting judgments of students, and that these judgements are frequently based on first impressions. Within the first week of school, students are assigned to reading groups or study tables by teachers who may be using very little information in making these decisions. In practice, this information is derived from both external and personal evaluations.

The external data involved in such grouping decisions sometimes include "objective" measures (e.g., previous grades, achievement test scores, etc.) and sometimes subjective information, such as input from principals, counselors, and other teachers on the individual or even members of his family (comparison with older siblings, family standing in the community, stigmatizing social factors, etc.). But teachers also rely on first-hand assessments in making decisions about students. An individual's early classroom performance, his attentiveness, and the extent to which he volunteers have a powerful effect on a teacher's early judgments of the student, as do his clothing, physical attractiveness, personal cleanliness, and the amount and frequency of his disruptive behavior. This is not to say that teachers willfully or maliciously stereotype students. Instead, school policies about grouping and the prevalent tracking system within and across classes force teachers to group children in many ways. Unfortunately, factors such as clothing, personal hygiene, and a child's social behavior—which have little or nothing to do with his intellectual ability—are often operative in the early decisions teachers make about students.

Although they point out many problems with Rosenthal and Jacobson's controversial Pygmalion study (1968), Brophy and Good conclude that these early judgments lead to long-range expectations and attitudes on the part of the teacher, which have subtle and significant consequences. Apparently such attitudes generate an expectation effect within the teachers which is sometimes realized as a self-fullfilling prophecy: the teacher expects the student to do poorly, and as a result of several complex interactional processes the student ultimately does poorly. A negative assessemnt of a child's ability, for example, may lead to a cushioning effect, even among well-meaning teachers. This tendency to "protect" those students rated as low by the teacher is often realized in the frequency of turns allotted to poorer students (Good and Brophy, 1971). Teachers sometimes attempt to avoid embarrassing a student, especially when they feel he is unable to answer a question. For this reason, a poor student may be asked fewer questions or given fewer opportunities to respond.

Moreover, the types of tasks delegated to "low" students are often easier than those delegated to "bright students." For instance, a low student might be asked to confirm or deny information in a yes/no question ("Did Junipero Serra establish the first missions in California?") or provide basic information in answer to a content question ("Who began the first missions in California?"). In contrast, a bright student might be asked a more complex question of process or inference ("Why were the missions built in California? What was life like in an early mission? How were the missions organized?"). Thus, although we as teachers believe we are protecting the low students from failure or embarrassment, there is evidence that we may also be short-changing them in terms of the educational opportunities we provide, or prevent them from having.

Another example of the cushioning effect is found in the length of time a teacher will wait for the response to a question before prompting the student, moving on to another person, or answering the question herself. In a study that sampled teachers' wait-times in science and mathematics lessons, Rowe(1969) found that teachers waited significantly less time for the poor students to reply to a question. In other words, slow students had to reply to questions more rapidly than bright ones. The study goes on to report that teachers apparently were surprised by these findings. This study also determined that teachers with very short wait-times were inflexible in the kinds of responses they allowed. On the other hand, wait-times of not less than five seconds combined with low teacher rewards had the effect of producing longer responses and more exchanges between children. The students were also more confident and tended to speculate more and provide more supportive evidence for their ideas. Is it possible that the benevolent desire to avoid embarrassing students in fact limits their educational opportunities to an undetermined extent?

So far we have seen that teachers form early and lasting impressions of students. These impressions are operative in the formation of teacher attitudes and expectations, which, in turn, are sometimes realized as inappropriate or prejudicial behavior. Furthermore, a teacher's classroom behavior can be unwittingly discriminatory in terms of the types of tasks allotted to a student, the frequency of such tasks, and the time he has in which to perform the desired response behavior. If extraneous factors such as a student's clothing and personal cleanliness can influence a teacher's perception of a child's ability, how and to what extent can a student's accent influence a teacher's perception of that child?

In order to answer this question, we need to examine the literature on accent variation and see how it relates to teacher attitudes. We might ask how differences due to language background affect teacher attitudes. More specifically, are negative expectation effects related to accentedness as they have been shown to be related to other student characteristics? Secondly, would such attitudes result in a cushioning (or other) effect that might limit a child's educational opportunities?

Attitudes Toward Language Variation

Several studies have identified differential personality judgments based on language variation. Both speaker and listener characteristics can influence the polarity of evaluations made about a tape-recorded stimulus. The studies by Lambert and his associates in Canada (Lambert, Anisfeld and Yeni-Komshian 1965; Lambert 1967; Lambert, Hodgson, Gardner and Fillenbaum 1960; Preston 1963; Tucker and Lambert 1969) established that the judgments people make about speakers just on the basis of vocal cues (i.e., tape recorded speech samples) are related to factors such as the sex, social class, and dialect of the speakers. They found that subjects gave consistent personality evaluations of the speakers whose voices they heard and that this consistency correlated with the social and linguistic characteristics of the speakers. Another Canadian study investigated personality evaluations made by bilingual French-English subjects about speakers tape-recorded in both English and French and found that the bilingual judges were influenced by the language spoken by the speaker. The ratings of the same speaker were significantly different for French and English, depending on the language heard

(Brown, 1969).

Researchers in the United States have reported similar results. Evaluations of the language as well as the personality of speakers representing a variety of regional and ethnic dialects have also been linked to social and linguistic characteristics of both listeners and speakers. Shuy and his coworkers at Georgetown University investigated the attitudes of college students in American universities toward the English speech of whites and blacks (Shuy 1969; Shuy, Baratz and Wolfram 1969). Their findings suggest that the more nonstandard varieties of English are evaluated more negatively regardless of the judges' language background. However, the intensity of the evaluations is less strong among the judges who themselves speak nonstandard varieties of English. Labov's (1966) study of the varieties of English spoken in New York City found them to be distinguishable in terms of the speakers' social class. In reviewing studies that used teachers as raters, Brophy and Good(1974) conclude that teachers too are negatively affected by nonstandard speech.

Williams and his associates at the University of Texas at Austin conducted a series of studies in which teachers were asked to evaluate the language and personality of Anglo, Black and Chicano children (Williams, 1970, 1973a, 1973b; Williams, Whitehead and Miller, 1971a, 1971b; Williams, Whitehead and Traupman, 1971). They used a matched-guise technique in which videotapes of the children were paired with audio tapes in various combinations, so that both visual and vocal cues were controlled. Their findings demonstrated a similar set of correlations between the characteristics of the speakers and those of the teachers. In the first place, teachers gave different evaluations of Anglo, Black and Chicano children. Anglos received higher ratings than the rest and Chicanos recieved lower ratings than the other two groups. Secondly, they found the ethnicity of their judges to be related to their judgments in an interesting way. On a group of attitude scales related to ethnicity and standardness, teachers of all backgrounds evaluated Black and Chicano students more negatively than Anglo students, but Black teachers were more positive than white teachers in their evaluations of both Black and Chicano children. Finally, they found that the ratings also varied according to the social class of the speakers. For example, among middle class youngsters of all three ethnic backgrounds, the Chicanos were judged the least confident and eager. The ethnicity-standardness ratings for the low and middle class groups were lower for both Chicanos and Blacks than for Anglos of either class.

Several recent studies which examine accent variations among Chicano speakers of English demonstrate that the same evaluative polarities noted above for standard/nonstandard varieties of English apply to the scale of least-to most-accented English. That is, the more accented Chicano speakers of English consistently receive more negative judgments on both personality and linguistic rating scales. And these judgments are based on vocal cues alone!

These studies use a variety of techniques for identifying the speakers heard, including the three which will be considered here: categorical distinctions, in which speakers represent either accented or nonaccented varieties on English; a modification of the matched-guise technique described above; and a scaled paradigm, in which the speakers are ranked by independent methods from least-to most-accented.

Ryan and Carranza (1975) asked Anglo, Black and Chicano female high school students in Chicago to rate personalities of male speakers of standard English and Spanish-accented English. While their design distinguished between home and school contexts and significant differences were found between the two, their more general finding, which is that the standard English speakers were assigned more positive ratings in all of the scales used in both contexts, illustrates the strength of this correlation.

Politzer and Ramírez (1973) report that both Chicano and Anglo children give more negative ratings to accented varieties of English than to standard English on a single-speaker matched-guise design. In another study employing the same technique, Arthur, Farrar and Bradford (1974) also found that more negative ratings on some evaluative scales were related to the more heavily accented varieties.

Galvan, Pierce and Underwood (1975, 1976) used both paired-comparison and criterion-referenced techniques to scale the speech of Spanish accented Chicano college students. They too found that judgments on both personality and language scales are related in polarity to the degree of accent apparent in the English of the speakers. Significantly, the judges were teacher candidates specializing in the teaching of secondary school English. Ryan and Carranza (1977) report on a study by Ryan, Carranza and Moffie (1977) in which they found increases in accentedness to be associated with increasingly negative reactions about personal and speech characteristics of the speakers. This was based on a sample of Anglo college student raters. Their scale was determined by two methods different from those used by Galván et al. (1975); however, Galván, Lodmer, Ochsner, Plummer, Telatnik and Walter (1977) speculate that degree of accentedness can be determined by a variety of methods with similar results.

Several conclusions can be drawn from these studies. First, people do consistently distinguish among accent varieties. Second, these differences in accentedness correlate in a disturbing way with the judges' attitudes toward the speakers (i.e., the more accented speakers receive the least favorable ratings). Third, even individuals who will be working intimately with language in the classroom (i.e., high school English teachers) are influenced by degrees of accentedness.

Future research should replicate studies of language attitudes and accentedness such as the Galván et al. studies (1975, 1976) and Ryan, Carranza and Moffie (in press) with more and/or different controls. Attitudes in different regions of the country should be investigated. One study underway examines this issue with respect to Texas and California (Galván et al., 1977). Teachers from different backgrounds should be included in future studies. For example, would teachers from different language backgrounds perceive accentedness in the same way as Anglo teachers do? Accent variation among speakers of other languages should also be investigated.

Some questions remain. How are these attitudes realized in teachers' classroom behavior? Also, what can we as teacher trainers do to monitor and perhaps alter these attitudes and behavioral patterns? These questions guide the discussion that follows.

Changing Teachers' Behavior

We have just seen that accent variations affect even those individuals who should be least affected by them. We have also seen that teachers' attitudes strongly influence their classroom behavior. Since it is possible that teachers' attitudes toward accented individuals may also influence their classroom behavior, the issue of teacher training needs to be addressed.

There is some indication that making teachers aware of their attitudes toward student characteristics, perhaps to include accentedness, may be impetus enough to begin altering their behavior (Brophy and Good, 1974). However, Tuckman, McCall and Hyman (1969) found that the mere provision of information by itself is not as effective in changing teacher behavior as when it is accompanied by details about their classroom conduct. In a study designed to assess the effects of various approaches to changing teacher behavior, four groups of high school teachers representing three treatments and a control group were compared. Tuckman et al. were interested, first, in determining whether teachers whose self-perceptions of their teaching behavior were different from external observations of their behavior, would alter (a) their perception, (b) their behavior or (c) both their perception and their behavior. Secondly, the study sought to evaluate three different methods of providing teachers with information about their classroom behavior.

The three treatments studied were audio tape recordings of the teachers' classrooms, training in Interaction Analysis (IA), and direct verbal feedback based on IA observations of their behavior. Teachers in the first group listened to unedited tape recordings of three different lessons, but received no critical commentary from the researchers. The second group was trained in a modified system of Interaction Analysis. The remaining group was provided with specific input from observers regarding their classroom behavior vis-a-vis IA. Although all the teachers in the study were monitored by trained IA observers, the difference between the second and third groups is that the third group received the interpretation of the results from an external source, while the second group did not. Although they were trained in IA procedures (Flanders 1970), there was no requirement that they analyze their own teaching. The control group received no feedack of any kind.

Tuckman et al. (1969) found that the verbal feedback treatment produced the most significant change in teaching behavior when compared to the control group, especially among teachers whose perceptions of their teaching differed greatly from an objective analysis. While this research does not address the question of the relationship between student characteristics and teaching behavior, its relevance to this review lies in its implications for changing behavior in the classroom.

Other studies have assessed the usefulness of various means of producing changes in teaching behavior. Jacoby (1976) discusses the positive results obtained by combining student evaluations of teaching (SET) with specific behavioral prescriptions for change. He found that teaching could be improved by identifying teachers' strengths through SET and then cataloguing the particular behaviors which those teachers felt had produced their high ratings in given categories. These activities were then prescribed for teachers who had been rated low in those categories. On subsequent SET reports the low-rated teachers showed improvement in these categories.

Several studies have tried to define the carry-over effects of training teachers to use observation instruments. Moskowitz (1968) found that training foreign language teachers (both pre-service) in the use of various systems of Interaction Analysis influenced both their attitudes and their classroom behavior. In reviewing eighteen projects that used IA to help modify teaching behavior. Flanders (1970) concludes that a program of initial attention to teaching activities, followed by practice in analyzing teaching behavior combined with performing it with feedback, tends to incorporate such behavior in teachers' repertoires.

In a study designed to assess the effectiveness of a "minicourse" on improving classroom discussion techniques, Borg (1969) found that teachers did in fact change their classroom behavior. By using a delayed post treatment measure, he also found that teachers retained most of the skills acquired in the mini-course. Other means of changing teaching behavior include videotape feedback (Olivero, 1972) or evaluation by outside observers using objective instruments such as the Instrument for the Observation of Teaching Activities (IOTA) (Bradley, Kallenbach, Kinney, Owen and

Washington, (1973). In a study which examined the use of two ESL observation instruments (one of which was used on the IOTA model), Bailey (1976) found that teachers benefit from having an active role in the evaluative process.

All of these approaches to improving teaching behavior attempt first to make teachers aware of their behavior in some way, and then to provide them with alternative behaviors. Although relatively little has been done as yet to investigate changing teachers' attitudes toward language variation, there is strong evidence that teachers' classroom behavior can be altered positively.

Further investigations of teacher attitudes and behavior are also needed. Observational studies of classroom interaction should be designed to document the behavior of those teachers whose attitudes toward accentedness have been found to be the most positive and the most negative. Following up on the Galván et al. (1976) report, pre and postmeasures of teacher attitudes with university coursework as the treatment need to be compared. Likewise, similar studies utilizing training with a feedback component as the treatment are needed to assess the various strategies for changing teachers' behavior.

The relationship between teachers' classroom behavior and teacher attitudes toward students has been considered. Second, research on accentedness has been surveyed which suggests that more heavily accented individuals are perceived more negatively by teachers. It was speculated that teachers' attitudes toward accentedness may be reflected in their classroom conduct. Next, findings were presented which suggested effective strategies for changing teachers' classroom behavior. Now it is necessary to consider the implications of this research for teacher training.

University Education of Prospective Teachers

In this essay we have seen that teachers' attitudes are often realized in inappropriate or problematic classroom behavior. We found that teachers not only perceive differences in accent but that they also express more negative attitudes toward more heavily accented individuals. The main conclusion that can be drawn from this information is that there is an obvious need to know more about this problem.

Nevertheless, it is our feeling that the university education of prospective teachers should include coursework which will make them aware of their cultural biases. The findings of the Galván et al. (1976) study suggest that there is a slight difference in attitudes toward accented speech between teachers who had taken courses in sociolinguistics and those who had not. While the obtained difference was not statistically significant, the absolute improvement is not known since no pretest measure was administered. It should be noted that since these results are inconclusive, further study is needed. However, our initial interpretation of the data suggests that coursework of a culturally broadening nature may help to make teachers aware of their attitudes. We concur with Brophy and Good (1974) that becoming aware of one's attitudes is a first step in changing one's behavior.

Based on this review we are prepared to make some recommendations about teacher training curricula:

1. Teacher candidates should receive courses in sociolinguistics, especially those dealing with language variation, and first and second language acquisition. Such courses would supplement exposure to minority culture already offered in many schools of education.

2. Student-teaching programs should continue to include a feedback component. There are two reasons why this is important. The first is that the student teaching experience seems to be an ideal time for instilling new awareness in teachers (Moskowitz 1968). The second reason is that there is little supervision of teachers after completion of their university preparation (Brophy and Good 1974; McNeil 1971). These factors accentuate the need for continued emphasis on supervision during teacher training.

3. There should be further use of objective instruments for analyzing classroom interaction utilizing Tuckman's (1969) findings with respect to feedback strategies. During their student-teaching experience teachers should receive direct verbal input bases on objective data about their classroom behavior.

To the extent that these three factors are already a part of the teacher training curricula, many institutions have in fact begun to address the question of teacher attitudes and behaviors. We would hope that as more is learned about accentedness and language variation in general, these specific issues would be incorporated into a prospective teacher's education.

In-Service Training

Ideally a teacher's education should not end with the credentialing process. Indeed, for dealing with the kinds of issues we have raised in this essay, mini-courses at the in-service training level would provide an effective vehicle for making teachers aware of their attitudes and behavior, and for effecting the kinds of changes which may be desirable. There are several reasons for considering in-service training as a means of dealing with these problems.

1. In-service training is pragmatically oriented. Workshops are normally geared to the application of theoretical models rather than to intellectual inquiry.

2. Such workshops offer a more intensive treatment of a topic in a shorter period of time than is provided in university courses. In-service training programs make it possible to reach teachers who have not had exposure to the kinds of culturally broadening activities described above. Regrettably, this group comprises the majority of teachers in the field.

3. Another advantage of in-service workshops is their specialization. Because they are usually designed by school districts to concentrate on one topic, it is possible to localize the orientation. For example, the cultural components of in-service courses would be very different in a Navajo reservation school and in Dade County, Florida.

4. Finally, in-service training programs can address the immediate problems teachers face in the classroom on a daily basis. They can provide teachers with problem solving strategies geared to their own classrooms, their own individual needs vis-a-vis their students, and any other "real world" concerns.

Given the framework just described, we can reconsider the issue of teachers' attitudes toward accentedness and their resultant behaviors. We can envision an in-service training program to include a sociolinguistic component which would involve language variation and accentedness as they relate to the specific community. Discussions and demonstrations could be used to help teachers become aware of stereotypical views on nonstandard dialects. The cultural component, which is already included in most districts' in-service workshops, would complement this linguistic training.

In-service training, however, should also include direct feedback to teachers. Easy access to videotaping equipment makes it possible for many school districts to provide teachers with unbiased information about their actual classroom behavior. The coding processes involved in Interaction Analysis and other observation systems also provide teachers with objective information about their behavior. If training faculty members in such systems is not feasible, independent outside observers can be called in to observe classroom interaction. Although it is more subjective, input from principals, supervisors, and peers has been shown to be useful in changing teachers' behavior. Peer visitations could be built in as the feedback component of most locally planned workshops. Finally, student evaluations of teaching should be considered in any in-service training program designed to help teachers improve their teaching.

In-service training programs that include linguistic and cultural information, and direct feedback to teachers, could do much to help credentialed teachers improve their classroom performance. As more information becomes available through research on teacher behavior and attitudes toward accentedness, our schools will be better prepared to help teachers deal effectively and fairly with linguistic minority children.

Notes

1. The term "salad bowl" was used by Bambi Cárdenas at a meeting on Chicano education held by the United States Commission on Civil Rights in San Antonio, Texas in March 1974.

References

Arthur, B., Farrar, D., & Bradford, B. Evaluation reactions of college students to dialect differences in the English of Mexican Americans. *Language and Speech*, 1979, *22*, 255-274.

Bailey, K. M. The use of two observation instruments in supervised ESL teaching. Master's thesis, University of California, Los Angeles, 1976.

Baird, S. J. Employment interview speech: A social dialect study in Austin, Texas. Unpublished doctoral dissertation, University of Texas, Austin, 1969.

Borg. W. B. The minicourse as a vehicle for changing teacher behavior--the research evidence. Paper presented at the American Education Research Association symposium, Los Angeles, 1969. (ERIC Document Reproduction Service No. ED 029809)

Bradley, R., Kallenbach, W., Kinney, L., Owen, V., & Washington, E. A design for teacher evaluation. *National Elementary School Principal*, 1963, *42*, 32-37.

Brophy, J. E., & Good, T. L. *Teacher-student relations: Causes and consequences.* New York: Holt, Rinehart and Winston, 1974.

Brown, B. The social psychology of variations in French Canadian speech styles. Unpublished doctoral dissertation, McGill University, 1969.

Flanders, N. A. *Analyzing teaching behavior.* Reading, Mass.: Addison-Wesley, 1970.

Galván, J.L.; Lodmer, E.; Ochsner, R.; Plummer,. D.; Telatnik, M.A.; and Walter, G. A comparison of the accented speech of seven Spanish-English bilinguals speakers. *UCLA Workpapers in Teaching English as a Second Language*, 1976.

Galván, J.L.; Pierce, J.A.; and Underwood, G.N. Relationships between teacher attitudes and differences in the English of bilinguals. *Proceedings of the Southwest Areal Language and Linguistics Workshop IV.* San Diego: California State University, 1975.

Galván, J.L. The relevance of selected educational variables of teachers to their attitudes toward Mexican American English. *Journal of the Linguistic Association of the Southwest*, 1976, *2*, 13-27.

Good, T.L. & Brophy, J.E. Analyzing classroom interaction: A more powerful alternative. *Educational Technology*, 1971, *11* (10), 36-41.

Jacoby, K.E. Behavioral prescriptions for faculty based on student evaluations of teaching. *American Journal of Pharmaceutical Education*, 1976, *40*: 8-13.

Labov, W. The social stratification of English in New York City. *Urban Language Series, No. 1.* Washington, D.C.: Center for Applied Linguistics, 1966.

Lambert, W. A social psychology of bilingualism. *Journal of Social Issues,* 1967, *23,* 9-109.

Lambert, W.; Anisfeld, L.; and Yeni-Komshian, G. Evaluational reactions of Jewish and Arab adolescents to dialect and language variations. *Journal of Personality and Social Psychology,* 1965, *23,* 84-90.

Lambert, W.; Hodgson, R.C.; Gardner, R.C.; and Fillenbaum, S. Evaluational reactions to spoken language. *Journal of Abnormal and Social Psychology,* 1960, *23,* 44-51.

McNeil, J. *Toward accountable teachers: Their appraisal and improvement.* New York: Holt, Rinehart and Winston, 1971.

Moskowitz, G. The effects of training foreign language teachers in interaction analysis. *Foreign Language Annals,* 1968, *1,* 218-235.

Olivero, J.L. *Self-evaluation via videotape feedback: One method for improving teacher performance.* Albuquerque, New Mexico: Southwestern Cooperative Educational Laboratory, Inc. 1972.

Politzer, R.L. & Ramírez, A.G. *Judging personality from speech: A pilot study of the attitudes toward ethnic groups of students in monolingual classrooms.* Stanford University, Center for Research and Development in Teaching, R&D Memo No. 107, 1973.

Preston, M.S. *Evaluational reactions to English, Canadian, French and European French voices.* Master's Thesis, McGill University, 1963.

Rosenthal, R. & Jacobson, L. *Pygmallion in the classroom: Teacher expectations and pupils' intellectual development.* New York: Holt, Rinehart and Winston, 1968.

Rowe, M.B. Science, silence and sanctions. *Science and Children,* 1969, *6,* 12-13.

Ryan, E.B. & Carranza, M.A. Evaluative reactions toward speakers of standard English and Mexican-American accented English. *Journal of Personality and Social Psychology,* 1975, 31, 855-863.

Ryan, E.B. & Carranza, M.A. Ingroup and outgroup reactions to Mexican-American language varieties. In H. Giles (Ed.), *Language, ethnicity and intergroup Relations.* London: Academic Press, 1977.

Ryan, E.B.; Carranza, M.A.; and Moffie, R.N. Reactions toward varying degrees of accentedness in the speech of Spanish-English bilinguals. *Language and Speech*, 1977, *20*, 267-273.

Saville-Troike, M. *Foundations for teaching English as a second language: Theory and method for muticultural education*. Englewood Cliffs, New Jersey: Prentice Hall, Inc., 1976.

Shuy, R.W. Subjective judgements in sociolinguistic analysis. In J.E. Alatis (Ed.), *Linguistics and the teaching of Standard English to speakers of other languages or dialects, No. 22*. Washington, D.C.: Georgetown University Press, 1969.

Shuy, R.W.; Baratz, J.C.; and Wolfram, W. *Sociolinguistic factors in speech identification*, Report No. MH 15048-01. Washington, D.C. National Institute of Mental Health, 1969.

Thompson, R.M. *Social correlates of regional pronunciation in Mexican-American English*. Paper presented to the Linguistic Society of America. Ann Arbor, Michigan, 1973.

Tucker, R.G. & Lambert, W. White and Negro listeners' reactions to various American English dialects. *Social Forces*, 1969, *47*, 463-468.

Tuckman, B.W.; McCall, K.M.; and Hyman, R.T. The modification of teacher behavior: Effects of dissonance and coded feedback. *American Educational Research Journal*, 1969, *6*, 607-619.

Williams, F. Psychological correlates of speech characteristics: On sounding 'disadvantaged'. *Journal of Speech and Hearing Research*, 1970, *13*, 472-488.

Williams, F. Some recent studies of language attitudes. In R.W. Shuy (Ed.), *Some new directions in linguistics*. Washington, D.C.: Georgetown University Press, 1973a.

Williams, F.; Whitehead, J.L.; and Miller, L. *Attitudinal correlates of children's speech characteristics*. Final Report USOE Project OEG-0-70-7868 (508). Austin: The University of Texas, Center for Communication Research, 1971a (ED 052 213).

Williams, F. Ethnic stereotyping and judgments of children's speech. *Speech Monographs*, 1971b, *38*, 166-170.

Williams, F.; Whitehead, J.L.; and Traupman, J. Teachers' evaluations of children's speech. *Speech Teacher*, 1971, *20*, 247-254.

Nonstandard Dialect: Research and Treatment
by John Edwards

The Status of Nonstandard Dialect

Thanks to the efforts of linguists and others, nonstandard dialect is seen more and more for what it is--a valid, rule-governed system which cannot be judged in terms of linguistic inferiority or superiority. This is, however, quite a recent development; the validity of dialect took longer to establish (where it has been established) than that of language. It is still possible to find people who agree that statements like "German is better than French" are ludicrous, but who would be uncertain of, or would actually accept, the proposition that (for example) "New England English is better than Alabama English." What is accepted at the language level is not always accepted at the dialect level--although, linguistically, dialect validity is a logical extension of language validity (see Trudgill, 1975). Still, the very term "non-standard", a nonpejorative label, represents a great advance over "substandard."

A second line of defense, as it were, against the equivalence of dialects has been that some are aesthetically more appealing. Thus, although dialect inferiority can no longer be justified on strictly linguistic criteria, it might rest upon aesthetic ones. Here, however, social psychologists have convincingly demonstrated that our perceptions of what is aesthetically pleasant are usually confounded with our knowledge and perceptions of speakers' social status. This is easily grasped at an anecdotal level: Stage a play in which a prominent surgeon speaks with a thick Bronx accent, and you achieve comedy. This only works because the audience knows something about both speech variations in English and how these customarily relate to speaker status. The social-psychological demonstrations here involved asking judges who did not know the speech community concerned to make ratings of the aesthetic quality of different languages and dialects. They were unable to find significant differences in these terms, between varieties which, for the members of the speech communities themselves, were clearly differentiated in terms of speaker status and prestige (see Giles, Bourhis, Trudgill & Lewis, 1974; Giles, Bourhis & Davies, 1975; see also Trudgill, 1983). Out-of-context aesthetic differences simply could not be predicted. Thus, as an inherent feature of dialect or language, aesthetic difference, like linguistic difference, cannot reasonably support evaluations of inferiority or superiority.

There is a third possibility here which, by eliminating the linguistic and aesthetic arguments, is seen to be the real basis for judgements about dialect difference. It is simply sociopolitical power, prestige, or status. The speech patterns of prestigious, respected, or majority-group individuals are the ones which are themselves respected and associated with favourable traits like competence and ambition; they form the "standard." Put in this way, it is easy to see that dialect judgements are the result of social and historical dynamics. Thus, if Marseilles and not Paris were the capital of France, if the English royal court had gathered at York instead of London, and if Houston were the capital of the United States, then received notions about standard French and English would not be what they are today.

This sort of discussion has animated what has become to be known as the linguistic "difference-deficit" controversy. The fact that linguistic and psychological evidence now supports the term "nonstandard" rather than "substandard" indicates that the difference position has, academically at least, won the day. There is, however, a danger that dif-

44

ference theorists are too optimistic about the likely results of their demonstrations. Within the academic community and, to a growing extent, within the educational field generally, difference has (quite rightly) triumphed over deficit. But, in the larger society, old established views are slow to change. Although politicians and other manipulators constantly talk of the need to "educate the public" and to "change people's attitudes," we know that these tasks are just about the most difficult to achieve. To expect a person or a group to change a longstanding opinion simply on the basis of reasoned, documented argument is to be very naive. Therefore, with regard to language and dialect, we should always be aware that ruling out linguistic or aesthetic deficit does not rule out what we may call social deficit. And, if society at large believes dialect A to be in some sense inferior or nonprestigious, then--given that we act upon our perceptions--dialect A is deficient for all practical purposes.

Therefore, the bulk of the linguistic and psychological work on dialect has had the effect, essentially, of ascertaining the basis of social judgement. It is, of course, extremely important to know that there is no linguistic or aesthetic foundation to ratings of dialect validity or "goodness" and to know that differential evaluations relate to differing perceptions of speakers, and have nothing to do with speech per se. But this only clarifies the issue; it certainly solves nothing. Furthermore, in my view, no solution to the social deficit of certain dialects is likely to occur in stratified communities. For, where you have status/occupational/prestige differences within society and where, also, you have dialect variation, the two are linked. Perhaps the most important feature of the linkage is the enshrining of a standard as "correct" in print. This ensures a continuous reinforcement of the standard. The linkage does not, of course, take exactly the same form in all societies. In America, for example, there is a wider range of acceptable accent than in Britain. A heart surgeon may have a Texas rather than an educated New England accent, and a president may betray his Texas, Georgia, or Massachusetts background. In Britain, surgeons sound remarkably similar regardless of their regional origins, and there is often little accent difference between Labour and Conservative leaders. This is because there is no overarching American R.P. (received pronunciation) as there is in the United Kingdom. However, even within the greater "acceptable" American accent range, there is only minor dialect variation.

Thus, there is no reason to think that nonstandard dialect is quickly going to lose a pejorative tone simply because of psychological and linguistic evidence. This simple fact--that social deficit will continue to be a feature of some dialects--is of the greatest importance in education. For, even assuming that we have teachers who no longer make the erroneous equation of standard with "correct," we must still consider the function of schooling in the larger social context, a context which may place the nonstandard speaker at a disadvantage.

Educational Treatment of Nonstandard Dialect

There are three aspects here which I shall touch upon: (a) nonstandard dialects of foreign languages, (b) nonstandard dialects within the same language, and (c) nonstandard dialects and bilingual education. It is the third which is the most relevant here, but the others are not unrelated.

When children learn a foreign language at school, in the traditional way (i.e., as another subject), there is usually little difficulty in deciding that the standard variant of that language is the desired goal. This is especially true when little thought need be given to actual face-to-face interaction with foreign speakers. Here, it can be argued that ability in the variety which is written is likely to be the most useful for most pupils. However, when there is a real possibility of using the language orally, the dialect question emerges. A North American example of this has to do with English Canadians learning French: should they be taught Quebec or European French? The matter would seem to be clearer if we restrict discussion to those English speakers living in Quebec, and clearer still if we restrict ourselves further to those learning French by "immersion." Yet even here there is room for argument about the type of French to be taught.

A second aspect has to do with the educational treatment of nonstandard-speaking youngsters in what has traditionally been a standard-reinforcing school. A familiar example is Black English in the United States. Given what we now know of dialect validity, but also being aware of the low status of Black English in a social sense, what should schools do? We know what schools always used to do--they insisted that students accommodate linguistically to standard norms that were thought to be correct (see Edwards, 1981a). Although often admitted to be harsh treatment, this was justified as being in the students' best interests. Since they came to school speaking incorrectly, it was clearly the role of education to improve their language. Nowadays, however, one can at least raise the argument that schools should do the accommodating, and there is no doubt that this is the logical extension of the linguistic and psychological findings on dialect. But logical extensions are possible only within systems of logic, and society at large is not such a system. Thus the counterargument is possible: schools should still teach the standard (to black youngsters, for example) because failing to do so would put children at a disadvantage when they leave the more enlightened world of the school for the one outside. However, this need not mean a return to the attempted stamping out of the child's maternal variety; rather, it can involve what many have termed "bidialectalism."

The school is now to acknowledge that there is nothing wrong with the nonstandard variety but, at the same time, indicate to the students the usefulness of repertoire extension. We have, then, a policy of addition rather than one of replacement. This is a delicate undertaking if we wish to avoid, however subtly, stigmatizing the nonstandard dialect. It has the the great advantage, though, of attempting to deal with linguistic matters realistically, for it represents an effort to inform the student along the lines indicated here in the first section. Bidialectalism need not involve any active teaching of the nonstandard variety nor, for that matter, does it require any species of language "drill" in the standard. It can be built upon: (a) the evidence that nonstandard-speaking children are, from an early age, able to comprehend and use the standard, (b) a real awareness, on the part of teachers, that the nonstandard is a dialect of equal linguistic validity to the standard, (c) the good linguistic sense of all speakers, who come to realize that different aspects of the repertoire are called for in different situations, and (d) teachers acting as standard-speaking models (among the many accessible to nonstandard-speaking children) (see Edwards, 1979).

Bidialectalism is, I believe, a realistic aim for schools since it represents the type of linguistic flexibility which we know people possess. The nonstandard speaker whose speech patterns change between home and office, and the variations we all use when speaking to spouse, children, milkman, boss, etc. demonstrate a linguistic ability which can support bidialectalism at school. However, just as these operate at a "natural" or unforced level, so school practice should not stigmatize either standard or nonstandard. A child, clearly, should not be penalized for speaking nonstandard dialect, but neither is there any educational value in having, as some have suggested, nonstandard reading material.

This brings me to the third aspect of nonstandard treatment at school, and the one of direct concern here--nonstandard dialect and bilingual education. Although many bilingual programs make provision for majority-language children, the major thrust in the United States has been towards minority-group children having access to education in their own language. Let us consider a Spanish-English bilingual program. For native English speakers, the issue becomes that discussed above as aspect (a): should these children learn a standard Spanish-- a norma culta--or a nonstandard variety? For the Spanish-speaking youngsters, the situation is that of aspect (b): studying through their own language, should they learn via standard or nonstandard? Two factors are important here. First, we know that most children's native Spanish will not be a standard one itself. Second, the very concept of a standard becomes confused, and we can at least consider the notion of regional standards. A Spanish speaking child in the Southwest may speak a variety which is, in the broader scheme of things, nonstandard. However, within what may be the large and concentrated area of the child's own speech community, this variety may in fact be "standard." This is not quite the same situation as may apply to a nonstandard-English-speaking child, for here, contact with standard speakers is likely, and therefore the maternal variety can easily be termed nonstandard. In the case of a minority language, however, all of the speakers of that language who are likely to be encountered by a child are probably going to be nonstandard users themselves. Now, if all speak a nonstandard dialect then the very concept of nonstandard itself changes. The issue is, of course, confused by the fact that not all the nonstandard speakers will necessarily use the same nonstandard Spanish.

In these circumstances, what is the most reasonable course for the school to follow? I believe that it is to treat the nonstandard Spanish as standard. Given the obvious differences (which obtain for all speakers) between oral and written language, this need not lead to any "cutting-off" of children's access to the wider, standard Spanish community; this will be effected through facility with standard written Spanish. I see little point, however, in promoting an oral "standard" which will not, in the lives of most children, have any marked benefits and which may, in fact, negatively affect in-group solidarity and speech community cohesion.

Bilingual Education, Group and Society

As soon as we talk of such matters as in-group solidarity and cohesion, we confront the issues of bilingual education and social dynamics. This is especially apposite in discussions of the use of nonstandard vernaculars since these often centre upon a role of education extending well beyond the school grounds -- the role, in fact, of assisting in the cause of an enduringly pluralinguistic society. The school, it is argued, can help maintain group identity, particularly through communicative language support. There is no doubt that schools typically do this; we have only to look at the ongoing function of the school within majority society to see that it acts as a processor, conveyor and supporter of group values and behavior. But how does this operate when the education is bilingual, when the school is in some sense a go-between for majority and minority interaction?

I have already written about this topic and, to avoid repetition, will only advert briefly to the major point here (see Edwards, 1976, 1977, 1980, 1981b, 1982, in press-a, in press-b). This is simply that schools are more a reflection of larger group relations than leaders of social change. It is an egregious mistake to think that we can use schools to maintain aspects of minority lifestyle (including language) when external support is lacking. The failure of Irish schools to revive Irish in society at large is perhaps the clearest contemporary example of this (see Edwards, in press-c). I do not of course, rule out the possibility of education assisting in larger social movements, but is must be pointed out that many proponents of bilingual education see the role of school as much more than assistance.

Let us suppose that bilingual schools for Spanish speakers do reflect accurately the desires of the community. A strong Spanish-speaking minority in which Spanish functions as the communicative language across a broad range of domains will naturally want to see school as one of these domains. In this sense the school--particularly if it operates in the vernacular of the community--acts exactly as do schools for majority populations (at least in terms of linguistic medium). Three points then suggest themselves, which I think will be reasonably considered by all but the most fanatical of linguistic nationalists: (a) will such a process lead to a prolonged "ghettoization" of a population or, to put it another way, is segregation the price of permanent pluralism?; (b) how strong is community support for such bilingual education (in its "maintenance" format)? Are there signs of a generational gap, with the younger community members showing increasing desires to move into the "mainstream"?; (c) how does the process resemble the efforts of other ethnic minority groups in the United States? (see Edwards, 1981, 1982, in press-b).

All of these points can be discussed together. The historical evidence suggest that minority groups in the United States have typically been more assimilationist than many apologists would like to believe (Drake, 1979, in press). The attractions of mainstream society--which presumably prompted emigration in the first place--prove formidable and lead to the shifts in language and behaviour of which we are well aware. It can be argued that, for such a large and often concentrated group as Spanish speakers, a best-of-both-worlds scenario can occur; the rewards of American life can be gained without loss of certain group markers. But is this argument historically shortsighted? Other groups also have started from positions of concentrated strength, and at least one other group, Franco-Americans, also have had continued access to the homeland and new infusions of immigrant strength. These groups typically had strong school, media, church, and society support for ethnic identity. Where is it now? It is more correct to say that it abdicated responsibility or was crushed by official mainstream pressure. It would seem, in fact, that even the strongest and most cohesive groups in America show patterns of increasing assimilation over time, with the exception of some whose lifestyles and wishes (often religiously oriented) demand segregation (see Fishman, 1966). Naturally, the time scale is different for different groups, but the outcome seems remarkably similar.

None of this, of course, means that we cannot support bilingual education. It does, however, necessitate placing bilingual education in a broader historical perspective, if only to avoid unfortunate excesses which history will render naive. Further, there is the possibility that a failure to come to grips with group dynamics, desires, and movement may result not just in programs which, in the long term, may be thought to leave identity essentially unaffected, but may also actually damage it. I have described elsewhere a French-English bilingual program which terminated, leaving in its wake a cynicism which extended beyond those features of identity which it specifically addressed (Edwards, 1976, in press-b).

Failure of bilingual education to alter patterns of group movement towards assimilation does not mean that the loss of identity is inevitable. Although this is the warning often given by proponents of bilingual education, it neglects an important distinction in ethnic group life--that between private and public markers of ethnicity. The history of ethnic group adaptation to life in America shows a gradual lessening in importance of public and visible markers, presumably because these interfere with desired movement into the mainstream and subsequent upward mobility. Private markers of identity remain, however, for precisely as long as they are wanted (they are not, it will be noted, susceptible to outside intervention or support). In this sense, support for language often involves two misunderstandings. The first is that language is essential to continued identity; the second is that communicative language (a public marker) is inseparable from symbolic language (a private one) (see Eastman, in press; Edwards, 1977, in press-b).

To cite again the Irish case, we can see that a strong and continuing sense of group or national identity need not rely upon possession of an ancestral language for regular communicative purposes. Yet, to proceed to the second and related point, it would be inaccurate to say that Irish has no significance for those who no longer speak it. It has a very real symbolic value and in that way is an important part of identity. In the United States, bilingual education programs have been set up in the belief that communicative language is all-important for identity, and that schools can meaningfully sustain it. This is misguided for it shows a lack of historical awareness and, very often, a lack of understanding of a group's adaptive patterns to a new life. I am not suggesting that Spanish is necessarily going to recede to a strictly symbolic medium in the near future. My point is simply that any sort of language planning (including programs of bilingual education) should involve a sense of perspective in both a historical and a cross cultural sense (useful recent treatments of matters discussed here may be found in Gleason, 1979, in press; Higham, 1975, 1982; Mann, 1979).

Future Directions

For bilingual education there remain many unanswered questions of implementation, technique, and evaluation. The role of nonstandard dialect is one of these, and it is also one which leads to a consideration of more important issues concerning the place of bilingual education in the assimilation-cultural pluralism debate. The linguistic validity of nonstandard dialect is proven, but this in itself says nothing about its uses at school. Group identity, language maintenance and ethnic markers--these are matters of the first magnitude.

I have noted before that, in the highly charged arena of minority education, these matters are often treated in an unobjective way which neglects large social and historical forces. Therefore, the most important aspect of further exploration is a disinterested examination which places bilingual education in its full context. I suggest that only when the historical, sociological, psychological, linguistic, and educational parameters are given due consideration will fully rational discussion of bilingual education be possible. This will, among other things, clarify the role of the nonstandard dialect at school.

References

Drake, G. F. Ethnicity, values and language policy in the United States. In H. Giles & B. Saint-Jacques (Eds.), *Language and ethnic relations*. Oxford: Pergamon, 1979.

Drake, G. F. Problems of language planning in the United States. In J. Edwards (Ed.), *Linguistic minorities, policies and pluralism*. London: Academic Press, in press.

Eastman, C. M. Language, ethnic identity and change. In J. Edwards (Ed.), *Linguistic minorities, policies and pluralism*. London: Academic Press, in press.

Edwards, J. Current issues in bilingual education. *Ethnicity*, 1976, *3*, 70-81.

Edwards, J. Ethnic identity and bilingual education. In H. Giles (Ed.), *Language, ethnicity and intergroup relations*. London: Academic Press, 1977.

Edwards, J. *Language and disadvantage*. London: Edward Arnold, 1979.

Edwards, J. Critics and criticisms of bilingual education. *Modern Language Journal*, 1980, *64*, 409-415.

Edwards, J. Psychological and linguistic aspects of minority education. In J. Megarry, S. Niset & E. Hoyle (Eds.), *World yearbook of education 1981: Education of minorities*. London: Kogan Page, 1981. (a)

Edwards, J. The context of bilingual education. *Journal of Multilingual Development*, 1981, *2*, 25-44. (b)

Edwards, J. Bilingual education revisited: A reply to Donahue. *Journal of Multilingual Development*, 1982, *3*, 89-101.

Edwards, J. The social and political context of bilingual education. In R. Samuda, J. Berry & M. Lafferriere (Eds.), *Multicultural education in Canada*. Toronto: Allyn & Bacon, in press. (a)

Edwards, J. (Ed.). *Linguistic minorities, policies and pluralism*. London: Academic Press, in press. (b)

Edwards, J. Irish and English in Ireland. In P. Trudgill (Ed.). *Language in the British Isles*. Cambridge: University Press, in press. (c)

Fishman, J. A. *Language loyalty in the United States*. The Hague: Mouton, 1966.

Giles, H., Bourhis, R., Trudgill, P. & Lewis, A. The imposed norm hypothesis: A validation. *Quarterly Journal of Speech*, 1974, *60*, 405-410.

Giles, H., Bourhis, R. & Davis, A. Prestige speech styles: The imposed norm and inherent value hypotheses. In W. McCormack & S. Wurm (Eds.), *Language in anthropology IV: Language in many ways*. The Hague: Mouton, 1975.

Gleason, P. Confusion compounded: The melting pot in the 1960s and 1970s. *Ethnicity*, 1979, *6*, 10-20.

Gleason, P. Pluralism and assimilation: A conceptual history. In J. Edwards (Ed.), *Linguistic minorities, policies and pluralism*. London: Academic Press, in press.

Higham, J. *Send these to me*. New York: Atheneum, 1975.

Higman, J. Current trends in the study of ethnicity in the United States. *Journal of American Ethnic History*, 1982, *2*, 5-15.

Mann, A. *The one and the many*. Chicago: University Press, 1979.

Trudgill, P. *Accent, dialect and the school*. London: Edward Arnold, 1975.

Trudgill, P. *On dialect*. Oxford: Blackwell, 1983.

The Dialects

Chicano Spanish: Varieties, Styles and Functions

by Rosaura Sánchez

Introduction

At a time when educators continue to report that bilingual students of Mexican origin (hereafter also called Chicanos) are dysfunctional in both Spanish and English and for that reason underachieving in school, it becomes necessary to distinguish between language competence and conceptual development. It is true that language is the essential vehicle through which we handle conceptual material and that linguistic form and conceptual content are inseparable. But it is equally true that an individual may be fluent in his native language and yet be illiterate. This individual might be classified as "dysfunctional" in an academic setting where he would be expected to read and write and yet no one would venture to analyze his problem as one of language. Whatever his age, this individual would be seen as having the capacity to become literate and develop those skills that he had heretofore not had the opportunity to develop; in fact the problem would be seen as arising from economic and social conditions were this a peasant in a monolingual country. Linguists and psychologists have long recognized the capacity of all human beings to acquire new skills given the appropriate conditions (Cole and Scribner, 1974). Literacy programs throughout the world, and especially those in Cuba after the Revolution, have demonstrated the capacity of individuals to acquire literacy skills given appropriate instruction (MDJ, 1974).

In the case of bilingual Chicano students, the focus on language by educators and politicians has been an easy way of evading the issue: the failure of our public schools to stimulate the development of conceptual skills in either English or Spanish for a large number of Chicano students (Keller & Van Hooft, 1982). If we recall that all human beings have the innate capacity to structure language or a semiotic system and that all school children come to school with a mental grammar for each language that they speak, then the school's task becomes that of further developing the grammar or grammars through the child's acquisition of concepts, vocabulary, and more complex language structures. These children are not dysfunctional at the age of six; they are ready to learn. They only become dysfunctional if they are academically and conceptually starved.

Bilingual students of Mexican origin often come from homes where Spanish is the dominant home language. Studies like those of Skutnabb-Kangas have indicated that migrant children (in her study, Finnish children in Sweden) who migrate after the age of 10, that is, after developing basic skills in their native language in their native land, do better in school than those who migrate at an earlier age and are forced to acquire a second language before developing a conceptual base in their first language (Skutnabb-Kangas, 1979). Clearly, Spanish-speaking students should be developing this conceptual base in Spanish before being mainstreamed and placed in classrooms where English is the medium of instruction. Instruction in Spanish, however, should be oriented toward the acquisition of cognitive skills and not toward the reinforcement of the school district's notion of "Hispanic" culture nor toward the eradication of nonstandard forms. As students acquire additional concepts and the necessary vocabulary and forms with which to verbalize these concepts, they also will augment their language repertoires with additional varieties of Spanish. Time allotted for language arts classes should be directed toward the development of cognitive skills in specific academic areas (geometry, math, history, geography, literature, government), thereby ensuring the acquisition of additional vocabulary and language functions within academic contexts. These lessons must be accompanied by intensive student practice in verbalizing the concepts and lexicon acquired.

The teacher's task should be to develop code shifters, individuals who are able to shift from one code or language variety to another whenever the situation, topic, addressee, or language function calls for it. For that reason, it is important that all teachers working with bilingual or bidialectal students become familiar with language variation in their own repertoire so that they can lead the students to become conscious of variation in their own speech. As students become aware that shifting within one language is a common process that they already practice, as does any native speaker in the world, they will be on their way towards the acquisition of additional codes and concepts, in one or both languages.

Chicano Spanish

The Southwest of the United States has a large Spanish-speaking population of Mexican origin. Although this population becomes increasingly English dominant and eventually English monolingual with younger native-born generations, the continual immigration of Mexicans to the United States, the concentration of the population in low-income urban residential areas, and occupational segregation have ensured the maintenance of the language not only among older and recent immigrants but among segregated barrio residents as well.

Spanish-language T.V. (S.I.N. = Spanish International Network) contributes significantly to the establishment of a U.S. Spanish-language network and to the notion of a Spanish-language community which transcends state and national borders while surrounded by a majority English-speaking population. Spanish-language radio, although local in nature, has a more immediate impact on radio listeners and serves as the major means of wider communication among housewives and workers, particularly in those shops and work sites where the radio is on continually. Spanish-language newspapers, wherever available, are an additional community link with Mexico and the rest of Latin America. Thus Spanish-language media, although not offering the opportunity to verbalize in Spanish since participation is primarily at a passive receptive level, has accomplished an important goal: language contact between Chicano listeners and Mexican and other Latin American speakers, however limited the viewing or listening time among younger Chicanos.

Media also offers receptive contact with the Spanish varieties of many Latin American nations, especially with a standard Mexican media Spanish. The inclusion of Argentinian, Venezuelan, Mexican, and Puerto Rican soap operas over T.V. has familiarized a number of Chicano viewers with the expression and particular intonations of these Latin American speakers.

This passive reception however does not significantly affect the oral production of most U.S. Spanish speakers just as the English standard variety broadcast over U.S. media does not produce significant changes in the speech of black English speakers. Spanish interaction is thus still limited for the most part to informal and intimate contexts where family and community patterns of speech predominate.

It is this informal and intimate Spanish that children and adolescents bring to school. Technical and more formal varieties often are lacking as there is little opportunity for contact with these varieties in daily interaction. With the exception of media and churches, there are few instances where formal varieties are the primary medium of interaction in the Southwest since English is the language of government, work, media, recreation, and school. There are thus few opportunities to develop Spanish-language skills for technical and formal functions.

What follows are some of the more salient characteristics of informal and intimate Spanish varieties, all of which can serve as the basis for the development of additional varieties and more extensive vocabularies as cognitive skills are developed in the language and as students are able to function in Spanish in broader contexts.

Spanish of the Southwest

The Spanish of the Southwest is a dynamic language with a great deal of diversity and its own internal organization and stratification. The language in some cases has suffered periods of isolation from the Spanish metropolis to the south and periods of intensive contact with newly arrived Spanish-speaking immigrants. Throughout its survival as a functional language of the Southwest it has changed and adapted in its contact with the dominant language of the land, but these changes have followed the structural organization and rules of the Spanish language. Its most salient characteristic is the adoption of a number of loan words from English, much as the Spanish language at one point adopted numerous Arabic terms and later numerous terms taken from the languages of American Indians. Clearly a functional, vital language must adapt and evolve with social changes if it is to survive. The incorporation of loanwords is a common phenomenon throughout the world whenever there are two or more language groups in contact. Generally the subordinate language will incorporate terminology from the dominant language. In the case of the Southwest, English initally incorporated the ranching and mining vocabulary used by Spanish-speaking cowboys and miners who settled in the area before the arrival of Anglo-Saxon settlers. Later as these settlers became the dominant force, it was the Spanish language that incorporated numerous terms. These loanwords from English are common in other Spanish varieties of the world. What is unique here is that the greater contact with English and the bilingual situation have made the borrowing process quantitatively greater in the Southwest.

Linguistically and demographically, the borrowing phenomenon is quite clear. Ideologically, it also is not surprising that the politically and economically prestigious language has had an impact not only on the lexical component but on the degree of code shifting as well. Only social and political change which improved the status of the Spanish language and allowed for regular infusion of Spanish language instruction and cultural events could ever change the linguistic situation and decrease the need for borrowing and code shifting. What is remarkable is that speakers from Latin American countries and from Spain generally lack an analysis of the situation and inevitably blame the Chicano Spanish speakers for their need to resort to loanwords. Nor is there any degree of realization that the Chicano Spanish speaker has found ways within his Spanish language system to deal with new situations that call for terms which he has never heard in Spanish and, more important, that this speaker has succeeded in forcing the English language into a Spanish mold rather than succumbing to use of the English language system.

Before exploring further the type of borrowing that has occurred in the Spanish of the Southwest since 1848, we will look first at the language diversity that is present in the speech of this population of Mexican origin, coming from various parts of Mexico and of long-and short-term residence in this country. The Mexican-origin population is spread throughout the country but concentrated in the Southwest, with a large community in the Pacific Northwest and in the Midwest. Although today over 80 per cent of persons of Mexican origin reside in urban areas and only between 7 and 8 percent of the Chicano work force are classified as farm workers by the census bureau, the rural roots of a large percentage of the Mexican-origin population are traceable within this century to Mexican rural communities or to farm-working families in the United States. Recent studies of Mexican women working in border runaway shops (las maquiladoras) and of undocumented laborers indicate a large rural to urban migration within Mexico before immigration to this country. Mexican urbanization undoubtedly will affect future Spanish varieties of the Southwest, but for now evidence of rural variants continues to be present in the speech of Spanish-speaking Chicanos throughout the Southwest, particularly in the language of second-and third-generation Chicanos who continue to speak the Spanish language. In some cases recognition of these rural variants has led to a conscious decision not to speak the language in front of strangers or persons considered to be "educated" and likely to laugh at rural variants.

The rural Spanish of the Southwest stems largely from rural varieties in Mexico. That both Southwest and Mexican rural varieties share numerous characteristics with the rural varieties of the rest of Latin America is no surprise since the original Spanish immigrants and their descendants who did not form part of the urban conglomerates developing in Latin America were to have similar agricultural, ranching, and mining experiences despite national and regional differences. Thus the weakening of voiced fricatives (estado-estáo; luego-loo-lo), the loss of final consonants (usted-usté), the simplification of clusters (doctor-dotor), the aspiration of sibilants (los-loh; nosotros-nohotros), the aspiration of the labiodental voiceless fricative (fueron-hueron), and various other phonetic changes which characterize rural varieties of northern Mexico and the Southwest can be found throughout the Spanish-speaking world.

The rural variety of popular Spanish is not homogenous throughout the Southwest, however. In some areas, particularly rural areas that have been characterized by isolation, archaic forms no longer current in urban speech are notable. Thus forms like "truje,""vide,""ansina," and "haiga" can be heard not only in New Mexico and West Texas but in Arizona, Colorado and Central California as well. Other rural varieties are characterized by phonetic and morphological variants. Consider, for example, the following sample recorded by Yolanda Róblez in Texas:

"... y tamién me gustaban los días que llovía porque esos días tamién este no teníanos que ir a trabajar y me la pasaba allí por las casas platicando con toda la gente pero más los ... especialmente los muchachos. Y tamién me gustaba en la noche porque nos juntábanos, un grupo nos juntábanos y nos sentábanos debajo de ese árbol."

Here Yolanda has recorded the events recalled by a Chicana student whose family was once part of the migrant stream. Both Yoianda and the student recorded were University of Texas at Austin students at the time of the recording.

In this particular sample, the shift of the first person plural morpheme in imperfect tense verbs is evident. This variant, as has been discussed before, occurs in verb forms with stress on the antepenult syllable ("esdrújulas") and includes the conditional, present subjunctive, imperfect subjunctive and imperfect indicative forms. In the case of the present subjunctive forms, stress shift has also occurred as a result of verb stem regularization.

Standard forms:	Popular rural forms:
imperfect: juntábamos	juntábanos

pres. subj.: volvamos	vuélvanos
Imperfect subjunctive: volviéramos	volviéranos
Conditional: volveríamos	volveríanos

These forms, however, do not exist in all rural speech varieties. Other rural verb variants exist also in urban popular Spanish. Before going on to a discussion of urban speech, consider the following composite sample which incorporates a number of rural variants noted in both Texas, New Mexico, and California recordings:

Cuando nohotros éranos chicos los juimos a las piscas a Tahoka. Yo no iba salida antes de mi pueblo y me gustó muncho el paseyo por otros rumbos. Mi apá trujo a toa la familia en una troca grande y allí atrás dormíanos y comíanos. Si no juera sido por esa troca no sé que biéramos hecho. Mi apá quería que studiáranos pero tenía que sacarnos por dos o tres meses cada año pa que le yudáranos. Mi apá me dijía: Mira, hijo, si yo biera ido a la escuela no andábanos acá afanando.

We will note first the phonetic variants in this sample:

a) Aspiration of sibilants: nosotros-nohotros decía-dijía
b) aspiration of initial f- : fuimos-juimos
   fuera-juera
c) lateralization of nasal: nos - los
d) epenthesis (insertion of a sound): insertion of palatal glide between
   a hiato (two vowels forming two syllables): paseo-paseyo
e) loss of intervocalic voiced fricative: toda-toa
f) Apheresis (loss of initial sounds): estudiáramos-studiáramos
                                          ayudáramos-yudáramos
                                          hubiera-biera
                                          hubiéramos-biéramos

The sample also includes the morphological -mos to -nos shift:
      éramos - éranos
   dormíamos - dormíanos
    comíamos - comíanos
  estudiáramos - studíaranos
   ayudáramos - yudáranos

The sample also includes an auxiliary variant noted in Texas: iba for había and the use of fuera for hubiera in imperfect subjunctive tenses:
      "Si no fuera sido"   for   "si no hubiera sido"
Also included in the sample is the use of the imperfect indicative for the conditional:
      Si yo hubiera ido a la escuela no andábamos acá afanando.
The use of both auxiliary forms was noted in the speech of Texas students who wrote:

Si fuera sabido, no hubiera venido.
Si fuera sabido, no fuera venido.
Si hubiera sabido, no hubiera venido.
Si sabía, no hubiera venido.

The sample also includes the archaic trujo and muncho with an epenthetic nasal. The apocope of "para" to "pa" is of course not only rural but urban as well, as is use of the loanword "troca," common throughout the Southwest and along the Mexican border.

As Chicanos migrated to urban areas or were able to reside all year in their urban homes, especially after World War II as mechanization reduced the need for farm workers, they took their rural speech patterns along. Contact with other urban residents and with incoming Mexican immigrants and the increased educational attainment of Chicano youth has undoubtedly affected the Spanish of the Southwest. In some cases these changes led to language shift and decisions to eliminate Spanish as the language of the home in order to give youngsters a better chance at school. In other cases it led to a dynamic bilingualism as children went from a Spanish language home environment to an English dominant school and work setting daily. Adaptation of English school terms to Spanish has been common among Spanish speaking students not only, as is often thought, because the lack of Spanish instruction did not allow for familiarity with the Spanish equivalent, but often because it was "smart" to do so. The more loans one coined the smarter one felt for not sticking to the "English only" rule while still dealing with the same subject. As contact with the English language increased and as individuals came to function primarily in English during a major part of the day, code-switching in the Spanish language environment ensued. English as the dominant language entered and often took over the domains previously controlled by Spanish. In some cases, both languages came to share the same domain, with parents often using Spanish and their children responding entirely in English.

Given the lack of instruction in Spanish, it was easier to resort to English when one discussed a technical or formal topic, since for that language function English was the frequent and often only language used. Code-switching, however, has never been limited to formal or technical functions. It often functions in intimate and informal situations where Spanish is the dominant language as a means of joking, verbal clowning, putting others at ease and establishing comradery among Chicanos. In a situation where switching is condemned by language purists, code-switching becomes an expression of group assertion and a rejection of linguistic norms established from outside the group.

Urban popular varieties share a number of phonetic variants with rural Spanish, although certain morphological and lexical variants from rural Spanish are absent here. A few morphological variants however are shared by both urban popular Spanish, as we shall see in the excerpts that follow from a dialogue presented by Alfredo Mancha of Odessa, Texas. As will be evident in the dialogue, urban and rural forms come together in an urban setting situated in a relatively isolated rural area. What is notable here is the incorporation of caló, a youthful urban style used primarily by Chicano males, with a number of loanwords common in the popular speech varieties of all Southwest Spanish speakers. Caló is characterized by lexical innovations, over-coding (metaphorical extensions of meaning), and the use of slang ("jerga") common in the slangs of other Latin American countries and said to derive from Romany, the Gypsy language.

Mancha's dialogue:

Un día andaba yo por la calle cuando me pasó un camarada en su carrucha. Me pasó y me pitó, pero yo no supe quién era hasta después de que paró.

"¿Qué pasó, Fred?" oyí yo después de que había backeado el carro después de que se había parado.

"¿Qué pasó?" le contesté sin saber quién era.

Entonces él abrió la puerta del carro y se aprendió la lucesita de adentro.

"¡Eeese Chivo! ¿Qué pasó? Le grité yo con mucho entusiasmo, "¿Qué andas haciendo, vato? ¿Qué pasó?," ya que lo conocí.

"Pos aquí nomás. ¿Y tú? ¿Cuándo llegates?"

"Pos nomás ando maderiándola. Apenas llegué ayer. ¿Pa dónde vas?"

"Pa ninguna parte. Aquí nomás ando maderiándola como tú. Súbete. Vamos a pasiarnos."

Y con eso me subí en la ranfla y nos fuimos a dar la vuelta. Anduvimos por el barrio watchando la movida, tú sabes, nomás jugándola fría. Watchamos a otros vatos que también andaban maderiando y watchamos también a unas chavas que también andaban nomás pasiándose. Periquiamos un rato y luego se nos metió a ir a echarnos unas cuantas heladitas.

"¿Para dónde vamos a pistiar?" le pregunté al vato como ya tenía mucho tiempo que no andaba yo por allá, "¿A dónde vamos?"

"Vamos al Holiday Inn, hombre. Allí tá de aquella para ir a pistiar."Entonces llegamos al "Holiday Inn."

"¿Está de aquella aquí, Chivo?" le pregunté yo como nunca había pistiado allí yo.

"¡Sí, hombre! Está a toda madre. Especially en los weekends cuando viene mucha gente," me contestó el vato.

"Qué de aquella," le digo yo patrás. "¡Shhiitt Yeeeaa!"

Y con eso nos metimos al congal. El lugar estaba poco grande. En una parte estaba un billar donde podías a vacilar pool si querías. En otra parte estaba la barra donde te servían vironga o wine o sodas. Estaba poco grande la bar y luego tenían un fregal de mesas en frente y, más por allá, otras al otro lado de donde bailaban unas go-go- girls cada vez y en cuando. Tenían una pianola y estaba bien oscuro para que se watchara de aquellas. Estaba a toda madre.

(The two friends begin drinking and talking to others; I will skip down to another part)

Y con eso pidimos otras dos. "Qué toda madre," pensé yo. Pasó un tiempecito, y después otras dos. Y luego, otras dos y otras dos, y otras dos.

"Chivo. ¿Qué...qué si ya no pudiéramos a pistiar aquí a gusto como dos carnales - así como estamos 'horita mismo?" le pregunto yo en un tono de vacil pero en seriamente también.

"¿Cómo...dices tú?" me dice porque de de veras no me había entendido como ya andábamos muy gastados los dos.

"I mean,...¿qué si 'tuviera así como cuando nos corrieron del parque nomás porque andábamos pistiando todo el tiempo? What would it be like si un perráo estuviera afuera whatchando over quien sale para persiguirlos?"

"No sé...yo creo... Pues no sé, pero tú sabes que no está así."

"Sí, ya sé, pero ¿qué si si ?"

"Pues...no sé, pero sé que estuviera bien gacho. Bien gacho de-a-madre." y lo dijo con una risita que me decía que no le gustaría. "Pero...¿por qué preguntas?"

(the two friends end up discussing the language of Chicanos)

"¿Cómo pasó que nosotros estamos hablando así como estamos hablando?" repetí yo para segurarme de lo que me había preguntado.

"Sí, ¿cómo pasaría que yo y tú hablamos como hablamos?"

"Bueno, pues...eso se puede ver por varias ventanas. Cada persona puede verla diferente porque cada uno es diferente. Pero con respeto a eso, sí hay una historia de como hemos llegado a hablar como hablamos ahorita mismo. Una historia que es realmente nuestra interpretación do lo que ha pasado en nuestras vidas por años y años y que se refleja en el modo de como hablamos nosotros."

"Interprecíón...o,o-he-he-he. Ya ni puedo hablar la fregada, he, he he. Interpretación. ¿Cómo dices tú, interpretación?"

"Bueno, pues cada uno tiene su modo de ver a las cosas así como dije. Pero como muchas veces somos iguales en muchos respetos - a veces comemos más o menos las mismas comidas, hablamos la misma o las mismas lenguas, vivemos en casas similares - tú sabes, cosas así. Los soul brothers con su soul food, nosotros con los parrales y las tortillas, tú sabes. Y como somos iguales en muchos modos, también munchas veces pensamos más o menos las mismas cosas. Y como pensamos igual en muchas veces, también formamos opiniones o puntos de vista de muchas cosas."

"Oyes, ¿cómo dices tú que en veces pensamos las mismas cosas?"

"O...pos, por ejemplo, ponle los farmworkers. Tú y yo y casi todos los camaradas pensamos que es bueno y que andan haciendo pedo - ¿verdad? Y también vemos que nosotros debemos de ponernos más trucha también - ¿verdad? No digo que no hay excepciones, pero sí digo que, como si alguien tomara un voto de opiniones en eso de lo de los farmworkers o de lo de nosotros, que nosotros vatos así como yo y tu saldríamos pensando más o menos las mismas cosas en esa vez."

"O dale pues. Al cabo que ya te entiendo cómo dices tú."

(this conversation is interrupted by another friend)

"Ah sí, ¿verdad? Te estaba platicando de cómo periquiamos nosotros así como periquiamos, ¿verdad Chivo?"

"O, a la brava."

"Bueno, pues, lo que estaba dijiendo yo era que nosotros tenemos un historia de como llegamos hablar así como hablamos y ahorita... chicano...No es español como el castillano, o como el que se habla en Mejicles. Pero nosotros ya también tenemos palabras nuevas, palabras como 'carrucha,' 'parquiar, 'deaquellonas'. Y así es que estas palabras y este modo de hablar son de nosotros. Nosotros vatos de aquí, del 'Chuco, de Los Angeles, o del valle."

"Sí, dale."

"Como sabemos nosotros, el guato de que nosotros hablamos en cualquier forma viene de nuestros jefitos. Y así es que para contar la historia de cómo hemos llegado hablar así como hoy día, tenemos que ver atrás con los jefitos do los de nosotros, a jefitos de ellos, y sas y sas hasta que ya no puédamos. Pero vamos a comenzar con los tiempos cuando había pura sangre india todo por aquí. Yo creo como en unos tiempos habían muchas tribas - tú sabes, tribes - que vivían por sierras y montañas así como todavía hay 'horita mismo en México - que no han cambiado casi nada por los años. Y de poco a poco se juntaron. Chansa pacá tuvieran porasos así como nosotros -"

"O, ese vato."

"No - a la brava -"

"Si, hombre. Yo sé. Nomás te estaba cabuliando. Dale, síguele."

(the conversation continues with a discussion of the history of Mexico and the Southwest.)

Mancha's dialogue is a linguistic gem because it allows us to see a sample of urban popular Spanish laced with a few rural variants, and interested by loanwords, codeshifting, popular slang, and caló. Within the popular speech of this speaker there are various stylistic shifts. Thus the speaker shifts from the standard *estuviera* to the popular *tuviera*, from the popular *carro* to the slang *carrucha* and on to the caló *ranfla*, from the standard *muchas* to the rural *munchas* and later to the familiar *un fregal*. There are at least three styles evident in the dialogue: representational, informal, and familiar.

Representational style (the usual narrative style characterized by the use of Standard forms):

"¿Qué pasó?" le contesté sin saber quién era.

Informal style (characterized by popular variants and used to establish a friendly, informal atmosphere):

"Pos aquí nomás. Y tú, ¿cuándo llegates?"

Familiar style (the endo-group style characterized by use of slang and caló which functions as an element of cohesion, uniting addresser and addressee as members of the same group): "Y con eso me subí en la ranfla y nos fuimos a dar la vuelta. Anduvimos por el barrio watchando la movida, tú sabes, nomás jugándola fría."

Within the familiar style, there is an additional subcategory which requires code-shifting and functions to call attention to the topic at hand, in this particular case, but could function in various other ways to produce a comical, satirical, or ironic effect or to produce understatement or even to make amends: In Mancha's dialogue, it merely calls attention to the seriousness of the proposed oppression:

"I mean,…que si 'tuviera así como cuando nos corrieron del parque nomás porque andábamos pistiando todo el tiempo? What would it be like si un perráo estuviera afuera watchando over quien sale para persiguirlos?"

Shifts in style occur at the phonetic and lexical level but rarely at the morphological level. Thus a speaker who shifts from *ahorita* to *horita* or from *pa* to *para* or from *decir* to *platicar* to *periquiar* will generally not shift from *vuelvamos* to *volvamos* nor from *salemos* to *salimos*, although, of course, it is quite possible. Shifts in style occur with shifts in speech acts and language function as well as with shifts in addressee and topic.

As is evident, there are a number of phonetic shifts that are common in all popular varieties of Southwest Spanish, whether rural or urban. The appearance of an epenthetic glide (oí - oyí), the diphthongization of hiatos (pasear - pasiar), the reduction of the diphthong ue to o in *pos* (pues-pos), the simplification of consonant clusters (respecto-respeto), the aspiration of the sibilant (diciendo-dijiendo), the loss of initial sounds (asegurarse-segurarse; estuviera-tuviera; ahorita-horita) and the closing of mid vowels in forms like *perseguirlo-persiguirlo* to follow the stem change in *persiguiendo* are all common forms in both rural and urban varieties of popular Spanish. The confusion of fricatives b- and g- before the semi-consonant w- is also common in popular speech (boato-guato).

Morphologically, the rural -nos verbal forms are not present nor are there any archaic verbal forms. But there is a common rural verb variant present: *llegates*. Recordings of other Chicanos and Mexicanos in Texas and California indicate that the form *llegastes* is common in popular Spanish, whether urban or rural. The variant *llegates* thus appears to be primarily rural. Consider the following forms:

Standard:	llegaste	dijiste	fuiste
Urban:	llegastes	dijistes	fuistes
Rural:	llegates	dijites	fuites

The second-person singular morpheme -s in standard Spanish changes to -ste in the preterit tense. This one exception is seemingly eliminated in popular Spanish where -s is added after the -ste suffix:

Standard: lleg-a -ste
Popular: lleg-a -ste-s

In rural Spanish the suffix is then reduced to -tes, perhaps through aspiration and loss. The fact that *llegastes* exists would tend to indicate that it is not a case of metathesis.

Another verbal variant common in popular Spanish is the vowel-shifted first-person plural form in -er verbs. Example: *vivemos*.

"a veces *comemos* más o menos las mismas comidas, *hablamos* la misma o las mismas lenguas, vivemos en casas similares - tú sabes, cosas así."

As is evident, the three infinitive forms (-er, -ar, and -ir) are reduced to two in the present tense:

Verb Form	Standard	Popular
-ar	hablamos	hablamos
-er	comemos	comemos
-ir	vivimos	vivemos

This vowel shift is simply a regularization of the tense rule. When we consider that the thematic vowel -e shifts to -i in the preterit, so that these forms become indistinguishable from -ir verb forms, then it is logical that the -ir verbs should indicate present tense by shifting the -i to -e:

Standard	Popular
salimos	salemos
dormimos	durmemos
venimos	vinemos
vivimos	vivemos

Note that stem shifts also occur in some cases.

The dialogue also includes a few loanwords, some of which are quite widespread and used in northern Mexico as well, like *carro* and *chansa*. Others are more particular to the speech of young Chicanos, like *watchando* (from *watching*), *porasos* (from *party* + augmentative suffix), and *backeado* (from to *back up*). In these cases the English term is adapted to Spanish phonetic and morphological rules. Loan translations are also common in the speech of young Chicanos, as in "jugándola fría" from "playing it cool." When in doubt, one can always coin one's own loan. In the case of *tribas* the speaker is unsure about his choice, and so he offers the English *tribes* immediately afterwards.

What characterizes this dialogue between two young males and their friends is the sprinkling of slang terms throughout the dialogue. The two domains--the street and the Holiday Inn bar--call for a familiar style and for the need to appear as "cool" and "hip." In only a few cases can the slang be termed part of the caló style for often those terms that one might associate with the speech of young *vatos* (dudes) have become part of general slang and are used by young and old, male and female alike. We would then have to classify caló as a subgroup of general slang, with caló being limited, in most cases, to the speech of males, particularly young males, and characterized by a particular lexical component and lexical innovations that are often incoporated later into general popular urban Spanish. Thus in this dialogue, few terms could be called strictly caló, although some are more generally associated with this urban style. In this dialogue, use of the demonstrative *Ese* for *tú* is a specific caló marker. Thus *Ese vato*, loosely translated as "Hey, you" or "Hey, guy," signals the beginning of a particular style and a particular relationship between the addresser and addressee. The term *vato* is becoming quite common and not strictly restricted to caló users. The term *ranfla* for *car* is also considered caló, according to my 'Chuco informants, as would be the case of *congal* for *bar*, *parrales* for *beans* and *vironga* for *beer*.

These few caló terms, like the other slang lexical terms to be reviewed, fall under one of six categories:

a) loanwords

b) metaphors - the use of one word or phrase denoting one kind of object or idea used in place of another to suggest a likeness or analogy between them.

c) metonymy - the use of the name of one thing for that of another of which it is an attribute or with which it is associated.

d) synecdoche - a figure of speech by which a part is put for the whole, the whole for the part, the specie for the genus, the genus for the species, the name of the material for the thing made.

e) phonetic and morphological adaptations of Spanish words, as in *Mejicles, escuelín,* as well as the use of homophonous substitutions.

f) the use of standard forms not common in the Southwest.

These associations and meaning extensions are of course determined by and operate within a specific speech community.

The caló term *vironga* is thus a loanword with an added suffix:
beer-bir-bir + onga

The suffixes -onga, -ón, onte, -ín, -cles, for example, are only a few of the humorous derivational suffixes used in slang. The term *ranfla* is probably another loanword, from *rumble*, possibly as in *rumble seat*. This would also be a case of syneedoche where the part (the seat) stands for the whole (the car). *Congal*, on the other hand, is a case of metonymy, where the Cuban dance associated with nightclubs and bars comes to stand for the place itself, with an additional -al ending added as in the term for shack, *jacal*. The term *parrales* is a bit more difficult to analyze since a *parra* is a grapevine and its fruit is the grape, not a bean. Perhaps it is simply a metaphor with "beans" being compared to "grapes," indirectly, through process of synecdoche, the whole (the vine) for the part (the grape).

Caló's penchant for innovation allows for the transformation of highly frequent words through the addition of nonsense suffixes or even for the substitution of one word for another provided it has a homophonous beginning and appears within a set phrase. Consider phrases like those below which do not appear in this dialogue:

"Ay nos vidrios" for "Ahí nos vemos."

"¿Ontables?" for "¿Ontabas? (i.e., ¿Dónde estabas?)"

"¿Qué pasión?" for "¿Qué pasó?"

Other cases of caló include the use of standard terms that are not common in the Southwest language commuity. Consider the following phrase:

"Le apañó la vaisa a la güisa."

Here "vaisa" is a loanword (from "vise") used metaphorically (as "hand") and güisa, a caló term for "girl." The verb apañar, on the other hand, is a standard form meaning "to take with one's hand" but the fact that it is not common in the Southwest qualifies it as an innovative term.

The other slang terms which appear are widespread and not limited to the caló style. These also follow the general categories established before. Carrucha, for example, is an adaptation of the loanword car which gives the word carro, and is then further adapted through the addition of the derrogatory suffix -ucha. The term carrucha exists in standard Spanish as well, but with the meaning "pulley." The word maderiando is a metaphorical extension of the term madera ("wood"), converted into a verb maderear to mean "to fool around" or in some cases, "to flatter." The term periquear ("to talk") from the noun perico ("parrot") is an association of the bird's speech attribute with human speech. Other terms like carnal ("brother" "friend"), bien gacho ("the pits"), a toda madre ("great"), vacil vacilada ("b-s"), hacer pedo ("to cause trouble"), and jefito ("little chief"- meant endearingly - for "father") are common in the popular Spanish of the entire Southwest and Mexico.

Caló and other slang terms are rich in figurative language, a fact that needs to be exploited in the classroom, since these terms can serve as the basis for developing skills in language analysis as well as allow teachers to develop language games where students can see the need and their ability to switch from one style or language variety to another, according to a number of social and linguistic factors present in the interaction.

The dialogue also includes a few cases of code shifting. The process involves shifts from one language system to another with all phonological, morphological, syntactic, and semantic rules within that system preserved. Even one-word shifts constitute acts of code shifting if the shift follows these rules. Loanwords which have been adapted to the grammatical system of the borrowing language are not cases of code shifting. Thus when the speaker in the dialogue says "después de que había backeado el carro," he is not code shifting, as backeado is a loan, adapted to the Spanish verb morphology and phonological system. But when the second speaker says, "Está a toda madre. Especially en los weekends cuando viene mucha gente," the shifts to especially and weekend are complete shifts to the English grammatical system. If the term weekend were pronounced with Spanish vowels and stress, (huiquén), then it would not be a shift, of course.

Codeshifting, as we already indicated, has numerous functions in the bilingual Chicano community. In this dialogue shifts occur not only as part of an informal comradery between two young male peers, but as a reiteration of the seriousness of a topic. This function is of course a direct result of the social and political dominance of the speakers of the English language. Syntactically, there is one case which allows us to see how both systems operate when the linguistic contexts of the two languages are not similar. Consider the following example:

"What would it be like si un perráo estuviera afuera watchando over quien sale para persiguirlos?"

The speaker has already introduced this unreal situation in Spanish. After reiterating the "what if" proposition in English, he decides to continue in Spanish. Note that the shifts occur at the clause level:

What would it be like/
si un perráo estuviera afuera/

watchando over/
quien sale para persiguirlos.

Interestingly enough, the speaker, faced with the inability "to borrow" both verb and particle ("watching over"), retains "over" as a code-shifted item. Thus lexical rules appear to be dominant in both borrowing and shifting. These surfaces structure restrictions at times appear to produce in both languages.

Conclusion:

Any partial attempt to describe variants occuring in the Spanish of the Southwest inevitably produces distortions since focusing on the variants often leads educators and linguists to forget four significant facts:

1) The Spanish of the Southwest consists primarily of standard forms.
2) All Spanish-speaking areas of the world include a number of regional and social language varieties, and all speakers of any language are able to shift from one style to another or from one variety to another.
3) Most of the variants discussed here are present in the Spanish of other Spanish-speaking nations.
4) Loanwords are present in all languages of the world. The Spanish of Latin America and Spain include a number of loanwords from English. Only the degree of borrowing in the Southwest is higher, given the more intimate contact with the English language.

Teachers need to remember that once one knows a variety of a language, it is easy to acquire a second variety of the language; in fact it is easier to do this than to acquire an entirely new language since one has only to master a few rules to be able to shift from one variety to another at will. It is thus easier to acquire a standard variety of Spanish if one already speaks a popular variety than to acquire the English language or another second language. The important thing is the acquisitition of cognitive skills in one's own language, whatever that may be. The acquisition of English is a secondary matter for that will come quickly once it is initiated. What will not come later, if it is neglected from the start, is the cognitive development.

The fact that language shift occurs in the Southwest with younger generations of Chicanos needs to be examined in the context of language maintenance, which also occurs in the Southwest given the social, residential, and occupational segregation of the Mexican-origin population that continues to exist. It then becomes indispensable that schools know the areas they are serving in terms of language shifts and language maintenance so that school programs may be planned with the sociolinguistic needs of that particular population in mind. Whatever the native language or bilingualism of the community, let us remember that the student population arrives at school with the capacity to develop its cognitive skills. Only the school system and ultimately the teacher are responsible for the failure of these students to develop both language skills and critical conceptual skills at ever higher levels. The school, of course, cannot effect social changes since the school itself is an arm of the social and political system in power. We ask merely that it teach our students to read and write and compute and verbalize at a high, abstract level.

68

References

Cole, M. & Scribner, S. *Culture and thought.* New York: John Wiley and Sons, 1974.

Keller, Gary D. & Van Hooft, Karen S. A chronology of bilingualism and bilingual education in the United States. In Joshua A Fishman and Gary D. Keller, (Eds.), *Bilingual education for Hispanic students in the United States.* New York: Teachers College Press, 1982.

Ministerio de Justicia. *La mujer en Cuba socialista.* Havana. Cuba: Empresa Editorial Orbe, 1977.

Skutnabb-Kangas, T. *Language in the process of cultural assimilation and structural incorporation of linguistic minorities.* Rosslyn, Va.: National Clearinghouse for Bilingual Education, 1979.

Chicano English
by Gustavo González

Introduction

The purpose of the present article is to explore some of the facets of Chicano English and attempt to link these to the practice of teaching in bilingual or ESL classrooms. The words "some" and "attempt" are used advisedly. As the reader will realize, the linguistic phenomenon called Chicano English has many sides to it, the majority of which remain to be identified and described. Add to this paucity of information the increasing need to put our knowledge to use for the benefit of our limited-English proficient population, and you have a most unenviable situation, one which offers much promise but which also has its share of difficulties.

Among the problems one encounters very early in the study of Chicano English is what Baugh (1984) has called "the anguish of definition" (p. 3). Fernando Peñalosa (1980) acknowledges the lack of clarity in the current conception of Chicano English when he states: "The term Chicano English is ambiguous in that it may refer to all the varieties of English spoken by the Chicano, or it may refer to varieties of English spoken only by Chicanos" (p. 115). Sawyer (1970) viewed Chicano English as an interlanguage, a transitory state in the Chicano's voyage toward standard English. To her, Chicano English represents ". . . an imperfect state in the mastery of English" (p. 19).

Sawyer's observation suggests that the deviations characteristic of this "imperfect state" are brought about by having Spanish as a first language. In her view, then, Chicano English consists of those errors attributable to a Spanish base. Metcalf (1974), while acknowledging the role of Spanish in the development of Chicano English, nevertheless insists that it is more:

A variety of English that is obviously influenced by Spanish . . . but that nevertheless is independent of Spanish and is the first and often only, language of many hundreds of thousands of residents of California. (p. 53).

More recently, Gingràs (1978) has proposed that Chicano English is

. . . a type of creolized dialect of American English. There has been simplification (in the direction of Spanish) in the surface segmental contrasts as well as simplification of the stress system found in other American English (AE) dialects. The vocalic system seems to be emerging from a basic five-vowel system to a somewhat more complex six-vowel system that is still simpler than other AE dialects have. (p. 12)

This view is supported by Godínez (1984), whose work on the phonology of Chicanos in East Los Angeles led him to conclude

. . . rather than being primarily determined by interference from Spanish, Chicano English--at least that spoken in East Los Angeles--represents an autonomous social dialect with distinct characteristics passed on by mutual processes and linguistic transmission. (p. 45).

The controversy is best summarized by Peñalosa (1981) in his article on issues in Chicano sociolinguistics:

The main theoretical dispute here appears to be whether Chicano English, the fluent kind spoken by many as their first language, is simply English with Spanish interference, or whether it is a social variety which represents not imperfect learning of Standard English, but rather competent learning of a variety of English current and standard in the community. (p. 8).

At present, the meager research evidence will support either interpretation.

The debate over definitions is an indicator of the complex language situation of the Chicano in the Southwest. The Chicano population is linguistically heterogeneous, spanning the spectrum to include monolingual Spanish speakers, monolingual English speakers, and varying levels of bilinguals. Some claim Spanish as their first and stronger language while others claim to be native speakers of English; still others claim to have spoken both from the early years, often with a resultant minimal proficiency in each language. For public school teachers charged with educating these children, attempting to meet the needs of this diverse group can lead to confusion and frustration. Since pupils are as likely to come from homes and environments where English is a second language and there is heavy influence from Spanish as they are to come from families and neighborhoods where English is the primary-and sometimes the only--language spoken, it is best to consider Chicano English as encompassing both extremes. This will enable us to address a greater number of characteristics of this language variety and consequently make the teacher more aware of the complexity that is Chicano English.

The sections that follow focus on two major types of features found in Chicano English: those directly attributable to Spanish and those not traceable directly to Spanish but still not characteristic of the "Standard" dialect of English. The former would generally be associated with speakers whose first language is Spanish and who are learning English as a second language; the latter would more likely include those persons for whom English is the first and often only language. Research on the Spanish-influenced variety is considerable, while similar efforts on the less creolized version have barely begun.

Phonology

According to Ortego (1970) and Metcalf (1972), the most prominent characteristic of Chicano English is its phonology. Speakers of Spanish-influenced Chicano English (SPICE) tend to substitute the sounds of Spanish for English sounds. Thus, by comparing the sound system of Spanish with that of English, we can project which English sounds are likely to cause difficulty for the Spanish speaker learning English as a second language. Those English sounds not found in Spanish will be substituted for by the closest Spanish phonological equivalent. It must be emphasized that this procedure identifies potential areas of difficulty; no claim is made that every contrast possible will manifest itself in the speech of every Spanish-background child, since other factors such as age, length of exposure to English, and the role of Spanish in the early years would need to be taken into account.

Consonants

Among the consonants, perhaps the most well-known and most often quoted difficulty is that involving [č] and [š]. Speakers of SPICE initially substitute [č] for [š], since [č] is part of Spanish phonology and [š] in not (except in some dialects). At the word level, SPICE renders "wash" as "watch," "mash" as "match," "wish" as "witch," "share" as "chair," and "cash" as "catch." As the child's exposure to English grows, he learns to articulate the new sound and to use it in words where [č] is appropriate. It is not unusual for children at this stage to say "schiken" for "chicken," "shursh" for "church", and "shildren" for "children."

The latter situation has been attributed to hypercorrection, a phenomenon in language learning in which the learner substitutes the new sound in places where the original sound ([č] in the above case) was needed. The problem is one of differentiation: not only does the child have to learn to articulate the new sound, he has to learn how it fits into the emerging English system, especially in contrast with [č]. Stated differently, speakers of SPICE have to make room for both sounds [č] and [š] and learn which words call for which sound. It is not merely a question of learning to articulate a new sound, but to learn to use it only in situations calling for it and not as an indiscriminate substitution for the original sound. The new sound has to be accorded the status of a phoneme in the new language.

Control of the [š] - [č] distinction in English in isolated words does not assure that the child will be able to maintain such a distinction at the phrase or sentence level. Since the longer phrase or sentence unit may contain other new English sounds upon which the child must also concentrate, the child cannot focus his complete attention to producing just one sound correctly. A child who can correctly produce the minimal pair distinction "witch" - "wish" cannot be expected to automatically produce the [š] - [č] distinction in sentences like "The witch made a wish" or "Which shoes should she choose?" While distinguishing minimal pairs at the word level is an important beginning step, teachers should be aware that it is only a beginning, that successful performance beyond the word level cannot be assumed on the basis of performance at the word level.

A similar situation occurs with the affricate pair [č] - [ǰ]. The voiceless affricate [č] is familiar to speakers of SPICE, since it is part of the Spanish phonological system. Not so the voiced affricate [ǰ]. Like [š], it is a new sound whose articulation and role within the English phonological system must be learned. The tendency is for SPICE speakers to substitute [č] for [ǰ], since it is articulatorily the closest consonant sound to it. Speakers making this substitution will say "match" for "Madge," "Lecher" for "Ledger," or "batch" for "badge." The substitutions appear to be limited to word-medial or word-final position. Hypercorrection does not seem to occur with this contrast.

A third consonant pair that can cause difficulty for essentially the same reason is [t] and [θ]. The Northern Mexico dialect of Spanish, the closest in form to that spoken in the United States, does not contain the apico interdental [θ] in its sound system. As with the two preceding cases, the articulation of the sound and its appropriate use needs to be learned. At the earliest stages of learning English, substitutions such as "tin" for "thin," "bat" for "bath," "boat" for "both," and "tick" for "thick" can be frequent. Unlike the earlier situation with the affricates, the substitutions here seem to occur in all positions.

The three instances above concern the incorporation of new sounds--new both in articulation and function (phonemic, or meaning distinguishing)--into an emergent English sound system whose base is Spanish. Somewhat more complicated for the language learner are situations in which sounds that exist in his first language are also found in the second language, but with a function different from that carried out in the first language. I am speaking here of sounds that may be allophones in Spanish but are used as phonemes in English. The difficulty here is twofold. Aside from the change in roles (allophonic to phonemic), there will be changes in the phonetic environments in which the sounds are articulated in the new system. In a set of allophones belonging to the same phoneme, the phonetic environment determines which allophone will be articulated.

The sounds [s] and [z] offer a good example. In English, the two sounds are phonemes, as evidenced by numerous minimal pairs including "rice/rise," "race/raise," "price/prize," "sink/zink," "face/phase," and "sue/zoo." They serve to distinguish meaning: in the preceding examples the meaning is determined by which of the two sounds is used. The same two sounds in the Spanish system have a different relationship to each other: they are variants of the same phoneme. The occurrence of the variants will be determined by the phonetic environment. In this instance, the voiced variant [z] will occur in Spanish before a voiced consonant. Words like "mismo," "rasgo," and "desde" will contain the voiced allophone [z], while words like "sapo," "peso," and "casas" will have the voiceless allophone [s].

A speaker of SPICE will experience difficulty articulating the voiced allophone [z] in environments different from those in which it is found in Spanish. Thus, for example, a choice in utterance-final position between [s] and [z] will be decided in favor of [s]. For the teacher, the task is to accustom the child to pronouncing the [s] and [z] in a variety of phonetic environments consonant with the phonemic status the sounds will enjoy in the new English system. Hypercorrection is to be expected here, too, as the new sound begins to establish itself. Also, since [s] and [z] are not in contrast in Spanish, the use of one in place of the other does not change word meaning in spite of sounding somewhat out of the ordinary.

Somewhat more complicated is the case involving the English phonemes /b/ and /v/, rendered phonetically as [b] and [v] respectively. Spanish has one phoneme corresponding to that pair, namely the phoneme /b/, but this is phonetically represented by two different sounds depending on the phonetic environment. One of these sounds is the [b], a voiced bilabial stop, which occurs at the beginning of an utterance [Ven acá, "Come here"] and after a nasal sound [envenenar, "to poison"]. The second variant [ƀ], a voiced bilabial fricative, occurs in all other environments, such as intervocalically [robar "to steal;" lavar, "to wash"], or as part of a consonant cluster [árbol, "tree;" abrir, "to open"].

Using the Spanish sound system as a base, SPICE will begin with the phoneme /b/ and its two variants [b] and [ƀ]. In developing mastery of the English sound system, the speaker of SPICE will need to become accustomed to using [b] as a phoneme, that is, to using it in contexts other than those called for in the Spanish sound system. This would include English words in which [b] is found intervocalically but which in Spanish would require [ƀ], such as, for example, "about," "robber," and "labor." To further complicate matters, the situation calls for adopting a new sound which is phonetically similar but not identical to the voiced bilabial fricative already part of the Spanish sound system: the voiced labio-dental fricative [v]. (This situation is thus different from that described earlier involving [s] and [z]). The speaker must learn to use the new sound in phonetic contexts once reserved for the [b]. A case in point is the combination of [n] + [v]. English words like "invite," "envy," and "involve" would prove problematic: the speaker would tend to subsitute [b] for [v] in these environments, following the pattern in Spanish.

Finally, the speaker must be able to contrast the established variant [b] with the newly-acquired [v] in such pairs as "boat"/"vote," "bat"/"vat," and "robe"/"rove." Since in English the occurrence of [b] and [v] is not dictated by phonetic environment, the learner has to pay special attention to assure that the appropriate sound is assigned to new words as they become part of his vocabulary. The English writing system will be of some assistance here since the letters "b" and "v" always represent the [b] and [v] sounds respectively.

Another case involving sounds that are phonetically similar and which differ in phonemic status in Spanish and English is that of [d] and [ð]. In English these two sounds comprise different phonemes, as in "den"/"then" and "dare"/"there." Spanish has one phoneme corresponding to this pair, the /d/, which consists of two phonetically determined variants. One of these variants, [ð], is identical in place and manner of articulation to the English sound. The second variant,[d],differs, from the English [d] in having an apico-dental (as opposed to apico-alveolar) point of articulation. Persons whose first language is Spanish may at first substitute the dental stop [d] for the alveolar stop [d]. They may also find it difficult to articulate the sounds in environments different from those of the Spanish system. For instance, a Spanish speaker, unfamiliar with the use of [ð] in utterance initial position, would be inclined to use [d] instead. The speaker of SPICE would be faced with learning to articulate a sound slightly different from one he already uses and with learning to use it contrastively with [ð]. This latter part would involve articulating each of the sounds in all contexts, in particular those that do not correspond to the environments in Spanish.

Consonant Clusters

Differences between the languages involving individual sounds and phonemes are only part of the difficulty. A second set of obstacles arises in the pronunciation of sequences of consonants, or consonant cluster. Here the difficulty originates not with the articulation of individual sounds but with their occurrence in unfamiliar locations or unfamiliar sequences with other consonants. In the first category would be included single consonants that can end words in English but cannot do so in Spanish. The rules of Spanish allow only [n], [l], [s], [r], and [y] to occcur at the end of words. All other single consonants in English would thus be unfamiliar to Spanish speakers in this environment, and prone to substitution or elimination by the novice English speaker, not on grounds of articulatory difficulty, but on unfamiliarity with their occurrence in this position.

Difficulties can arise with respect to articulating sequences of consonants in certain environments. In word-initial position, for example, English consonant clusters *sp-*,*st-* ,*sn-*, *sl-*, *sm-*, and *sf-* (*spin, stick, skin, snow, slide, smile, sphere,* respectively) would violate Spanish sound sequence patterns. To bring these sequences in line with what is expected in Spanish, the Spanish speaker would likely add an /e/ at the beginning: *espin, *estick, *eskin, *esnow, *esmile, *esphere. Doing so breaks up the unacceptable clusters into patterns found in Spanish. The same can be expected of words involving three-consonant clusters *spr-*, *spl-*, *skr-*, and *str-* (*spring, splash, scream,* and *string,* respectively).

Consonants clusters occurring in word-final position are also novel to Spanish; recall that only certain single consonants are allowed to end words. English allows sequences of two, three, and even four consonants to end words. Among the most common of these, and examples of words in which they appear, are the following (sequences are given in phonetic symbols):

Two-Consonant sequences
-ft: left, draft, shaft
-sk: risk, disk, mask
-sp: crisp, clasp, grasp
-pt: slept, kept, crept
-čt: pitched, reached, matched
-kt: act, tracked, lacked
-lө: health, wealth, stealth

-bd: robbed, mobbed, sobbed
-gd: dragged, snagged, lagged
Three-Consonant sequences
-fts: lifts, gifts, rafts
-skt: asked, masked, risked
-rts: hearts, parts, starts
-rst: first, cursed, burst
-nčt: crunched, bunched, drenched
-rkt: worked, marked, sparked
-spt: grasped, lisped, rasped
-lpt: helped, scalped, gulped
-ŋkt: thanked, spanked, gulped
-rnd: burned, leaned, turned

One consequence of the difference in allowable consonant sequences is, of course, modification of word-final consonant sequences through reduction or elimination. A more serious consequence involves the effect of such reduction on the production of certain morphemes, for example, the past tense and the plural. Past tense forms that end in -bd (robbed), -pt (slept), -rct (reached), -skt (asked), -rkt (worked), -nkt (thanked), -rnd (burned) are likely to be reduced by dropping the morpheme marker. The learner would thus produce a present-tense form while intending to use a past-tense form of the verb. The teacher might interpret this to mean that the learner has not conceptually mastered the difference between the present and past tenses.

Vowels

Conflicts arising over differences in the vocalic systems are fewer in number but equally important. Speakers of SPICE should experience difficulty with the following English vowels:

/I/: The sound of English "bit," "sit,' "lip." It is articulated slightly lower than the Spanish /i/ of "Piso' and is less tense. Spanish speakers would tend to substitute the /i/ for /I/ so that "bit" sounds like "beat," "sit" like "seat," "lip" like "leap," and so on. The new sound will require practice in its articulation as well as in its contrastive use with the /i/.

/ae/: This English sound is articulated in the front part of the mouth slightly lower than the /e/. The /ae/ is very common in English, occurring in "bat," "cat," "rat," "mat," "sat," and "pat." The closest Spanish sound to this is the [E], similar to the English /e/. The tendency is for beginning students of English to substitute [E] for /ae/, resulting in the production of bet for bat, set for sat, met for mat, and so fourth. Hypercorrection is to be expected with this pair as with others, reversing the substitution pattern mentioned above.

/U/: This sound is found in English words like book, took, shook, brook. The SPICE speaker will tend to substitute the Spanish /u/ for the /U/; the resultant pronunciation would not cause confusion in meaning but would be considered "accented speech" by English speakers. A similar situation arises with the mastery of the English "schwa" /ə/: the Spanish speaker will tend to substitute the Spanish /a/, but doing so creates only difficulties related to accentedness and not to distinguishing meaning.

Grammatical Difficulies

Needless to say, the influence of Spanish on English is not limited to the phonological level. Spanish speakers learning English may experience difficulty at the clause level as well. The examples that follow, taken from the work of González (1976) and Cohen (1976), are representative of problem areas beyond the word level.

Lack of Subject-Verb agreement:

> The cat **are** going to stay up.
> And the mother **have** an apple.
> The father and the little boy **is** fishing.

Omission of copula (to be)

> And they...to old.
> This...a school.
> She...carrying her.
> He...sleeping with a bear.

Incorrect present participle in progressive

> They're play.
> He's hammer a nail.

Pronoun: number

> There's a big tree with leaves on **them.**
> **They're** long the grass.

Pronoun: case

> The mother, **he's** eating the apple.
> He have a hammer in **her** hand.
> He brush **her** teeth.

Pronoun: omission

> The cat doesn't want to get... down.
> Then... puts this in the pants.
> ... is washing the hair.

Mass vs. Count Noun confusion

> a cloths   a popcorn   **a work**

Inappropriate use of **some**

> I see **some** dress.
> There's some pants and **some** shirt.

Adjective: Inverted order

> There's a mother **white** and there's a girl **negro.**
> There's two white boys and a man **white.**

Misplaced adverb

> What's that **again** called?
> This boy had **once** a cat.

Prepositions: Substitutions for **at**

> He's pointing **on** a cat on a treetop.

He's smiling **to** the cat.
He's pointing **from** the cat.
The boy is pointing the finger **in** the cat.

Prepositions: substitutions for **on**

Putting a towel **in** his head.
He write **in** the paper.
The mother has a girl **up** her.
One day that teacher took her **to** a trip.

Prepositions: substitutions for **in**

He's up **to** heaven.
They're **on** the store.

Negation: double negative

That little kid don't have no shoes his own.
I don't know no stories.

Interrogatives: incomplete or incorrect form.

How…you call these?
What **we're** going to do?

Although the preceding types of deviations have been documented, attempts to trace all of them directly to Spanish have been less than successful. Some, such as the misplaced adjective, leave little doubt of the source; others, such as the difficulty involving prepositions, are not as easily attributed to Spanish, except in the most general of terms. At present, we can only report their occurrence in the speech of some Chicanos and leave explanations of causality to future scholars of Chicano English.

Suprasegmentals

Stress. It is a well-established fact that Spanish has a relatively simple system of word stress: one syllable per word is stressed and the rest are left unstressed. The English involves at least one and, in some analyses, two additional stress levels per word. Persons accustomed to the Spanish word-stress system will tend to superimpose this on the newly acquired English words, resulting in a conversion of syllable stress to either "stressed" or "unstressed." In words of two or three syllables, the effects of this modification are not noticeable. However, when words of four and five syllables are encountered, and all but one syllable is unstressed, the influence from Spanish is quite evident.

Examples of the above include words such as "conversation," "computation," "opportunity," "discrimination," and "manufacture." The speaker of SPICE would be prone to stressing only one syllable (the capitalized sequence in the examples below):

converSAtion
compuTAtion
opporTUnity
discriminNAtion
manuFACture

This seems to be one of the most difficult areas for the speaker to isolate and acknowledge, and as a result is one of the most persistent influences from Spanish. The stress pattern is often heard among SPICE speakers whose pronunciation is otherwise flawless. (See Gingràs (1978) for further information on Chicano English stress patterns.)

Intonation

Though little is known empirically about Chicano English intonation patterns (especially those found in the speech of fluent Chicano English speakers), there have been some observations made regarding this descriptively elusive aspect of Chicano speech. Metcalf (1979) considers intonation to be one of the most distinctive characteristics of Chicano English, adding that "Chicano English adds a 'Spanish accent' to a local Anglo variety" (p.9). He makes it clear that this characteristic is not limited to Spanish speakers with an imperfect control of English:

> The curious thing about this Spanish accent is that it is often heard from people who have no ability to speak or understand Spanish, people who are monolingual as well as perfectly fluent in English. (p.1)

Penfield (1984), in her analysis of natural spontaneous conversations between Mexican Americans, developed a set of generalizations describing how prosodic features in "Standard Anglo English" differ from those of Chicano English. She concludes that differences in prosodic patterns " . . . may cause misunderstandings or awkwardness at least" (p.57). As an example, she points to the Chicano English speaker's inclination to end statements on pitch level 2, which in Anglo English is taken to mean that the speaker has not yet concluded his statement. The communication act takes on an air of uneasiness, the Anglo speaker expecting the Chicano to conclude the statement, and the Chicano wondering why the Anglo does not contribute his part to the interaction.

These types of misunderstandings, especially those involving Chicano children in the classroom, need to be documented more extensively. Do the different intonation/stress patterns affect the educational process, the transfer of learning from teacher to student? If so, to what extent? More importantly, what can be done to train teachers to be sensitive to and accepting of different intonation/stress patterns in the speech of Chicano students so that the students are not discouraged from participation in school activities? The answers are not readily apparent, given our current state of knowledge of Chicano English.

Chicano English: A Sociolinguistic Perspective

The concept of Chicano English encompasses a range of linguistic abilities, from the most limited and heavily Spanish influenced to the most advanced and near native. The preceding sections have described the speech of Chicanos who were attempting to master the English language, who were trying their best to duplicate the English of native speakers around them and, to the extent possible, to rid themselves of the Spanish accent in their English.

But Chicano English is not limited to imperfect stages of development en route to a native command of English. Chicano English also includes the conscious, deliberate use, among some speakers under certain circumstances, of Spanish features in one's English. Although the details of such linguistic behavior remain to be fully explored, it is clear that its purpose is to poke gentle fun at those whose command of English is lacking, usually a third party identified only as "La Raza." Partakers in this activity thus have (or consider themselves to have) an adequate mastery of English. A speaker of Chicano English still struggling with particular sounds, syntactic patterns, or intonation features of English would not be likely to engage in this type of activity. The other members of this group must be well aware that the speaker making the substitutions is doing so not out of inabililty with English, but to make fun of how "La Raza" speaks English or how he himself may have spoken the language at one time. The other members of the group also must have an adequate command of English, otherwise the point is lost, as some members may take the kidding to be an insulting reflection of their own limited ability in English.

The above reflects my own experience growing up in a Chicano community in South Texas. Among members of my family, the type of activity described was quite common. "University" was pronounced (junibérsiti), "college" was rendered as (kólic), and "love" became (laf). At the morphosyntactic level, utterances such as the following have been produced deliberately:

"Is more better for me."
"Forget it about it."
"Put attention."

The items may come from phonological, syntactic, intonational, or stress differences between the two languages and are indistinguishable in form substitutions made by Spanish speakers attempting to master English. Curiously, this type of linguistic behavior has been observed only among Texas Chicanos, as was reported earlier (González, 1984). It also has been observed to occur primarily with adults, although it's quite possible that younger speakers also have the facility. Undoubtedly, much research remains to be done in this fascinating area.

Chicano English and the Classroom Teacher

The ESL/bilingual classroom teacher whose class contains Chicano pupils needs to be aware of the wide heterogeneity of ability in English represented by her/his students (González, 1984). This awareness will enable her/him to approach the assessment of English language abilities cautiously and on an individual basis. Differences between the two languages can identify or help explain possible areas of difficulty. Knowing the specific area of language involved (phonology, syntax, etc.) will enable the teacher to develop appropriate activities.

The current debate regarding the status of Chicano English (e.g., whether the language variety is a separate dialect of English, and imperfect stage on the road to fluency in English, or some position in between) should serve to underscore the complexity of the linguistic situation of the Chicano in the Southwest. At one end of the spectrum there are those students whose English shows unmistakable signs of Spanish influence and who have a good command of Spanish. At the other end will be those with fluency in English, but whose speech is tinged with an accent, and who know little or no Spanish. The teacher's unenviable task is to deal with both extremes and all levels in between. Her/his task is not the teaching of this variety called Chicano English, but its recognition and acceptance. The primary concern should be the acquisition of knowledge. The teacher's acceptance of Chicano English, while simultaneously adding a standard variety to the Chicano's linguistic repertoire, can do much for the student's self concept and can greatly enhance the learning environment of the classroom.

References

Baugh, J. Chicano English: the anguish of definition. In J. Ornstein-Galicia (Ed.), *Form and function in Chicano English*. Rowley, Mass.: Newbury House, 1984.

Cohen, A. D. The English and Spanish grammar of Chicano primary school students. In J. D. Bowen & J. Ornstein-Galicia (Eds.), *Studies in southwest Spanish*. Rowley, Mass.: Newbury House, 1976.

Gingràs, R. *Rule transfer and innovation in the phonology of a California Chicano English dialect*. Paper presented at the TESOL Convention, Mexico City, 1978.

Godínez, M., Jr. Chicano English phonology: norms vs. interference phonomena. In J. Ornstein-Galicia (Ed.), *Form and function in Chicano English*. Rowley, Mass.: Newbury House, 1984.

González, G. Some characteristics of the English used by migrant Spanish-speaking children in Texas. *Aztlán*, 1976, *7*, 27-49.

González, G. The range of Chicano English. In J. Ornstein-Galicia (Ed.), *Form and function in Chicano English*. Rowley, Mass.: Newbury House, 1984.

Metcalf, A. A. Mexican American English in southern California. *Western Review*, 1972, *9*, 13-21.

Metcalf, A. A. *Chicano English. Language in education: theory and practice, No. 21*. Arlington, Va.: Center for Applied Linguistics, 1979.

Ortego, P. D. Some cultural implications of a Mexican American border dialect of American English. *Studies in Linguistics,* 1970, *21*, 77-82.

Penfield, J. Prosodic patterns: some hypotheses and findings from fieldwork. In J. Ornstein-Galicia (Ed.), *Form and function in Chicano English*. Rowley, Mass.: Newbury House, 1984.

Peñalosa, F. *Chicano sociolinguistics: a brief introduction*. Rowley, Mass.: Newbury House, 1980.

Peñalosa, F. Some issues in Chicano sociolinguistics. In R. P. Durán (Ed.), *Latino language and communicative behavior*. Norwood, N. J.: ABLEX Publishing, 1981.

Sawyer, J. B. Spanish-English bilingualism in San Antonio. In G. G. Gilbert (Ed.), *Texas studies in bilingualism*. Berlin: de Gruyter, 1970.

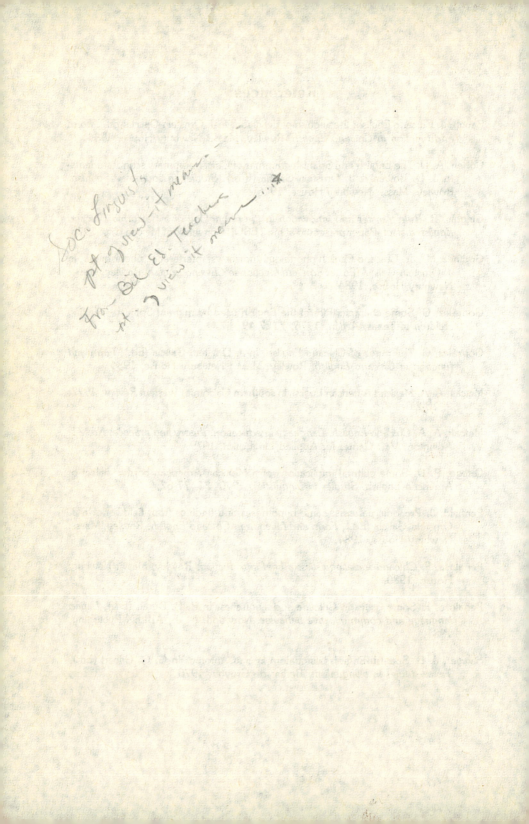

Soc. Linguists
pt. I view — it means —
From Sec. Ed. Teachers
pt. I view it means

Code-Switching and Intuitive Knowledge in the Bilingual Classroom

by Adalberto Aguirre, Jr.

Introduction

The question most often asked by teachers of bilingual children is: "What does it mean when bilingual children alternate languages in ongoing discourse?" On the surface level, such bilingual speech production is an indication that the speakers have some knowledge of more than one language. On a deeper level, it is an indication that the speakers have a set of linguistic competencies that permit them to alternate languages in a meaningful and communicative manner. In short, when teachers ask about language alternation they are simply recognizing that the speakers they are hearing are bilingual, and that linguistic exchanges between bilingual speakers are often not characterized by language compartmentalization of one language from the other.

Our purpose in the following pages is to provide an overview of language alternation in bilingual speech, and its utility to teachers in bilingual classrooms. We will examine the use of language alternation, or code-switching, as an assessment strategy in the bilingual classroom and its association with a teacher's intuitive knowledge for language behavior in bilingual children.

Code-Switching

Code-switching has become a common term to describe those speech situations in which (Hymes, 1974; St. Clair & Valdés, 1980; Lance, 1970):

a. speakers alternate between two or more languages, varieties of a language, or even speech styles;
b. speakers alternate between two different language codes within the same discourse, implying that the speaker is conscious of the switch;
c. speakers alternate between two different language systems because of the environment (e.g. the presence of a speech partner with whom the speaker prefers to speak in another language) or topic of discussion.

For example, Denison (1968) in his study of a trilingual Italian community, Sauris, discovered that he could outline those factors involved in the selection of one or the other of the three languages: German, Italian, Friulian. The factors identified by Denison fall into four general components that are associated with language selection:

1. situation: formality/informality of the setting.
2. genre: spontaneity versus non-spontaneity of conversation.
3. participants: age, sex, etc.
4. topic: personal/impersonal, technical/non-technical, etc.

Thus, in Sauris, according to Denison, to achieve greater or less formality, or a different style of interaction, one simply changes language.

A review of the code-switching literature suggests that one can identify two major concerns with the study of code-switching. On the one hand, a focus on the social uses of code-switching has resulted in analyses regarding the rules of speaking, or communicative competence, for bilingual speakers (Lipski, 1980; Valdés, 1980). These rules of speaking have been examined by observing bilingual speakers participate and

84

interact in social activities that require linguistic performance. By outlining the association of such rules with on-going social interaction, the attempt has been made to observe
the decision process by which speakers select the appropriate code (language), and
how code selection contributes to the maintenance of social interaction. For example,
one finds that a social dimension such as *social distance* affects code selection: choice
of Haitian French or Creole in Haiti marks role and topic shifts with a setting.

On the other hand, a concern with the linguistic features in code-switching has led
researchers to examine those linguistic environments in which code-switching takes place
(Valdés-Fallis, 1976; Sridhar & Sridhar, 1980; Pfaff, 1979). By uncovering linguistic
regularity in the production of code-switching, studies in this area have attempted to
develop the idea of a third type of grammatical knowledge for bilingual speakers that
permits for the ordered alternation of languages. For example, a study that took an
early look at the presence of syntactic constraints on code-switching among bilingual
Mexican American speakers in California was done by Gumperz & Hernández-Chávez
(1970). They found in their analysis of code-switching the operation of certain syntactic constraints: adverbial constructions may be switched, "Vamos next week," but not
as interrogatives, "When vamos?"; a switch may occur at a noun phrase only after
a determiner, "Se lo dí a mi grandfather," but not as, "Se lo dí a my grandfather";
an adverb may be switched before an adjective, "Es very friendly," but not "Es very
amistoso."

In summary, code-switching is an activity that is instrumental in maintaining bilingual
social interaction, and indicates an ordered linguistic process at work that facilitates bilingual communication. Code-switching then is not random linguistic speech production - that is, code-switching is not simply language mixture, but speech production
that is the result of ordered linguistic selection. Code-switching is also not an indication
that the speaker is linguistically incongruent with his social surrounding. Thus, code-
switching is an active process of negotiation that insures a high degree of linguistic and
social congruency within a given social context (Aguirre, 1978; Miller, 1984).

Code-Switching in the Bilingual Classroom

Even though code-switching has attracted much sociolinguistic and psycholinguistic
attention, the role of code-switching in the bilingual classroom has been subject to limited
attention. One obstacle that has limited the attention paid to code-switching as a
classroom strategy has been due to the conceptual complexity in deciding what type
of code-switching will be most productive in the classroom. For instance, while Jacobson (1975,1979) is a leading supporter of code-switching as a teaching strategy in the
bilingual classroom, he is also careful to point out that his concern is only with *intersentential* code-switching. That is, Jacobson's concern is with the alternation of both languages
in separate and independent utterances that reinforce the sociolinguistic knowledge
the student possesses for each language. According to Jacobson (1981), any use of
intersentential code-switching in the bilingual classroom should be done with the following
concerns in mind:

1. the extent to which the native language must be developed in order to succeed in
learning a second language;
2. the extent to which the home language should be used in school to develop a positive
attitude toward it;
3. the extent to which first language maintenance in the primary grades would not

interfere with the transition to English in post-primary education;

4. the extent to which the use of both languages would lead to an understanding of the bilingual functioning of some sectors of our society;
5. the extent to which school subjects could be learned through two language media.

González (1972), however, argues against the use of code-switching in bilingual classrooms. Underlying González's argument are the following observations;

1. children can learn a second language while maintaining their first language, but allowing code-switching deprives the child of the opportunity to practice using the two languages as separate modes of communication;
2. code-switching in the bilingual classroom encourages the student to use the stronger language (usually English) rather than attempting new linguistic expressions in the weaker language;
3. the use of code-switching prevents the teacher from identifying language areas in need of remediation.

González & Mesa (1980:133) agree with Jacobson's view of code-switching: "Code-switching of the intersentential type can and should be used in teaching, while intrasentential code-switching should be accepted (as should any variety of language the child brings with him) but should not be used by the teacher. In addition, the teacher should assure that when the child does engage in intrasentential code-switching, the word switched to English is in his repertoire." In summary then, language alternation is regarded as a valuable tool in the bilingual classroom when it occurs in separate and independent linguistic environments. In contrast, language alternation that occurs within the same sentence, while regarded as a sociolinguistic feature in bilingual speech, is viewed as an impediment to the development of independent bilingual language use. Thus, the concern is not so much with the presence and occurrence of code-switching in the bilingual classroom, as much as it is with what form is assumes.

While it is not our purpose in this paper to examine much further the use of code-switching in the bilingual classroom, we must note that its presence in the bilingual classroom is both obvious and unavoidable. Placing the pedagogical issues aside, teachers in bilingual classrooms encounter code-switching in their student's speech at both the intrasentential and intersentential level. It is necessary that teachers in these situations regard code-switching as a communicative strategy. By doing so, the teacher in the bilingual classroom may be able to use his/her own intuitive knowledge about bilingual behavior to develop a sociolinguistic profile of the bilingual student. In what follows, it is important to note that we will be referring to teachers in bilingual classrooms as persons who are themselves proficient bilingual speakers, and who are indigenous to the areas their bilingual students originate from.

Discourse Alternatives in the bilingual classroom

All persons possess a base of intuitive knowledge that is reflective of their own life experiences, and which is used to infuse order into the meaning of everday life. In a sense, this base of intuitive knowledge enables persons to believe that things 'make' or 'do not make' sense. Thus, persons experience order in their everday life if people and events are as they are assumed they should be (Aguirre, 1981; Boulding, 1981).

We have already noted that bilingual speakers are able to alternate languages in a manner suggesting an on-going process of ordered selection. Let us assume that this process of ordered selection is dependent on a bilingual speaker's base of intuitive knowledge for bilingual behavior. Let us further assume that this base of intuitive knowledge expands in correspondence to a bilingual speaker's ability to approach a state of linguistic balance for his/her two languages. However, a prerequisite for approaching a state of linguistic balance is active participation in bilingual social contexts. Thus, one's base of intuitive knowledge for bilingual behavior will expand correspondent with one's level of linguistic balance and participation in bilingual contexts. As a result, simply speaking two languages is not sufficient to permit the development of a base of intuitive knowledge for bilingual behavior.

We must assume that teachers in bilingual classrooms are bilingual and proficient in those languages their students possess. For teachers in bilingual classrooms not to be bilingual would render both the classroom context and interactive behavior meaningless. In a sense, while the school structure may in itself impose some order into classroom behavior, both teacher and students would be operating with a base of intuitive knowledge that would create abiguity in the interpretation of behavior. In other words, in order to establish a relative level of understanding for carrying out classroom lessons, there must be a high level of correspondence between a teacher's and student's base of intuitive knowledge.

Let us assume that all of the preceding assumptions are operative in the everyday life of the bilingual classroom. How then can one use, as a teacher, intuitive knowlege to enhance the learning of children in bilingual classrooms? Let me outline some observations that are reflective, rather than inclusive, of what is possible within the bilingual classroom.

a. If code-switching is employed properly in the bilingual classroom it will promote the functional separation and specialization of language use. For instance, the teacher in the bilingual classroom may listen to students' code-switching in order to identify *what* is being switched and *how* it is being switched - such as, word repetition across languages, translation of same sentences across languages, etc. If the teacher's intuitive knowledge tells him/her that the child possesses a similar linguistic ability in each language, then the teacher may then want to alternate languages with the student in order to build on sentence complexity and word power.

b. The teacher's intuitive knowledge may tell him/her that a bilingual student is mixing languages in a manner that communicates confusion - e.g. the language alternation is incongruent with what is socially and linguistically permissable given the social context. The teacher may then be able to separate simple language confusion from complicated problems tied to language learning. The teacher could then employ code-switching to teach the student how to transfer concepts, and their linguistic symbols, from one language to the other. The goal would be to use code-switching to develop within the student's linguistic knowledge two separate symbol systems and their appropriate meaning.

c. The teacher can use his/her intuitive knowledge for code-switching behavior to develop criteria for separating meaningful from meaningless code-switching. That is, the bilingual teacher may be able to identify those speakers whose code-switching is reflective of participation in bilingual contexts from those speakers who have learned how to code-switch as part of some social activity (Gumperz & Hernández-Chávez, 1970). The former will usually be proficient bilinguals, while the latter will be limited in use of both languages. The teacher may then develop sets of classroom lessons that are bilingual in goals and which depend on some reinforcement outside of the classroom.

The preceding observations are only those associated with the use of intuitive knowledge for code-switching by the teachers with bilingual students. The attractiveness of this approach is that it takes into consideration the limited time available to teachers for making a lengthy and complete assessment of a bilingual student's language use and language ability. This approach enables the teacher to develop a sociolinguistic profile of the bilingual student given the teacher's intuitive knowledge for social and linguistic profile highlighting global, rather than particularistic, features in a student's bilingual behavior. Since the educational process is, in general, oriented toward students' global rather than particularistic learning features, this approach is compatible with what is both possible and probable in the school classroom.

While this approach enables the teacher to assess through observation a student's bilingual ability, it does not serve as substitute for developing learning materials. This approach simply permits the teacher to make an evaluation of a student's bilingual ability under conditions that are not conducive to a lengthy sociolinguistic evaluation. As a result, the teacher is able to respond to a student's needs by quickly developing classroom lessons that focus on problematic areas in the student's language development.

Summary

The controversy will no doubt continue as to what role code-switching should play in the bilingual classroom. It is worth noting that regardless of what view one subscribes to, code-switching is a reflection of sociolinguistic negotiation in everyday bilingual behavior. Its presence is simply a recognition of the fact that more than one language is capable of defining events and persons.

Secondly, we have observed that not all forms of code-switching are regarded as acceptable in the bilingual classroom. It is commonly accepted that code-switching of the intersentential variety is the most effective because it provides for the development of language compartmentalization. In other words, language alternation in bilingual classrooms must be meaningful in itself and not simply reflect a language choice. That is, the alternation must communicate meaning and be tied to co-occurring social and linguistic features in the social context.

Finally, the primary obstacle to the meta-theoretical approach discussed in this paper is the limited number of teachers in bilingual classrooms who are proficient bilinguals. The student is at risk in these classroom situations because the teacher is unable to comprehend the manner in which the student is negotiating his/her social and linguistic identity. The teacher's limited comprehension will usually encourage him/her to identify learning problems that are assumed to be reflective of language problems, but which are not reflective of the student's actual learning needs. The unavoidable outcome is that classroom structure will become a barrier to sociolinguistic interaction and exchange between teacher and student.

References

Aguirre, Jr. A. In search of a paradigm for bilingual education. In R. Padilla (Ed.), *Bilingual education technology*. Ypsilianti, Mi: Eastern Michigan University Press, 1981.

Aguirre, Jr. A. *An experimental sociolinguistic study of Chicano bilingualism*. San Francisco: R & E Research Associates, 1978.

Boulding, K. Human knowledge as a special system. *Behavioral Science*, 1981, *26*, 93-102.

Denison, N. Sauris: A trilingual community in diatypic perspective. *Man*, 1968, *3* 578-592.

González, G. Analysis of Chicano Spanish and the problem of usage: LA critique of Chicano Spanish dialects and education. *Aztlán*, 1972, *3*, 223-231.

González, G., & Maez L. To switch or not to switch: The role of code-switching in the elementary bilingual classroom. In R. Padilla (Ed.), *Theory in bilingual education*. Ypsilanti, Mi: Eastern Michigan University Press, 1980.

Gumperz, J., & Hernández-Chávez, E. Cognitive aspects of bilingual communication. In H. Whitely (Ed.), *Language use and social change*. London: Oxford University Press, 1970.

Hymes, D. *Foundations in sociolinguistics: An ethnographic approach*. Philadelphia: University of Pennsylvania Press, 1974.

Jacobson, R. The implementation of a bilingual instruction model: The NEW concurrent approach. In R. Padilla (Ed.), *Bilingual education technology*. Ypsilanti, Mi.: Eastern Michigan University Press, 1981.

Jacobson, R. Can bilingual teaching techniques reflect bilingual community behaviors? - A study in ethnoculture and its relationship to some amendments contained in the new bilingual education act. In R. Padilla (Ed.), *Bilingual education and public policy in the United States, V.I.* Ypsilanti, Mi.: Eastern Michigan University Press, 1979.

Jacobson, R. The bilingual's two languages: Duplication or compartmentalization? Paper presented at the annual TESOL meeting, Los Angeles, March 1975.

Lance, D. The codes of the Spanish/English bilingual. *TESOL Quarterly*, 1970, *4*, 343-351.

Lipski, J. Bilingual: code-switching and internal competence: The evidence from Spanish and English. *Le Language et l'Homme*, 1980, *42*, 30-39.

Miller, N. Language use in bilingual communities. In N. Miller (Ed.), *Bilingualism and language disability: Assessment & remediation.* London: Croom Helm, 1984.

Pfaff, C. Constraints on language mixing: Intrasentential code switching and borrowing in Spanish/English. *Language,* 1979, *55,* 291-318.

St. Clair, R., & Valdés, G. The sociology of code switching. *Language Science,* 1980, *2,* 205-221.

Sridhar, S., & K. Sridhar. The Syntax and psycholinguistics of bilingual code mixing. *Canadian Journal of Psychology,* 1980, *34,* 407-416.

Valdés, G. Is code switching interference, integration, or neither? In E. Blansitt, Jr. & R. Teschner (Eds.), *Festchrift for Jacob Ornstein.* Rowley, Massachusetts: Newbury House, 1980.

Valdés-Fallis, G. Code switching and language dominance: Some initial findings. *General Linguistics,* 1976, *18,* 90-104.

Educational Issues and Practices

The Role of Chicano Spanish in the Early Grades: Clarification of the Issues
by Robert D. Milk

Introduction

A great deal of heat has been generated by debates surrounding the proper role of regional and local varieties of Spanish in bilingual education programs. Because feelings run quite high on this issue, discussions have at times been characterized more by acrimonious exchanges than by thoughtful insights. This article represents an attempt to redirect the discussion away from the issue of code selection (i.e., who should speak what in the classroom) towards the more central issue of what should, in essence, be the one fundamental concern of formal schooling in the early grades—namely, strengthening of the cognitive underpinnings of that dimension of language proficiency that appears to correlate most strongly with academic success. The basic argument to be developed is that it is the quality of interaction and the cognitive content of educational programs—not decisions related to code selection— that are the key variable leading to optimal realization of academic potential among Mexican American children. If this argument is valid, then, viewed from a strictly pedagogical perspective, the question of which variety of Spanish should be used for instructional purposes in the early grades becomes somewhat superfluous. Seen from this perspective, the issue of code selection is relegated to its proper place. i.e., to discussions dealing exclusively with certain aspects of language development. By removing this issue from the agenda, other matters related more directly to the maximizing of educational benefits for children enrolled in bilingual instructional programs can thus be addressed. –

The Role of Chicano Spanish in Educational Programs

Discussions surrounding the proper role of nonstandard varieties in education over the past decade have tended to revolve around three core positions (Wolfram & Fasold, 1974; Wolfram & Christian, 1979; Valdés, 1981): a) eradication of the "marked" nonstandard dialect, b) an additive approach whereby the standard dialect is added to the existing linguistic repertoire of nonstandard speakers, and c) an attitude modification approach, whereby negative social attitudes toward marked varieties are assailed, and efforts are directed toward reeducation of the public regarding the nonsuperiority, linguistically speaking, of one variety of language over another. Valdés (1981) correctly points out that it is not uncommon for persons espousing one of these positions (Typically "b") to advocate classroom procedures that reflect more exactly a totally different position (typically "a"). Thus although identifying these three positions may be a useful exercise for delineating contrasting philosophical orientations, the question can be raised to what extent these positions provide any practical guidelines for considering concrete questions related to code selection during the teaching/learning process. In other words, aside from the general principle "to respect the home language of the child," are there clearcut differences implied in terms of specific techniques for classroom practice by each one of these three positions? If not, how useful is the distinction for the *practitioner* in resolving core problems related to the instruction of children whose first language is a nonstandard variety of Spanish?

In discussion the role of Chicano Spanish in educational programs, two areas of confusion frequently emerge. The first confusion that penetrates many discussions is caused by a failure to distinguish between language used as a vehicle for developing concepts (i.e., Spanish as a medium of instruction), and language development *per se*.

The second confusion that surrounds many discussions related to the role of Chicano Spanish in education is very aptly pointed out by Valdés (1981). For years, many practicing members of the Spanish-speaking profession have failed to distinguish between: a) teaching Spanish as a native language, b) teaching Spanish as a foreign language, and c) teaching standard Spanish as a second dialect (Valdés, 1981, p.6). The precise nature of this confusion, however, operates differently at different levels. At the high school and college levels, the most serious problems are created by confusion between the needs and goals of students for whom Spanish is a native language and those for whom it is not. At the elementary school level, however, this is not, in most bilingual programs throughout the Southwest, a real source of difficulty. The difficulty resides, rather, in the tendency to conceptualize the Spanish language issue around the question of code selection, instead of around the more fundamental question of language proficiency. In other words, the problem centers around the tendency to frame the debate in terms of Chicano Spanish vs. standard Spanish, rather than in relation to matters that are more centrally related to academic learning—viz., fostering the cognitive base for successful literacy development. Thus, the nature of the questions asked with respect to the role of Chicano Spanish may be as much a source of the problems as anything else. What I am suggesting is that perhaps the key question is not "What is the appropriate role of Chicano Spanish?" but "What can be done in the classroom to more effectively develop the underlying cognitively, related dimension of language proficiency in bilingual children?" It is to this latter question that we now turn.

Developing the Cognitive/Academic Dimension of Language Proficiency

Cummins (1980, 1981) has made a distinction between two separate dimensions of language proficiency, one that involves cognitively demanding tasks, as well as to communication through more decontextualized channels (such as reading and writing). The importance of this distinction for our discussions is derived from Cummins' assertion that the first dimension (which he labels Basic Interpersonal Communication Skills-BICS) is code-specific, whereas the second dimension (Cognitive/Academic Language Proficiency-CALP) is not. The implications of this distinction for children who speak a regional variety of Spanish are profound. The issue of code selection is relevant only to the first dimension, clearly, the wider the linguistic repertoire of the child, the greater the possibilities for communicating with persons outside the primary associative group of that individual. With respect to the second dimension, however, the issue of code selection becomes irrelevant. The important issue is how to provide learning experiences that make increasing cognitive demand on the student, as well as how to succesfully initiate the student into literacy. For language-minority children in the United States, there is abundant evidence to suggest that the appropriate language through which to accomplish these educational goals is the primary language of the child, be that what it may.

In what kinds of activities should children be engaged in the classroom inorder to stimulate this development of the underlying nonlanguage-specific dimension of language proficiency? Cummins suggests that all learning activities can be identified along two separate continua: a) the extent to which the activity is cognitively demanding/undemanding, and b) the extent to which it is context embedded/context reduced.

(Conversation is an example of an activity that is context embedded; talking over a telephone and reading a text without pictures are examples of activities that are to some extent decontextualized.)2 Ulimately, the kinds of learning activities that would do most to foster CALP (and to develop literacy-related skills) are presumably those that are increasingly cognitively demanding and increasingly context reduced. This would include problem-solving activities as well as activities that foster what Penfield and Ornstein (1981) call "advanced inquiry processes." Of course, many learning activities are not intrinsically at one end of the continuum or the other for these two dimensions; the teacher is clearly empowered to adapt activities to make them increasingly demanding from a cognitive standpoint and/or increasingly context reduced. A skillful teacher will learn to make appropriate demands on his/her students with respect to the learning activities in which they are engaged in order to constantly foster the development of this vital dimension of language proficiency.

Distinguishing Between Oral and Written Channels of Communication

The primary fallacy behind attempts to treat Spanish language development in the early grades from a perspective of "standard Spanish as a second dialect" (SSSD) is that the focus for language development becomes largely structure-based, and, in many cases, instruction in grammar comes to dominate this segment of the curriculum. This directly contradicts research evidence that "planned instruction in grammar in the elementary grades is unlikely to enhance either knowledge of grammar or expressive abilities of children" (Allen and Brown, 1979).

A second concern with respect to SSSD is related to its efforts to make young children consciously aware of structural differences between different varieties of Spanish through special drill techniques. There is a fear that these efforts may be counterproductive over the long run since the techniques that are commonly used may have the undesired effect in many children of discouraging language use of any kind. An effective program of oral language development, critics point out, demands that an environment favorable for language use be maintained at all times.

A third reason for rejecting formal instruction in standard Spanish as a second dialect in the early grades is that clearcut structural differences between Chicano Spanish and standard Spanish have not been systematically identified. In fact, viewing the issue of dialectal diversity in Spanish from a language variation perspective (as does Floyd, 1981), there are reasons to consider structural diversity in the spoken Spanish of the southwest not as a manifestation of several discrete language varieties, but, rather, as rule-governed variation influenced by both external factors (including regional, historical, and socioenvironmental variables) and internal factors (including developmental and systemic variables).

An important point remains to be made—the three concerns that have just been raised regarding SSSD in the early grades are each valid *only with reference to the oral channel*. They do not represent an argument against the development of "standard Spanish" among children participating in bilingual programs. The teaching of standard Spanish is, by definition, a central part of literacy development. During reading, children are exposed to a register which differs in fundamental ways from spoken language. (This is true to a greater or lesser extent, for *all* children, not just children who happen to speak a "nonstandard" variety of language.) Likewise, development of writing skills requires children to learn a new register of language that is different, to a greater or lesser extent, from the way they speak. Thus, the arguments presented above against explicit formal instruction in standard Spanish in the early grades relate exclusively to the oral channel of communication, and not to the development of literacy skills.

The Social Significance of Code Selection

Numerous issues related to the role of Chicano Spanish in bilingual programs have been raised in this article. Up until this point, the issues have been discussed strictly within a pedagogical framework, with no consideration accorded to the social dimension of these issues. Perhaps the most succinct summary of this article's central theme is that the matter of code selection is not the key *pedagogical* issue of bilingual education pracitioners that it sometimes has been made out to be. Having made this argument, however, it would be misleading to conclude the article without acknowledging the intense *social* significance of issues related to code selection in bilingual programs. It is doubtful that any educational program can be successful if it violates strongly held community norms regarding appropriate language use, particularly with regard to language(s) of instruction in the schools. In addition to community attitudes, other factors that are likely to influence code selection include: a) goals of the program, b) long-term educational aspirations, and c) relative status of the language varieties of the community.

For the most part, however, these social variables are not under the immediate control of classroom practitioners. At the level of day-to-day performance of instructional tasks, the fundamental language-related question that remains for the practitioner is: "What can I as a teacher do to provide the kind of language-rich, cognitively demanding educational environment that will lead to optimal development of academically related language proficiency?"

NOTES

1 This article deals solely with issues related to the appropriate variety of Spanish for bilingual programs in the early grades. It does not deal with the parallel issue related to the appropriate variety of English for ESL instruction within bilingual programs. The assumed target population is children whose primary language is a local or regional variety of Spanish—clearly, only one segment of the population currently being served by bilingual programs.

2 These ideas were suggested by Cummins in response to a question by a teacher following a presentation at the University of Texas at San Antonio during Spring, 1981.

REFERENCES

Aguirre, Jr. Adalberto & Dennis Bixler-Márquez. A sociolinguistic assessment model for Bilingual Education: A case study. *NABE Journal, 1979, IV (2)*, 1-17.

Allen, R.R. & Kenneth Brown (eds.). *Developing Communication Competence in Children*. Skokie, Ill.: National Textbook Co., 1976.

Cummins, J. The entry and exit fallacy in bilingual education. *NABE Journal*, 1980, *IV*(3), 25-60.

Cummins, Jim. *Bilingualism and Minority-Language Children*. Toronto: The Ontario Institute for Studies in Education, 1981.

Floyd, Mary Beth. Language variation in Southwest Spanish and its relation to pedagogical issues. G. Valdés et al. (eds.), *Teaching Spanish to the Hispanic Bilingual Student:. Issues, Aims, and Methods*. New York: Teachers College Press, 1981.

González, Gustavo & Lento Maez. To switch or not to switch: the role of code-switching in the elementary bilingual classroom. R. Padilla (Ed.), *Ethnoperspectives in Bilingual Education, V II: Theory in Bilingual Education,* 1980.

Jacobson, Rodolfo. Can bilingual teaching techniques reflect bilingual community behaviors? - A study in ethnoculture and its relationship to some amendments contained in the new bilingual education act. R. Padilla (ed.), *Ethnoperspectives in Bilingual Education Research, Volume I: Bilingual Education and Public Policy in the United States,* 1979.

Penfield, Joyce & Jacob Ornstein-Galicia. Language through science: An integrative model. R. Padilla (ed.), *Ethnoperspectives in Bilingual Education Research, Volume III: Bilingual Education Technology*. Ypsilanti, Mich. : Eastern Michigan University, 1981.

Ramírez, Arnulfo, Robert Milk, & Alexander Sapiens. In press. Attitudes toward varieties of Spanish among bilingual pupils from Texas and California. *Hispanic Journal of Behavioral Sciences, 1983,* 5(4), 417-429.

Valdés, Guadalupe. Pedagogical implications of teaching Spanish to the Spanish-speaking in the United States. G. Valdes et al. (eds.), *Teaching Spanish to the Hispanic Bilingual: Issues, Aims, and Methods*. New York; Teachers College Press, 1981.

Valdés, Guadalupe. Anthony Lozano & Rodolfo Garcia-Moya. *Teaching Spanish to the Hispanic Bilingual: Issues, Aims, and Methods*. New York: Teachers College Press, 1981.

98

Wolfram, Walt & Ralph Fasold. *The Study of Social Dialects in American English.* Englewood Cliffs, N.J.: Prentice-Hall, 1974.

Wolfram, Walt & Donna Christian. *Dialogue on Dialects.* Washington, D.C.: Center for Applied Linguistics, 1979.

Nonstandard Dialects in Bilingual Education: The Read-Aloud Strategy in Children's Literature

by Marie E. Barker

Introduction

This paper is divided into two sections; the first part states the case for the use of nonstandard dialects in bilingual education. The second proposes the reading aloud of Spanish children's literature as a viable strategy for language development in the bilingual classroom.

Nonstandard Dialects in Bilingual Education

For those whose home language is a nonstandard dialect of Spanish, it carries all the meanings and overtones of the home, family, love, and friendship that the standard variety carries. It is the instrument for living, for thinking, and for feeling of many Spanish-speaking children in our schools. It is also the best instrument for learning, a fact recognized and accepted in bilingual education.

As instruction in two languages, bilingual education carries on the teaching/learning process by using English and Spanish for any or all parts of the curriculum. Unless the home language is used, education cannot be properly considered bilingual. The home language, more often than not, is a nonstandard dialect of Spanish.

As the key to equal access to educational opportunity, bilingual education helps the child make the transition from home to school more easily by reducing the difference between the language and culture of the home and that of the school. The use and acceptance of the home dialect helps children feel loved, accepted, and respected. This in turn translates into positive self-concepts and children who are motivated to learn with optimism and confidence in their abilities, children who feel adequate and are not frightened by difficult school tasks.

Fishman (1966) tells us it is a proper function of the school to accept, not to destroy, the learner's native dialect but to assist him to acquire such additional dialects as may be of value to him. In this way the learner has access to different dialects for use in specific context. On the one hand, the nonstandard or home language for group identification, for school learning in the early stages, for conversation at will with family and friends, and other social functions such as writing letters to friends and relatives. On the other hand, the standard colloquial is the tool for greater use and accessibility to the intellectual heritage of his culture and society.

Bilingual education offers the learner the opportunity to add other dialects and the language of the textbooks while allowing him to keep his own. For example, it provides for the development of a second dialect of Spanish to children who speak nonstandard dialects through a Spanish language arts approach, thus ensuring the same continuity in language development that native English-speaking children experience in a monolingual English curriculum. Spanish language arts programs, like English arts programs, are designed to extend and refine children's use of language and aid the development of expression skills commensurate with their level of intellectual and emotional development.

Since language is recognized as the means for representing thought and as the vehicle for complex thinking (Chazan and Cox, 1976), the importance of allowing children to use and develop the language they know best becomes obvious. Whereas this common-sense approach is self evident to linguists and language teachers now, it was not so clear before the advent of bilingual education in the United States (Valdés et al, 1981). It was not too long ago when Spanish-speaking children in Southwestern schools were not only *not* taught in their nonstandard dialects but even their Spanish proficiency was denied; it was simply not recognized as being in existence. It was overlooked and ignored not only by most classroom teachers but by the Spanish teaching profession at all levels (Gaarder et al, 1972). All Spanish-language instruction was delivered through second-language teaching methodologies and in "Castilian," the prestigious dialect, to both the native and the non-native speaker of Spanish alike.

It is a well-documented fact (Gaarder et al, 1972) that native-Spanish-speaking children, on the one hand, were deprived of cognitive learning through the only language they knew and were taught their own tongue as a foreign language. On the other hand, since many did not know English, they received instruction in regular English language classes along with native speakers when in fact they needed English as a second language.

In today's enlightened times, language-minority children should be allowed to use and maintain their nonstandard dialects for school learning in the bilingual classroom. They can use the dialects they understand to explore, interpret, and construct meaning, and are therefore better able to remember and manipulate complex concepts presented in texts written in the standard dialect. Bilingual education teachers can help children reach the maximum level of cognitive growth by facilitating language development and verbal interaction in the native tongue while developing proficiency and cognitive transfer in the standard vernacular of the school--English--the language required for ultimate success in American society.

Not only is the relationship between well-developed language and cognitive growth critical to future success, but so is the ability to use oral and written language effectively since it is often considered the mark of a well educated individual. The decisions in our schools to promote children from one grade to the next is based on whether or not they are able to communicate that they have learned the information and concepts required: in the early grades children do so by expressing themselves orally; in the upper grades the emphasis is placed on written performance (U.S. Commission on Civil Rights, 1975).

Finally, the fact that verbal ability is one of the three basic measures used on college entrance examinations underscores the importance of well-developed language skills for future educational opportunity.

Bilingual education has triggered worldwide attention on the linguistic phenomenon that is bilingualism and the concomitant assets that accrue from it (Cummins, 1979). More specifically, recent research on the effect that the level of development of the mother tongue--the first language--has on second-language acquisition, presents implications for maintaining formal instruction in the first language. Recently Cummins has hypothesized that "there may be threshold levels of linguistic competence which bilingual children must attain, both in order to avoid cognitive deficits and to allow the potentially beneficial aspects of becoming bilingual to influence their cognitive growth" (Cummins, 1979). By threshold level he means the point in language development when children have attained sufficient competence in a language to function in it and where it allows cognitive development to proceed at a normal pace. Cummins also hypothesizes on what he calls "Developmental Interdependence: the level of second language competence which a bilingual child attains is partially a function of the type of competence the child has developed in the first language at the time when intensive exposure to the second language begins." Cummins defines developmental interdependence as a language phenomenon in which competency in the second language, English, is, to a certain degree, dependent on competency in the native language, Spanish (Cummins, 1979).

If Cummins' hypotheses are true, given what is known about the interrelationship of language and cognition, then efforts must be intensified to raise the Spanish-language competence of children in bilingual education classes. And what better way to do it than through children's literature?

The benefits of early exposure to literature have been well documented. As compared to young children who do not have stories read to them, children who do (have stories read to them) have the potential to develop more sophisticated language structure, accumulate more background information, develop an awareness for story structure, and have more interest in learning to read (Morrow, 1984).

Spanish Children's Literature and the Read-Aloud Strategy

Why children's literature? Why the read-aloud strategy? The answers are found in the following pages.

When parents or teachers read literature aloud to children, it exposes them to more common forms of language. Many Spanish-speaking students in bilingual education classrooms speak nonstandard dialects of Spanish. Much of it is learned at home and in the neighborhood with friends. Constant correction or intervention is neither helpful nor recommended; it can leave the impression with children that they must choose between language forms of books and teachers over those of friends and relatives. Research shows that listening to stories and responding to them orally through discussion or dramatization can help students adopt a more standard dialect at school (Fisher and Elleman, 1984). When students themselves read stories aloud, they are actively participating in the educational process: they learn to pronounce words clearly and to enunciate distinctly by projecting the voice aloud. They learn to read with expression that can come only from understanding what they read. It makes them feel good to hear Spanish literary forms, which they may or may not fully understand, and the messages which they convey that flow from the same cultural value system. These are psychological spin-offs that contribute to their feelings of security and good self concept. When stories or plays or poems are dramatized, they also aid in the development of memory, a very prized instrument for learning.

Reading aloud in Spanish-speaking countries is a common school activity in which children learn to read with expression and feeling. Even though it is a reading-aloud activity, it is known as "la escuela del buen hablar" (school for good speaking), according to (Ada, 1980), on the assumption that if you read aloud well, you are a good speaker and practice makes perfect. Schools in the United States, on the other hand, do not emphasize oral reading; instead they encourage students to read silently in order to increase comprehension. We see the result of this school practice on oral speech at professional meetings where papers are literally read in a monotonous and incredibly boring manner (Ada, 1980). It is suggested that teachers provide reading aloud practice at least once a week for those who are able to read independently and reading aloud by the teacher for children of all ages.

Reading aloud introduces students to new words. Children learn new words by hearing them *spoken* in a meaningful context. It is suggested that the teacher first screen each story, poem, or play for words that will be new to the pupils and then help children use context clues to comprehend the meanings of those works. For example, few children would not grasp the meaning "goloso" in the story of "La Cucarachita Martina y el Ratoncito Pérez" (Masses and Almendros, 1969):

. . . El ratoncito, que era muy *goloso*, sintió la tentación de probarlo porque tenía hambre. . .

Teachers can make a list of unknown vocabulary words before teaching the piece. Students not only will hear it once or twice but as often as necessary to accomplish the following: read it, recite it, retell it, tell it in their own words, dramatize it, etc.

Reading aloud introduces children to more complex sentence structure. Children develop spoken language by imitating what they hear. By accident and design, much of the language children heard at home and at school does not have complex sentence structure. For example, managerial classroom instructions such as "Voy a pasar lista" (I'm going to call roll), "Levanten la mano" (Raise your hand), etc. require sentence structures referred to by Cummins (1983) as Basic Interpersonal Communication Skills (BICS) and are on a very simple level of language. By contrast, as is illustrated in the poem below, poetry can aid in the development of the more sophisticated structures, Cognitive Academic Language Proficiency (CALP) also attributed to Cummins (1983):

Romance de don Gato

Estaba el Señor don Gato
en silla de oro sentado,
calzando media de seda
y zapatito calado,
cuando llegó la noticia
que había de ser casado
con una gatita rubia,
hija de un gato dorado
Don Gato, con la alegría,
subió a bailar al tejado;
tropezó con la veleta
y rodando vino abajo;
se rompió siete costillas
y la puntita del rabo.
Ya llaman a los doctores
sangrador y cirujano;
unos le toman el pulso,
otros le miran el rabo;
todos dicen a una voz:
--¡Muy mal está el señor Gato!
A la mañana siguiente
ya van todos a enterrarlo.
Los ratones de contento

se visten de colorado;
las gatas se ponen luto,
los gatos, capotes pardos,
y los gatitos pequeños
lloraban: ¡miau!
           ¡miau! ¡miau! ¡miau!
Ya lo llevan a enterrar
por la Calle del Pescado.
Al olor de las sardinas
don Gato ha resucitado.
Los ratones corren, corren,
detrás de ellos corre el Gato.
           Canción popular

The language of literature differs from the ordinary common form of language because it implies a language that carries musicality, rhythm, sensory images, and beauty of description; it is language that speaks of intrigue, tensions, character, anger, happiness, sadness, etc. in creative ways that are not simply expositive, like language in school books. By definition the language of literature is embellished, rich, and varied, the perfect place to learn new language sentence structure.

Reading aloud exposes students to different styles of written language. Written language is more than transcribed talk. An author's narrative description of a setting will differ from the way the author writes dialogue between two people. As students listen to stories read to them, they develop a sense of the subtleties and variations in written language. They can then use that language when they write their own stories, poems, and reports. Students also can keep journals in which they record their feelings and experiences.

Conclusion

Language development for Spanish-speaking students in bilingual classrooms can be hastened and enhanced through reading aloud of Spanish children's literature. While reading aloud to students is common in early childhood and primary grades where children are not yet able or just beginning to learn the skills to read alone, it all but disappears in the upper elementary grades as children acquire the skills to read independently. Given the multiple benefits that can accrue to the Spanish-speaking child from reading Spanish children's literature aloud on a daily basis, it is a strategy no bilingual education teacher can afford to underutilize.

References

Ada, A. F. Informal lecture at The University of Texas at El Paso, Summer 1980.

Burt, M., & Dulay, H. Should we teach children syntax? *Language Learning*, 1973, *23*, 245-258.

Chazan, M., & Cox, T. Language programmes for disadvantaged children. In V.P. Varma & P. Williams (Eds.) *Piaget, psychology and education: Papers in honour of Jean Piaget.* Itasca, Ill.: F.E. Peacock, 1976.

Cummins, J. Conceptual and linguistic foundations of language assessment. In S.S. Seidner (Ed.), *Issues of language assessement (V.2): language assessment and curriculum planning.* Ill.: Illinois State Board of Education, 1983.

Cummins, J. Linguistic interdependence and the educational development of bilingual children. *Review of Educational Research,* 1979, *49*(2), 233.

Español, segundo grado, lecturas. México, D.F.: Secretaría de Educación Pública, 1972, 133-134.

Fisher, C. J., & Elleman, B. The read-aloud remedy. *Instructor,* January 1984, 66-68.

Fishman, J. A. *Language loyalty in the United States.* The Hague: Mouton, 1966.

Gaarder, B., et al. Teaching Spanish in school and college to native speakers of Spanish. *Hispania,* 1972, *55*, 619-631.

Krashen, S. D. *Principles and practice in second language acquisition.* New York: Oxford/Pergamon Press, 1982.

Masses, R.R., & Almendros, H. *Había una Vez.* Cultural Centroamericana S.A./Editorial Vasco Americana, 1969.

Morrow, L. M. Reading stories to young children: Effects of story structure and traditional questioning strategies on comprehension. *Journal of Reading Behavior,* 1984, *16*(4), 273-287.

U.S. Commission on Civil Rights. *A better chance to learn: Bilingual bicultural education.* Clearinghouse Publication #51, 1975.

Valdés, G. Pedagogical implications of teaching Spanish to the Spanish-speaking in the United States. In Valdés et al. (Eds.), *Teaching Spanish to the Hispanic bilingual.* New York: Columbia University, Teachers College Press, 1981.

The Hispanic American in English Composition Classes

by Maureen A. Potts and Willard P. Gingerich

Introduction

It has long been an hypothesis among those of us who teach writing courses with a significant minority population that the minority students have greater difficulty achieving written literacy than do their Anglo counterparts. This assumption is almost always made about our Hispanic students, particularly in those areas of the country where they tend to cluster in large groups--like New York, Southern California, and the Southwest. Teachers have based their impressions on the high number of Hispanic students who are funneled into remedial or basic writing courses and on their high rate of failure. In desperation, many teachers have searched the literature on the subject only to find that most of it addresses the problems of the ESL student, or the true bilingual who has achieved a fairly high level of written literacy in his native language.[1] The students we are discussing in this paper, however, the kind that we find in our remedial composition classrooms in increasing numbers, are not truly bilingual in that they do not possess written literacy in any language, including Spanish. It is these students that the system most often misapprehends, assuming as we do that because they are products of English schools, they therefore enter University English classes on an equal basis with their monolingual peers. Before the specific writing needs of these "interlingual" students can be addressed, we first need to remind ourselves of the language and cultural heritage they bring with them to the composition classroom.

To begin with, Hispanic-American beginning or basic writers' possess a wide and confusing range of language competencies. To what extent they speak Spanish as a first language, are bilingual (or "interlingual"--codeswitching continously between English and Spanish), or speak a specifically local dialect of both Spanish and English is not clear, even to the students themselves. When asked if they are bilingual, they have difficulty answering. Usually, these students are not themselves immigrants but are the children or grandchildren of immigrants whose parents probably speak Spanish in the home but whose previous education has been in English exclusively. Since such students are not foreign students (they are, for the most part, American citizens), they are not eligible for specially funded ESL programs, and for all practical purposes we presume they enter our composition classroom on equal footing with monolingual, non-Hispanic students.

Studies done by the authors and other researchers suggest that the Hispanic basic writer does indeed manifest many of the problems that are common to all basic writers, including native speakers. They have a limited vocabulary, and their syntax is rudimentary, often garbled. Indeed, some of these students have no control over the simplest of English sentence structures, but when asked to write in Spanish, they exhibit the same lack of skills. Further, they possess no real strategies for composing discourse units larger than sentences, their language is largely oral, and their reading skills are often 5-6 years below grade level. They have poor motivation, little or no concept of study skills, and usually possess records of failure in their other courses as well as in English.

In addition to the above, however, the Hispanic writer also has a set of unique problems. He brings to the classroom language skills that are largely oral as does his non-Hispanic peer, but, in addition, he has two oral systems to manipulate, or if, as some insist, he has one, it is a mixture of English and Spanish, sometimes referred to as "Spanglish." Years of discrimination have generally convinced him that Spanish is an inferior language, and, by extension, an expression of an inferior culture. Consequently, many of the Hispanic students we attempt to teach have no real language identity they feel comfortable with at the level of academic discourse, no oral mastery which will serve them in the context of the university. It is difficult for us, at present, to assess the extent to which this situation impedes the writing abilities of our Hispanic students, but we do know it has a profound effect on them.

One of the earliest but mistaken assumptions we have made about the writing problems of these Hispanic students is that language interference is the major cause of their poor writing abilities, e.g., writing "these" for "this" because in Spanish "this" sounds like "deez." More and more, research is telling us that this scenario is simply not the case. Studies at Pan American University in Edinburg, Texas in 1978 concluded that only a small number of errors in the writing of Hispanic students appeared directly attributable to Spanish interference (Amastae, 1981). And our own studies at The University of Texas at El Paso indicate that while Hispanics enroll in our basic writing course in numbers disproportionate to their total enrollments in the freshman year, once in the course they do no worse than their non-Hispanic peers; in fact, they do slightly better (Gingerich and Potts, 1984). We do not mean to assert, however, that the dual language situation of the Hispanic student does not affect his/her writing. In an excellent article on Spanish language interference on written English, Betty Rizzo and Sanitago Villarne state, "it is not possible to claim that any particular error in writing can be better understood by exclusively applying knowledge of the Spanish language, but it is one perspective, among others, which may help." They go on to enumerate instances in which Spanish pronunciation causes spelling errors ("birtually" for "virtually") and where Spanish grammar and idiom transfers into English as "error." The student who writes, "She didn't do nothing about nothing" is doubling his negatives, a perfectly acceptable practice in Spanish, and the next student who writes, "In the publics schools, as far as I can see, seems like nobody cares about the students," is making her adjective agree in number with its noun. (The "s" on "public" was probably carefully added after proofreading.) The authors conclude that "it is valuable to both teacher and student to recognize why a student writes as he does, and why he commits certain characteristic errors. When the teacher percieves that the student is not committing errors out of ignorant willfulness or willful ignorance, he will begin to show a necessary respect for and interest in where the student has been and what he has been learning before his arrival in the present class." There also are characteristic errors a Hispanic may commit because he is applying the logic of Spanish syntax, grammar, or usage to English structures as in the case of run-on sentences which tend to be far more tolerated (therefore not "run-on") in Spanish than in English. But many of these errors are on the surface only (and immediately obvious to any competent bilingual teacher) and do not fully account for the far more serious writing problems that the Hispanic basic writer exhibits. As we have suggested above, many of these problems he shares with his non-Hispanic peers, and research has not yet satisfactorily or reliably defined the sets of problems (other than the surface idiomatic ones suggested by Rizzo and Villarne) peculiar to the Hispanic basic writer. Working on the temporary assumption, then, that both the Hispanic and non-Hispanic basic writer have many of the same problems, we would now like to suggest some possible teaching strategies to help them overcome their difficulties with writing.

Reading

One of the main reasons the above described students have such problems with written language is that they are not print oriented to standard written English. For whatever reasons they have not developed a habit of reading and, as a result, their intuitive grasp of English syntax is largely oral, hence the codeswitching and interference problems. Such students often come from homes that do not have books and magazines lying around and where there is little encouragement from parents to read. An informal survey of our own freshman basic writers at The University of Texas at El Paso (UTEP) indicates that they do little reading outside of absolutely required texts in their other classes. As a result, they have come to associate reading with difficult study and because they have no reading strategies, they do not do it well. Consequently, they get poor grades, which makes them dislike reading, which precipitates a vicious circle. In an attempt to break into this circle, at UTEP we have intitiated a combined reading and writing course for our very weakest basic writers. The reading component consists of a reading lab in which students bring to class reading material they think they will enjoy, and then they sit there and read it. Once every two weeks they may seek help from the reading instructors who are always present at the lab. When asked to write a response to his work at the end of the semester, one student wrote:

> Throughout the semester, I have read 6 books. That was more than I have done in my four years of high school. It was easier to do than I had expected and I even enjoyed most of the reading. Next time I have the need to read a book, I will not hesitate to do so and try and make it fun.

This student's description of his reading habits was fairly typical for most of the students in the class. An extreme case was the student who admitted at the end of the course that he had never read a book in his life, and now he had read two. Because of their poor, in some cases nonexistent, reading habits, the more formal structures of written English are foreign to them and must be consciously taught. Before we can expect such students to begin generating correct formal written English sentences, they must begin reading and they must develop the reading habit. More and more we are realizing that so much of our grasp of language--oral or written--is intuitive. While formal instruction in rules and grammar patterns may help, to achieve any degree of proficiency students must be saturated with exposure to the written language. Only then will they begin to internalize the proper patterns of standard written English. Students who write "freshment" for "freshman," "I thing as an individual" for "I think as an individual," and "I would have had a better chance of pasting the course" for "I would have had a better chance of passing the course" are not used to seeing the proper forms on the printed page. Their grasp of the language is largely oral, and they are writing what they hear, not what they have seen in print.

But how do we get such students to read? Daniel Fader's *Hooked on Books* (1976) offers some useful strategies. Fader describes an English classroom situation in which students learn to read with books they enjoy before they are forced to grapple with more difficult texts. He insists that "pleasure and enthusiasm must be the first goal of the English teacher." Students, particularly the kind we are discussing here, will never read on their own unless they can be convinced there is some pleasure in it. We can set up our classroom to create a reading environment for them, but they must carry their engagement with books outside the classroom and into their everyday lives before they can hope to become fluent with standard written English. Fader suggests having newspapers, magazines, and paperback books present in abundance in the English classroom and encourages the teacher to spend a large amount of class time reading and discussing. While it is true that there are reading strategies we can teach our students to help them read better (Burmeister, *Reading Strategies for Secondary School Teachers*, 1974, 1978), in the long run they must become immersed in the dialect of standard written English. Quite apart from improving reading speed and comprehension, this immersion will improve vocabulary, give them ideas for writing content, and reinforce the appropriate patterns of standard written English.

Another strategy we would suggest in an attempt to help the Hispanic move away from interference problems is oral reading. We would not recommend having students read aloud in class as their performance can be disastrous and acutely embarrassing. Reading privately to the instructor, however, or into a tape recorder for later review by student and instructor together can be immensely helpful. In such sessions, the instructor should always keep in mind the student's sense of inadequacy and insecurity with standard English patterns. He will not easily forget the ridicule he has experienced in his previous educational career and will not react positively to excessive criticism.

Sentence Combining

A second strategy that has proved most successful in reinforc ing appropriate English syntactical patterns and overcoming interference problems for the Hispanic basic writer is sentence combining. There are many texts available on the market--most notably Frank O'Hare's *Sentencecraft* (1975), Rippon and Meyers *Combining Sentences* (1979), Daiker, Kerek and Morenberg *The Writers Options* (1979), and Bill Strong's *Sentence Combining* (1983) and *Sentence Combining and Paragraph Building* (1981). In addition, Strong has recently come out with two more texts that are particularly suited to the basic writer *Practicing Sentence Options* (1984) and *Crafting Cumulative Sentences* (1984), both published by Random House. Of all the above possibilities, I would suggest the last two as most appropriate for the Hispanic basic writer from junior high school up. Both emphasize sentences as part of a paragraph, and both encourage the student to move on to his or her own creative writing at the end of the section. All of Strong's texts have an advantage over most on the market because he graduates his exercises from simple patterns to more difficult ones and tries to lead the student from isolated sentence structures in to matters of rhetorical context.

Sentence combining has its limitations in that students do not generate their own content, but by manipulating and combining existing kernels, they learn about the resourcefulness of the English language. They soon come to understand that even though there are many possible wrong ways to put an English sentence together, there are also many right ones; further, some combinations although right, are not as effective as others in relation to surrounding sentences. Sentence combining is also a marvelous way to show students that some parts of the sentence can move around while others cannot and that there are grammatical reasons for this phenomenon.

In other words, sentence combining gives the student exposure to variations in English syntactical patterns and encourages him or her to experiment with them. It is amazing how quickly students catch on and begin to internalize the structures they manipulate. All the grammar exercises in the world will not teach English syntactic patterns so quickly or so thoroughly. And if the instructor must teach grammar, sentence combining is an excellent way to do it. When a particular combination does not "work"--the student usually describes it as not sounding right--the class can explore why and the instructor can introduce the grammatical concept as an explanation. This way, the students learn their grammar in the context of a specific problem, not part of an isolated exercise. Finally, sentence combining also teaches students that they can change and restructure their sentences. One ot the most common preconceptions a basic writer holds is that once he starts a sentence, he is committed to it, no matter how convoluted it emerges. Sentence combining convinces the basic writer that it is acceptable, indeed admirable, to scratch out the beginnings of a try at a sentence and start again.

We would not advocate an entire semester of an English class given over to sentence combining once students understand what it is all about. The best way to integrate sentence combining into an English classroom is to explain the procedure to students, let them experiment, and then spend 15-20 minutes at the beginning of each class working with clusters. For Hispanic writers who may be even less familiar with idiomatic patterns of standard written English, it might be best to intensify sentence combining work at the beginning of the semester until they begin to feel at ease with the process, see they can do it, and start to experiment. Once they gain confidence in manipulating English sentences through sentence combining, it is then easy to lead them into using the same patterns in their own sentences. Done properly and with regularity, the carry-over into students' own compositions is remarkable, much more than could ever be accomplished through grammar drill and fill in the blank type exercises.

Free Writing and Journals

While sentence combining gives students confidence with writing at one level, it is also necessary to move them on to confidence in creating fuller compositions. One of the best ways to overcome the initial fear of composing an essay is to use warm-up exercises called free writing. Peter Elbow (1973) calls this type of writing "automatic writing," "babbling," or "jabbering" exercises. The idea is to write continuously for a set period of time, say 10 minutes at first and then gradually move to 15 or 20 minutes. Instruct students to write whatever comes into their heads, even if they have to write "I have nothing in my head." They should not stop to look back, to cross something out, to wonder how to spell something, or to worry about sentence structures. The only requirement is that they not stop. This kind of writing may seem pointless at first, but it does get the pencil moving across the paper without fear of censure. Students are so geared to not making mistakes that their major concerns when they are composing is spelling and grammar. This is not to say that spelling and grammar are not important. They are. But such considerations come well along in the composing process, at the editing stage, not in the preliminary warm-up and thinking stages.

In addition, free writing can also be used to explore a topic or to brainstorm it in writing. Have your students write for 10 minutes on the subject at hand, stop and do some physical stretch exercises, sit in groups of two or three and share what they have come up with, and then go back to free writing for another 10 or 15 minutes. Tell them to let their minds wander over the subject and write whatever occurs to them about it. They and you will be amazed at how much they have written and how much they have to say about the topic. From the pages of material they have generated they can now begin to sort and arrange, focus on one aspect, see the germ of an essay emerge, or discard the whole business and start again. Both student and teacher should remember, however, that the audience for this type of writing is the writer himself. Free writing is simply a method of getting ideas down on paper, of exploring and gathering and discarding, of getting the creative juices stimulated and flowing. Like sentence combining, it is a means to an end, not an end in itself, and properly used it can be an invaluable strategy for the basic writer to learn. Consequently, the student should be allowed to write in any kind of hieroglyphics he wishes and should never be censured for sloppiness or disorderliness. At this stage, sloppy is okay.

Some instructors use free writing more systematically by having students keep journals. In these journals, students are required to produce on a regular basis (four to five entries per week) self-expressive pieces of writing that are unstructured and ungraded. Students are encouraged to explore their own ideas in writing, react to their environment or events around them, whatever, so long as they keep writing and writing and writing. The great advantage to this exercise for the basic writer is that it, like free writing, gives the student an opportunity to practice writing without the threat of a grade and encourages fluency. One of the most serious mistakes we make as writing teachers, suggests James Britton (1975), is to think we have to grade everything our students write. While the industry of composition teachers who do this is commendable, it is energy that is often self-defeating. Students soon learn avoidance strategies, like the student who bragged to us that the best advice he ever gave to his younger brother on entering a composition class was to write as little as possible. That way, he told him, "you'll make fewer mistakes." Finally, journal writing makes available to our students an invaluable tool--the ability to use writing to probe, to explore, and to learn.

The Composing Process

One of the fundamental mistakes made by most teachers who deal with Hispanics and native English speaking, basic writers is to assume that their first need is drill in grammar. This approach makes the student work endlessly at exercises on the assumption that first they need to get the words right, and then the sentences, and only then can they move on to write a full paragraph. The course usually goes into a holding pattern at this point as students are drilled about topic sentences and supporting material and are then allowed to write paragraphs. Rarely are such students encouraged to write full essays, the instructor assuming that since their grasp of the written English language is so flawed they cannot possibly execute a complete composition. Instructors who adopt the above approach assume that we learn to compose linearly, that we progress from learning words to sentences to paragraphs to essays. We now know that this progression is simply not true. The best way to learn to compose is to compose, to write full essays, not parts of one. If the expression is mundane, if the ideas are halting, if the product is riddled with fragments and garbled sentences and spelling errors, at least the student has written a full piece of work. Supplemented with sentence combining, errors tend to take care of themselves over time if students deal with them in the context of their own writing.

The best approach recent research has given us in regards to dealing with all writing instruction--including, indeed particularly for, the Hispanic basic writer--is to consider writing as a process, not a product. Taught from this point of view a novice writer would approach his task in the following manner. First he would free write his way through the preliminary stages of this thinking (assuming the topic has been assigned) and would talk to his peers in group sessions about the topic. Then he would consciously consider the rhetorical context for the piece--such matters as whom the writing is intended for, the occasion for the essay (not a class assignment!), and what effect or purpose the writer wishes to achieve with the audience. Then he might begin organizing his material from the free write into some kind of structure. For beginning writers, we have found that this is the stage they most often ignore. They do not realize that a piece of writing must be consciously organized, that it does not just happen by itself. Once this fact has been pointed out to them, they seem to grasp it quickly, however, and with practice soon start to produce structured writing.

From this beginning structure (preliminary outline?) the student can then be led through several drafts, each one working on matters of further content development and organization until both teacher and student feel the paper is taking shape. Then, and only then, should matters of grammar and usage become important. With a final editing and proofreading stage, the paper is ready for the instructor to evaluate. More and more we are beginning to understand that the writing process is a terribly complex procedure involving countless decisions on many levels. The basic writer usually approaches the task by attempting to generate content, organize, worry about spelling and grammar and punctuation, be concerned about inane expression and wordiness, all at the same time. No one can possibly keep all these considerations in mind simultaneously. It is the job of the instructor to encourage multiple drafts, to break into the writing process at each stage to give feedback, and to suspend judgment on such matters as style and grammar until well on in the process.

The above approach may seem too ambitious for the students we are discussing in this paper--those who have only a halting command of standard written English-- but in our experience, requiring beginning writers to write works far better than grammar drills in helping them to achieve written fluency. The writing instructor must have patience and a high tolerance for chaos at first, but the writing will come together if the student is encouraged and is allowed to make mistakes. No one ever learns to swim by paddling around in the wading pool.

In conclusion, it seems that at this time research has not yet told us whether the Hispanic basic writer has his own unique set of problems, let alone how to deal with them. One area of further research that we speculate may yield some interesting answers is that of cultural stress. A number of anecdotal and impressionistic factors lead us to suspect that classroom attitudes toward English and English writing may be a significant factor among Hispanic students. An extreme case is the adult student who failed our basic writing course four times--in spite of the fact that she lived almost all her life in the United States, had gone through the public schools, spoke English with perfect fluency, and was obviously bright. She told us she is sure her problems with written English are psychological and the consequence of having been physically punished for speaking Spanish in grade school. More typical are the Hispanic students who describe memories of hostility and anger toward English when they were told by elementary teachers that they could no longer use Spanish in their classrooms, hostility which would often be expressed only as secret, passive resistance. On the opposite side, the ease with which an occasional multilingual Dutch or German or Spanish student sometimes passes through our writing programs further suggests that language itself is not an issue at all, that the sociocultural context of the Hispanic student living in our society and the subtle racism and isolation that often occurs may be a secret, living presence in our classrooms. Of course, the examination of attitudes is difficult and would have to be coordinated with more concrete data on such matters as socioecomonic status, the degree of bilingualism and language identity, sex, and educational level of parents. Future research, then, needs to examine the stress factors involved as the Hispanic basic writer attempts to learn standard written English.

For the moment, however, it appears that what works with the non-Hispanic basic writer works equally well with the Hispanic since most of their problems are the same. Having acknowledged this fact, we would still suggest that writing instructors can do a great deal to break into the vicious circle of inferiority many Hispanics feel about their language situation. Such students can be convinced that their own dialect, whatever its blend of colloquialisms from both English and Spanish, is an acceptable way of communicating in certain situations. Learning standard written English merely involves mastering another dialect, not the "correct" one, and is useful in manipulating one's way through the various demands of American society. In the process of learning this dialect, however, students should never be allowed to forget the richness of their own native dialect and the culture of which it is an expression. Learning the conventions of standard written English should not mean that the student feels he has to reject an inferior language and culture. It is this assumption that, unfortunately, our public schools have too often fostered in the past, and has led, we suspect, to feelings of guilt and betrayal and anger among many of our Hispanic students. If there is any one thing we can do as composition teachers for the Hispanic basic writer, it is to recognize and respect his dual, sometimes even confused, language situation and attempt to foster an informed, sympathetic attitude toward his struggle to learn standard written English.

Notes

1 The authors have compiled an extensive bibliography of material available on the Hispanic bilingual student, We have included here a much shortened version. The complete bibliography will be submitted upon request to those interested.

2 We use the term "basic writer" as first defined by Mina Shaughnessey in *Errors and Expectations* (1977) to denote the student with the writing problems described in this paragraph. Those who are truly bilingual, or who achieved a high rate of written literacy in Spanish, soon pick up English syntax and usage and readily learn to compose. They do not have the same problems as does the Hispanic basic writer we are describing in this paper.

3 For specific ideas on the use of the journal in the composition classroom see Donald Stewart, *The Authentic Voice: A Pre Writing Approach to Student Writing* (1972), Michael Paull and Jack Klegerman, "Invention, Composition, and the Urban College" (1972), Daniel Fader, *Hooked on Books* (1976), and Toby Fulwiler, "Journal Writing Across the Curriculum" (1980).

References

Amastae, J. The writing of Hispanic students. In B. Cronnel (Ed.), *The writing needs of linguistically different students.* Los Alamitos, California: SWRL Educational Research and Development, 1981. (ERIC Document Reproduction Service No. D 210 923)

Arapoff, N. Writing as a thinking process. *TESOL Quarterly,* 1967, *1,* 33-39.

Britton, J., et al. *The development of writing abilities (11-18).* Urbana, Ill.; The National Council of Teachers of English, 1975.

Burmeister, L. *Reading strategies for middle and secondary school teachers* (2nd ed.). Menlo Park, Ca.; Addison Wesley, 1974, 1978.

Cronnel, B. (Ed.) *The writing needs of linguistically different students.* Los Alamitos, Calif.: SWRL Educational Research and Development, 1986. (ERIC Document Reproduction Service No. ED 210 923)

Daiker, D., et al. *The writer's options: College sentence combining.* New York: Harper and Row, 1979.

De Avila, E. A., & Duncan, S.E. The language minority child: A psychological, linguistic, and social analysis. In J. E. Alatis (Ed.), *Georgetown University Round Table on Languages and Linguistics.* Washington, D.C.: Georgetown University Press, 1980.

Durán, R. P. (Ed.) *Latino languages and communicative behavior.* Norwood, New Jersey: ABLEX Publishing, 1981.

Elbow, P. *Writing without teachers.* New York: Oxford University Press, 1973.

Fader, D. *The new hooked on books.* New York: Berkeley Publishing, 1976.

Fulwiler, T. Journals across the disciplines. *English Journal,* 1980, *69*(9), 14-19.

Gingerich, W., & Potts, M. The performance of Hispanic students at the University of Texas at El Paso in basic writing courses. *Border Issues and Public Policy Working Papers 11.* El Paso: The University of Texas at El Paso, The Center for Inter-American and Border Studies, 1984.

González, J. Bilingual education: Issues for the 80's. In J. Alatis (Ed.), *Georgetown University Round Table on Languages and Linguistics.* Washington, D. C.: Georgetown University Press, 1980.

Krashen, S. *Writing: Research, theory and application.* Los Angeles: University of Southern California, 1984.

Matthies, B. A non-native speaker of English learns to write--somehow. *The Canadian Modern Language Review,* 1980, *36,* 713-723.

Nattinger, J. Second dialect and second language in the composition class. *TESOL Quarterly,* 1978, *12,* 77-84.

Ney, J., & Fillerup, M. The effects of sentence combining on the writing of ESL students at the university level. Study report from the English department, Arizona State University, Tempe Arizona, 1980. (ERIC Document Reproduction Service No. ED 193 961)

O'Hare, F. *Sentencecraft.* Lexington, Ma.: Ginn and Company, 1975.

Paull, M., & Kligerman, J. Invention, composition, and the urban college. *College English,* March 1972, 651-59.

Peñalosa, F. Chicano multingualism and multiglossia. In E. Hernández-Chávez, A. D. Cohen, & A. F. Beltrán (Eds.), *El lenguaje de los Chicanos: Regional and social characteristics used by Mexican Americans.* Arlington, Va.: Center for Applied Linguistics, 1975.

Powell, B. ESL and composition: A report. *TESOL Newsletter,* 1980, (14), 3.

Rippon, M., & Meyers, W. E. *Combining sentences.* New York: Harcourt Brace Jovanovich, 1979.

Rizzo, B., & Villarne, V. *Spanish language influences on written English.* Source unknown, 62-71.

Shaughnessey, M. *Errors and expectations: A guide for the teacher of basic writing.* New York: Oxford University Press, 1977.

Sheorey, R. *Investigation of the problems in second language discourse and its pedagogical implications in the teaching of English as a second language at the advanced level.* Unpublished doctoral dissertation, The University of Texas at Austin, 1978. (BEBA 05405 8201).

Solé, Y. The Spanish/English contract situation in the Southwest In E. L. Blansitt, Jr. & R. V. Teschner (Eds.). *Festshrift for Jacob Ornstein.* Rowley, Ma.: Newbury House, 1980.

Stewart, D. *The authentic voice: A pre-writing approach to student writing.* Dubuque, Ia.: William C. Brown Company, 1972.

Strong, W. *Sentence combining and paragraph building.* New York: Random House, 1983.

Strong, W. *Sentence combining: A composing book* (2nd. ed.). New York: Random House, 1984.

Strong, W. *Practicing sentence options.* New York: Random House, 1984.

Strong, W. *Crafting cumulative sentences.* New York: Random House, 1984.

Zamel, V. Teaching composition in the ESL classroom: What we know from research in the teaching of English. *TESOL Quarterly*, 1976, *10,* 67-77.

Intersentential Codeswitching:
An Educationally Justifiable Strategy
by Rodolfo Jacobson

Introduction

Data concerning bilingual instructional methodology are still scarce, although some bilingual educators have recently come to realize that it is no longer enough to support bilingual education in principle but that there is a need to gain greater specific knowledge as to what actually works in a bilingual classroom. The question as to how one teaches bilingually must be addressed if he/she wishes to argue that bilingual education is preferable to monolingual education when teaching children from homes where a non-English language is the usual means of communication. This of course involves coming to grips with the kind of language distribution that is desirable for the classroom. Should the teacher switch back and forth from the school language to the home language, either randomly or by means of consecutive interpretation techniques? Should the teacher separate the two languages such that certain subjects are taught in L1 and others in L2? Or rather, should the teacher alternate between the two languages by controlling its distribution by the adherence to a structured pattern that allows the child to learn through both languages? This latter approach is now gaining recognition and beginning to generate research data of significance.

Language Distributional Practices--a Brief Survey

The few references available on the topic of language distribution in bilingual education (Andersson & Boyer, 1970; Cordasco, 1970; Gaarder, 1975; U.S. Commission on Civil Rights, 1975) have stressed the need for keeping home and school language separate from one another, either by assigning different time slots for either language or by using one language to teach, say, Social Studies, Art, Music and Physical Education and the other language, to teach Math, Science and Health. This strict separation of languages may be considered the most widely supported method of bilingual instruction, although the literature does not include a single study that proves the superiority of the *language separation approach* over other methods of bilingual instruction. Educators who support this conventional method of instruction object strongly to the *flipflopping approach* whereby the teacher alternates "randomly" between the school and the home language to overcome comprehension hurdles that some home language dominant children experience when taught in the school language, e.g.

T: This is a seed, ¿entienden? We plant it en la tierra para que eche raices. To make it grow fast, we water it. Le echamos agua and then the plant grows a stem and leaves.
¿Qué más tiene la planta?

ST: Hojas and a flower.

T: Have you all seen plants with leaves and flowers?

ST: (no response)

T: ¿Han visto Uds. plantas con hojas y flores?

ST: Yes.

Obviously, the meaning is conveyed to the children but the intrasentential switching may here interfere with the teacher's language development objectives. The conventional bilingual educator objects equally to the *concurrent translation approach* where everything that is said in the school language is also said in the home language. In this approach, the child can achieve academically, i.e. learn the subject of a lesson, without ever acquiring English. The preceding science lesson would go something like this:

T: This is a seed. Esta es una semilla. We plant it in the soil to develop roots. La sembramos en la tierra para que eche raíces. To make it grow fast, we water it. Para que crezca rápido, le echamos agua. The plant then grows a stem and leaves. La planta produce entonces un tallo y las hojas. What else does a plant have? ¿Qué más tiene la planta?
ST: Tiene hojas y una flor.
T: Have you all seen plants with leaves and flowers? ¿Han visto todos Uds. unas plantas con flores?
ST: Sí, maestra.

Recent studies in bilingual methodology by this writer have led to the development of a different type of language alternation approach, one which avoids the randomness of the flipflopping and the redundancy of the concurrent translation. The *New Concurrent Approach* makes use of intersentential, or rather interthought group codeswitching, such that certain segments of the lesson are taught in L1 and others, in L2. The alternation is initiated by the teacher only and as the result of a response to a given cue that he/she identifies in the class. The teacher switches languages only if he/she can rationalize, on linguistic, educational or attitudinal grounds, that the alternation at a given point will improve the quality of the lesson. The two languages are distributed at a ratio of 50-50 and the transitions from one to the other language are smooth enough never to disrupt the continuity of the lesson. The preceding samples could be adapted to the NCA Method as follows:

T: This is a seed. We plant it in the soil to develop roots. To make it grow fast, we water it. Después que la planta ha echado sus raíces y la hemos regado bastante, produce un tallo y las hojas. ¿Qué más tiene la planta?
ST: Tiene hojas y una flor.
T: Muy bien, tiene hojas y a veces tiene también flores. Have you ever actually seen plants with leaves and flowers?
ST: Yes, in my backyard.

The first switch to Spanish occurs after three complete sentences have been uttered in order to expose the child to a number of grammatical structures in English as the science concept is taught. The continuation of the lesson in Spanish allows for conceptual reenforcement and lexical enrichment (plantas, raíces, regar, tallo, hojas). The second switch, back to English, occurs at the end to explore the child's actual experience. The child's Spanish answer is however first acknowledged and expanded to ensure him/her that the answer was correct. This structural approach to language distribution, it is here argued, serves the parallel development of both languages necessary for the academic achievement of the bilingual child.

Critical Assessment.

On the basis of the methods surveyed in the preceding section, bilingual instructional methodology consists of three different approaches, i.e. (a) the conventional approach (language separation by time or topic), (b) the unstructured approach (flipflopping or concurrent translation) and (c) the structured approach (new concurrent approach). Neither the conventional nor the unstructured approach have been formally tested in regard to their relative effectiveness, but even before assessing them more rigorously, some shortcomings are evident in all of them, thus making it quite difficult for the teacher to select one and not the others.

(a) The conventional approach: If the language separation is based on the time factor, it is highly improbable that any teacher can teach all school subjects twice, once in the school language, English, and once in the home language, say Spanish. One of the languages will have to give and, because of the need to attain the proficiency level in English, the child will not receive the amount of instruction of Spanish that the bilingual program requires (e.g. preview-review). On the other hand, if the language separation is based on the content factor, there is no convincing argument available to single out a school subject as more appropriate for the teaching in Spanish and another, for the teaching in English. Furthermore, once a decision, arbitrary as it may be, is made, say, to teach Social Studies in Spanish and Math or Science in English, lexical and even conceptual deficiencies are noticeable when the subject matter is discussed in the language other that the one in which it was taught.

(b) The unstructured approach: If the language alternation is accomplished by means of mixing the two languages or, at best, by some variety of intrasentential codeswitching, the child is not exposed long enough to any one language to derive from the teacher's talk the grammatical, semantic and lexical rules of English nor Spanish. As a matter of fact this approach may increase the child's difficulty to tell one language apart from the other, although the conceptual meaning of whatever is taught may be understood by him/her. On the other hand, if the language alternation is accomplished through sentence-by-sentence translation, comparable to the consecutive interpretation technique in court procedures, all incentive to acquire the school language is lost as the child will phase him/herself out when the unfamiliar language is spoken as the lesson content can be fully understood by simply listening to the teacher's familiar home language version. In this latter approach a child may achieve academically without ever becoming proficient in English.

(c) The structured approach: The New Concurrent Approach developed by the writer during the last seven years in South and South-central Texas attempts to correct the above shortcomings. It has been defined in the literature (Jacobson, 1978; 1981; forthcoming;) as an approach through which the bilingual teacher teaches the school curriculum (except language arts) in the child's two languages concurrently, that is, switching from one to the other language as the teaching/learning situation may require. Each switching instance shall be pedagogically justifiable in light of four criteria:

(1) The languages are distributed at an approximate ratio of 50-50;
(2) The teaching of content is not interrupted;
(3) The teacher is conscious of his/her alternation between the two languages; and
(4) The alternation accomplishes a specific learning goal.

The structured alternation allows for the parallel development of both languages and avoids the concerns raised in regard to time and content. English and Spanish are distributed evenly and every school subject--except language arts--is taught in meaningful, justifiable alternation patterns. The teacher remains in each language long enough--at least for one sentence but most often for much longer--to allow the child to derive from each exposure the pertinent linguistic structures and, by the same token, to recognize one series of sentences as English and the other as Spanish. The redundancy of translations is avoided completely as nothing is actually translated. Simply, the lesson is taught in two languages but without breaking up the continuity of the lesson plan. Finally, the guidance provided in terms of language choice by the teacher leads the child effectively to internalizing a strategy that characterizes every bilingual person, that of alternating between two languages as the social situation may so demand. In order to determine whether the NCA (New Concurrent Approach) Method actually contained the advantages listed above, the presentor submitted to the U.S. Department of Education a proposal for the funding of a Title VII Demonstration Project in Bilingual Methodology that would permit the comparison of two bilingual methods on a longitudinal basis, in order to gather hard data on the relative effectiveness of the approaches used in teaching groups of comparison and treatment students. The Project that is now in its second year of implementation is described briefly in the following section.

The Title VII Demonstration Project in Bilingual Methodology.

The project was proposed, basically, to compare two bilingual instruction methods, the New Concurrent Approach (NCA) and the Language Separation Approach (LSA). Two schools of San Antonio's Southwest Independent School District are participating, one of which serves as the comparison school and the other as the treatment school. In 1981-82 a kindergarten and a first grade were identified in two of its schools in order to implement the NCA Method in a treatment school and LSA Method in a comparison school. The LEP (Limited English Proficiency) children admitted to these grades moved up to grades 1 and 2 during the current year and will be in grades 2 and 3 during 1983-84, so that their progress over three years of primary schooling can be assessed and the effect of the methodological variable be measured qualitatively and quantitatively. Each classroom operates with a certified bilingual teacher and a bilingual aide who work together in a teamlike setting. Although the major teaching responsibility lies with the teacher, the aide also teaches occasionally under the supervision of the teacher, the program coordinator or both. The Project is receiving the necessary funds to purchase equipment and to supplement district materials, so that the children have in their classes everything to make the learning experience a challenging one. The following three methodological settings describe the language distributional features of the Project.

(a) Home language development and second language acquisition: The development of Spanish Language and the acquisition and/or further improvement of English is an ongoing process during the three years of the program. At the kindergarten level it is however most obvious how the groundwork is laid for the children to function successfully in each of the methodological settings. Based upon the work of Jim Cummings and his associates (Cummins 1979, 1980) the program design gives particular attention to the development of the vernacular and the attainment of the threshold level in the child's first language. Ninety percent of the teaching at the pre-primary level is therefore in Spanish allowing only 10% of time for ESL instruction. There is almost no difference at this level of instruction between the comparison and the treatment groups except for the fact that, whereas the ratio of 90-10 is kept invariably for the latter, it is gradually modified for the former to arrive at a ratio of 75-25 by the end of the kindergarten year. The decrease of the home language and the increase of the majority language is the conventional procedure in bilingual programs and conveys to the child an implicit judgment concerning the relative values of his/her two languages which is avoided in the distributional pattern of the treatment groups.

(b) Language Separation Approach (LSA) on the basis of school subjects. An arbitrary choice is here made to teach Math, Science and Health in English and Social Studies, Art, Music and Physical Education in Spanish to all comparison students. The decrease-increase pattern is continued so that by the end of Grade One, 50 percent; by the end of Grade Two, 75 percent; and by the end of Grade Three, 100 percent of the instruction is in English. It is predicted that even with the reduction of Spanish over the three years of the program, the children will have reached their threshold level in the first language and perform academically well as they move to the end of the program. It is also predicted that, because of the decrease in the use of Spanish, their Spanish language proficiency will however suffer and, by the same token, will the attitude to the use of Spanish at school. The children's academic achievement, especially in the subjects taught in English, will be good but not superior.

(c) New Concurrent Approach (NCA) in content teaching only. The New Concurrent Approach (NCA) Method is used in all content classes. Accordingly, language alternations are always teacher-intiated. They are never shorter than one sentence but usually as long as 10 sentences or above depending on the length of the thought group or any other important reason for the switch. The switches occur in response to cues that the teacher identifies in the classroom. Some of these cues are from the broader area of Classroom Strategies, others from such areas as Curriculum Language Development, or Interpersonal Relationships.[1] Language arts proper is taught in the language to be developed further or upgraded. In the content areas, the ratio of distribution remains stable from grade 1 to 3 at 50-50 or as close to it as possible. A positive attitude toward both languages is stressed at all times as is the favorable attitude to the child's ethnic heritage but avoiding any feeling of marginality. In other words, bicultural education is made to go hand-in-hand with bilingual education. It is predicted that the children will develop both languages fully and improve their self-identity considerably. They will not only reach the threshold level in the first language, but be motivated to speaking the vernacular whenever its use is appropriate. It is also predicted that the children will achieve academically extremely well; as a matter of fact, better than the comparison groups. Finally, the treatment groups will have acquired the sociolinguistic knowledge to address people as warranted by the situation and to judge situations according to appropriateness for code selection.

ANALYSIS OF FIVE NCA CLASS SEGMENTS

Final conclusions concerning the success of the Project must await its termination. Some tentative findings can however be reported at this point already. An analysis of five class segments consisting of lessons taught in the NCA Method shall be described and its relevance to the potential outcome of the Project be briefly referred to.

(a) Description of corpus

Five class segments consisting of a total of 3,844 words have been recorded on audiotapes. The recordings represent two Math classes, two Social Studies classes, and one Science class. The first and second grade teachers conducting the classes are both regular teachers in the treatment school and experienced in the use of the NCA Method. Both teachers have been working in the Project since its beginning (Fall 1981), although one of them was assigned to the comparison school during the first year, whereas the other had been teaching at the treatment school both years. Ms. AG taught one of the Math lessons and Ms. EGR the remaining lessons of the total inventory of which 1,785 were Spanish words and 2,059, English words. This distribution of the two languages adjusts itself well to the program design as Spanish was spoken 46% of the time and English, 54%. The deviation of only 4% in favor of English is considered insignificant.

(b) Teacher talk

The teachers alternated between languages 39 times, an average of 7.8 alternations per lesson. The exact breakdown has been as follows:

Class Segment	Subject	Teacher	# of alternations	Topic	Grade
I					
II	Math	AG	5	Whole and halves	1
III	Social Studies	EGR	2	Addition	2
IV	Social Studies	EGR	8	Security, occupations	2
V	Science	EGR	7	Community helpers	2
		EGR	7	Insects	2

The shorter samples of teacher's talk range from one to 29 words. Only in one instance a sentence in English contains, for purposes of emphasis, a Spanish clause when Ms. EGR says:

(1) That's right, we did talk about looking both sides, viendo para los dos lados. (III, B/C:1)

Although this is an instance of intra-sentential codeswitching, it is worth noticing that, the English sentence structure had already been completed. All the remaining short utterances consist of one, two, three or six complete sentences. One incomplete sentence can be interpreted as an unsuccessful question technique to elicit the child's response.

(2) T: ....They have...
   ST: No.
   T: They have wings. The butterfly can fly. (V, F:1-3)

The longer uninterrupted samples of teacher talk surpass one hundred words and occasionally reach the 300's or 400's. There is usually only one such very long intervention in each class segment except for III where there are three:

Class segment	Words	Language	Words	Language	Words	Language
I	464	English				
II	336	English				
III	120	English	217	Spanish	356	English
IV	276	Spanish				
V	129	Spanish				

There seems to be no preference for any one language for these longer interventions as four of them are in English and three in Spanish. Obviously, one is here dealing with multiple number of sentences in one single language, so that the child's language exposure becomes almost like the one in a monolingual class. The teachers set, as expected, the pattern for language choice. Children violate the agreement only six times saying a total of sixteen words in the unelicited language:

III, E: 14-17 T: Otra persona más, Richard.
   ST: In the army.

T: ¿Qué?
ST: *In the army. Trocas*
III, F:32-33 T: Here is -- let's watch her -- Mrs. Wonderful. Come on.
ST: *A doctor.*
V, B:4-7 T: Spiders. Anything else, Jorge?
ST: *Gusanos.*
T: What?
ST: Worms.
V, B:8-10 T: Alex.
ST: *Cucarachos* [!] (laughs)
T: Spring bugs, cockroaches, ah?
V, G:1-3 T: ¿Quién puede decir ésta palabra? ?A ver, ésta palabra?
ST: *Ms. EGR may I go...*
T: No, nosotros estamos acá.....

This represents 4.03% of the children's utterances. Otherwise, they have followed strictly the convention of responding in the language in which they have been addressed, allowing hereby the teacher to select the language of instruction each time.

(c) Student talk
Children in the lower primary grades do not engage in a great deal of talk and limit themselves, almost exclusively, to answering questions in incomplete sentences; e.g.

(3a) T: No, we are not coloring wholes, we are coloring halves. All right. Now, we have another object down at the bottom, what's its shape?
ST: Pear
T: Pear, good. What color is around it?
ST: Green.
T: OK, is it green?
ST: Brown. (I, B, 38-44)
or
(3b) T: ....¿Quién más me puede decir lo que dijeron la vez pasada? Ramona ¿Qué hacía tu papá entonces?
ST: Es cajero.
T: oh, es cajero. Alex.
ST: Trabaja en guerra. [!]
T: ¿En guerra? ¿Está, ... es militar tu papá?
ST: Soldado.
T: Gracias, Felipe. ¿Es soldado?
ST: Sí.   (III, E:8-13)

The word count of children's responses as compared to teacher talk amounts in view of the shortness of their answers to only about 11.5% of class talk. Whereas children uttered a total of 397 words, teachers said 3,447. In some classes however children seem to talk more than in others as the following table illustrates:

Alternate	MATH (I)	MATH (II)	SOCIAL STUDIES (III)	SOCIAL STUDIES (IV)	SCIENCE (V)
A					
B	1	14			
C	23	10	12	4	17
D	6	---	0	12	13
E	6	24/395 = 6.08%	6	8	0
F	6		11	7	5
G	------		25	6	17
H	42/809 = 5.19%		44	3	8
I			65	0	12
J			0	------	0
K			----	40/585 = 6.8%	5
L			163/1,012 = 16.11%		14
M					17
N					5
O					0
P					0
Q					10
					1
					4

					128/1,033
					= 12.39%

The grammaticality of the responses is often difficult to determine as most of them are limited to one or two words. However, these very short responses fit grammatically into the sentence pattern used by the teacher to elicit the response, e.g.

    (4) T: ....First they drew what?
        ST: (They drew) a line.   (I, B:7-8)

or

    (5) T: If something real bad happens to you, what do we call that?
        ST: (We call it) danger.   (III, D:18-19)

or

    (6) T: Las cositas negras que vemos aquí mucho, ¿cómo se llaman?
        ST: (Se llaman) arañas.   (V, A:15)

The grammaticality of the responses is more obvious when longer utterances are used. The following longer than 2-word responses are in the corpus:

    (7) Sumar el 3 y (el) 2   (II, A:8)
    (8) ¡Qué se paren cuando pasa un carro!   (III, A:3)
    (9) Mirar a los dos lados   (III, A:5)
   (10) Para cuando la luz está roja.   (III, C:2)
   (11) They could be dead.   (III, D:13)
   (12) Trabaja en los botes.   (III, E:4)

(13) Trabaja en (cosas de) guerra. (III, E:9)
(14) By taking you to the house. (III, F:4)
(15) Taking us to the city. (III, F:6)
(16) They take you wherever you want to. (III, F:9)
(17) Take the bus. (III, F:42)
(18) By driving them to the hospital safely. (III, F:52)
(19) Ganando la guerra ayuda a la gente. (III, G:5)
(20) Le habla y le dice que como que (necesita que le traigan) una tierra. (III, G:14)
(21) Cuando tenemos un bebito, nos puede cuidar. (III, G:30)
(22) Cuando están mal(os). (III, G:33)
(23) Cuando le da calentura. (III, G:36)
(24) How about you? (IV, A:3)
(25) It's big. (IV, E:4)
(26) It's softlike. (IV, E:6)
(27) Las hormigas tienen más que cuatro. (V, E:7)
(28) La hormiga tiene ocho. (V, E:10)
(29) Mrs. EGR, may I go? (V, G:2)
(30) Some of the masters have four right here. (V, J:6)

Only five responses are minimally deviant but seem to be attributable to child language rather than lack of language proficiency due to other-language dominance. Also note that of the responses (7), (13), (20), (22), and (26), four are in Spanish and only one in English.

None of the responses reflect lack of comprehension as children answer all questions asked and provide meaningful clues to what is discussed in class. This assessment is of course made only on the basis of the children who responded. To conclude, the children's responses, in spite of their brevity, are grammatical and do reflect comprehension. Obviously, alternations occur, with very few exceptions (4 percent), only when triggered by the teacher. No mixing nor intrasentential codeswitching is noticeable in the entire corpus.

Disscussion.

The cited segments of five content classes as transcribed from the audio-tape recordings have shown that the children are exposed to sufficiently long speech samples in both languages each time that a teacher talks. The child has no difficulty in upgrading English when English is spoken and upgrading Spanish when Spanish is spoken. The alternation patterns of the NCA Method lend themselves to develop both languages in a parallel fashion as content is taught. The parallel development of English and Spanish is tied closely to the recognition that Spanish is as prestigious as English and that any school subject can be learned regardless of the language in which it is taught. The shortness of the children's responses is not language-specific; hence, it cannot be blamed on bilingual education nor on this particular method (NCA). More likely, it is the result of children's shyness in a formal class situation. Increased child talk could be accomplished by more innovative strategies that call for greater participation of children in the learning process.

The parallel language development is evidenced by the grammaticality of almost all the responses, whether they are single words, phrases, clauses, or full sentences. The five deviancies cited above are cases in point. The omission of the second occurrence of the definite article *el* is an interference from another potential structure, *sumar 3 y 2 [7].* The absence of *cosa de* or *asuntos de* is a child language deletion [13]. Sentence [20] is the most deviant one as it is almost incomprehensible without the insert *necesita que le traigan.* The child did not have the necessary vocabulary to get his message across. *Cuando están malos* instead of *cuando están mal* is a common colloquialism [22] and the use of *softlike* in [26] instead of *kind of soft* shows the child's familiarity with morphological processes. None of the deviancies represents interlanguage interference.

There is only one attempt made by a child to answer in English, whereas the question was in Spanish (III,E:15 and 17). This shows that the children feel equally competent in the two languages and it does not matter whether they respond in one or the other language. The adherence to the language choice pattern set forth by the teacher is almost total. The few exceptions (see above) can be explained as out-of-school experiences, like *dale*(III, F:33) and *doctor* (III, G:22), subconscious switches, like *gusano* (V, B:4) and *Ms. EGR may I go?* or humor, like Anglo-accented *cucaracho* [!] (V, B:9).

Intrasentential codeswitching is avoided by the children in the entire corpus and so is all kind of language mixing. In the very few cases where the child thought of the word or words in the other language first, he/she would stay entirely in that language, e.g. Ms. EGR may I go?, a doctor but not Sra. EGR, may I go or *un* doctor.

The children have developed interlinguistic flexibility as they alternate between languages with apparent ease. Obviously, the teacher's language switch does not present a comprehension hurdle. It is as if both language controls were constantly open so that the child might function in either language at all times. Regardless of his/her alertness to the switch, he/she captures the message that is conveyed. In other words, the alternation does not disrupt the continuity of the lesson. The learning of the subject matter goes on regardless of which language is spoken at a given moment. Hence, the child who is motivated to do well in class does not let him/herself phase out when one of the languages is spoken as he/she would then miss an important part of the lesson. In sum, the NCA Method may very well be the answer to how to teach the minority child bilingually as it brings together three very important objectives, i.e., dual language development, attitudinal growth, and academic achievement.

To return briefly to the Title VII Demonstration Project in Bilingual Methodology, the writer envisions an important feedback from it in that it will provide, after its third year of implementation, qualitative and quantitative data on the merits of the NCA Method. Plans are presently underway to replicate the Project and to make its results available to a larger audience. The adaptation of NCA to other hispanic or non-English settings might become a future goal, if and when the mentioned data support the tentative findings described in this paper.

Conclusion.

The preceding analysis and discussion of five class segments taught in the New Concurrent Approach Method by especially trained bilingual teachers shows that the reservations held by many bilingual educators in regard to language switching in the classroom do not hold for this type of language alternation method. This approach does NOT promote language mixing nor confusion as the children learn to keep the two languages apart from one another, distinguish them clearly and comprehend all parts of the lesson as evidenced in the transcriptions. It does NOT encourage failure to acquire English as the child cannot anticipate when alternations occur/nor whether the same topic will be taught in his/her dominant language at a later point. Rather, it enables him/her, as he/she learns the school subject, to develop further the home language and to become at the same time proficient in the language of the majority. Having become literate in both languages, the child can now achieve academically according to aptitude and do well in the broader society.

Notes

1 For greater detail please see Jacobson, R. The new concurrent approach. In R.V. Padilla (Ed.), *Biingual Educaion Technology, V. III. Ypsilanti, Mich.: Eastern Michigan Univiersity, 1981.*

References

Anderson, T., and Boyer, M. *Bilingual schooling in the United States.* Austin, Tx.: Southwest Educational Development Laboratory, 1970.

Cordasco, F. *Bilingual schools in the United States: A sourcebook for educational personnel.* New York: McGraw-Hlll, 1970.

Cummins, J. Cognitive/academic language proficiency, linguistic interdependence, the optional age question and some other matters. *Working Papers in Bilingualism,* No. 19, 1979.

Cummins, J. The entry and exit fallacy in bilingual education, *NABE Journal,* 1980, 4, 25-59.

Gaarder A. Bilingual education: A mosaic of controversy. In H. LaFontaine et al. (Eds.), *Bilingual Education.* Wayne, N.J.: Avery Publishing, 1978.

Jacobson, R. Codeswitching in South Texas: Sociolinguistic considerations and pedagogical applications. *LASSO-Journal,* 1978, *3,* (1), 20-32.

Jacobson, R. Beyond ESL: The teaching of content other than language arts in bilingual education. In Bauman and Sherzer (Eds.), *Working papers in sociolinguistics.* Austin, Tx.: Southwest Educational Development Laboratory, 1979.

Jacobson, R. The implementation of a bilingual instruction model: The new concurrent approach. In R. Padilla (Ed.), *Bilingual education technology, V. III.* Ypsilanti, Mi: Eastern Michigan University, 1981.

Jacobson, R. The role of the vernacular in transitional bilingual education. In Valdman et al. (Eds.), *Issues in international bilingual education: The role of the vernacular.* New York/London: Plenum, 1982.

United States Commision on Civil Rights. *A better chance to learn: Bilingual-bicultural education,* Clearinghouse Publication No. 51. Washington, D.C.: Government Printing Office, 1975.

Dialects and Initial Reading Options in Bilingual Education

by Dennis J. Bixler-Márquez

Introduction

The use of nonstandard varieties of English and Spanish in bilingual education as media of instruction continues to be a controversial issue, politically as well as pedagogically. Most of the research available on the role of dialects in initial reading instruction focuses on black English, with scant information available on Chicano English. The literature on the use of Chicano Spanish in education is oriented primarily toward secondary and post-secondary education. This chapter will concentrate on grades K-3, since most transitional bilingual education programs operate in those grades. The K-3 range also constitutes the span of time normally devoted to the acquisition of literacy in Spanish, oral development in English, and the transfer to English reading instruction.

Assumptions About Dialects and Instructional Options

Certain assumptions frame the relationship between dialects and the instructional options available to promote the acquisition and development of literacy. A predominant assumption is that dialects have no place in the classroom. Edwards (1984) stresses that such an assumption leads to instruction that fails to recognize and capitalize on the wealth of linguistic resources available for learning and teaching. It is important to note that the exclusion of the ethnic child's language in the classroom is tantamount to a personal and cultural rejection, which contributes to the development of a low-self concept in the student. In turn, low self-concept is usually associated with low academic achievement. The language and culture of the linguistically different child must be accepted, along with the child (Cárdenas, 1984). Educators must find ways of using his/her background for language and cognitive development. Indeed, several avenues exist for the treatment and/or utilization of dialects in the bilingual education classroom. These will be discussed later.

A second assumption is that spoken and written language are the same. Kress (1979) indicated that written language is organized in sentences, whereas oral language tends to occur in "complexes of clauses." Wolfram, Potter, Yanofsky, and Shuy (1979) argue that differences between written and spoken language exist among speakers of standard English as well as dialect speakers. All students usually encounter printed matter with syntactical, morphological, and phonogical patterns that are not part of their usual oral production. Thus, speakers of nonstandard varieties of Spanish and English will frequently encounter differences between oral language and printed matter, even when they have mastered the standard of these two languages.

Horowitz (1984) suggests that teachers need to consider that orality and literacy may differ for particular social groups, such as speakers of a nonstandard dialect. Differences between orality and literacy are accentuated to the extent speakers of a nonstandard dialect such as Chicano Spanish are members of a low socioeconomic group. Teachers, when selecting or modifying initial reading methods and techniques, must heed these differences in oral and formal language. The selection of an initial reading option for children who speak a non-standard variety of Spanish and/or English may rest on the reading-language relationship model to be followed (Horowitz, 1984 and Goodman, 1982). For example, some bilingual education programs teach initial reading simultaneously in Spanish and English. These programs follow a model in which oral language development in the second language is not considered a prerequisite to the acquisition of literacy in the second language.

A third assumption is that reading is just decoding, matching sounds with symbols. Oral reading includes both, though in initial reading, decoding and its accompanying difficulties receive far more attention that comprehension in the average classroom. This is usually the case with most synthetic methods for initial reading, such as the phonetic method, syllabic method, etc. However, it should be kept in mind that learning to read includes the extraction of meaning from printed matter, not just the production of sounds corresponding to symbols.

Language differences can cause some decoding, as well as some comprehension, problems for the beginning reader. However, Goodman and Flores (1979), in an account of reading behavior of bilingual children, suggest that the phonological differences are superficial, and that the reading process of bilingual children is still relatively proficient.

Reading behavior in which oral speech is substituted for written speech is common among both speakers of standard English and Spanish. If it does not interfere with comprehension, it should not be treated as a decoding problem. The reader is simply integrating the printed material with his/her semantic referents. Such a rendition may include features normally associated with the oral language of the reader, sometimes dialectal. Goodman (1973) provides a comprehensive discussion of the application of miscue analysis to reading instruction for the reader interested in this facet of reading.

A fourth assumption, perhaps the most controversial, is that speakers of a dialect are unable to comprehend the written standard. The research available in the field of reading indicates that the standard language is generally well understood by speakers of a nonstandard variety. Some dialectal differences can cause problems, but as Edwards (1984) indicates, their importance has been exaggerated: "The prescriptive attitudes toward language constitute a far more potent force in education failure than the actual differences." How a teacher identifies and treats dialectal differences seems to be a critical factor in determining reading success for speakers of a nonstandard dialect.

In the diagnosis of reading difficulties, teachers should be able to identify and differentiate dialectal features from developmental and linguistic interference errors. Also, they should avoid confusing learning disabilities such as aphasia and dyslexia with dialectal differences. The accurate identification and positive treatment of reading difficulties is a very important factor in promoting the acquisition and development of literacy.

Instructional Approaches

Somervill (1975), in a review of alternative solutions for the use of nonstandard dialects in the teaching of reading, has identified five major instructional approaches. These approaches are partially transposable to the issue of Spanish and English dialectal variations in bilingual education. Their application to bilingual education will be different, however, since Somervill's work addresses primarily the role of Black English.

In transitional bilingual education the first option is to teach initial reading in standard Spanish, followed by standard English at the transfer stage. On the average, the transfer from Spanish to English reading instruction is supposed to occur around second or third grade in a transitional program, assuming a child started the program at the normal entry level, kindergarden or first grade.

Bilingual education programs rely almost exclusively on commercially produced reading series and supplementary materials available only in standard Spanish. Some school districts with exemplary bilingual education programs have developed standard Spanish reading materials with more culturally and lexically relevant content. These strategies have proved effective, for as Joag-deu and Steffensen (1980) indicate, bicultural students have a better rate of reading comprehension with materials in their own culture than with materials from the second culture in the curriculum.

A substantial number of bilingual education programs in the nation have produced positive academic achievement results (Zappert & Cruz, 1977; Troike, 1978.) These successes suggest that significant progress can be made with the standard Spanish reading materials. The advantages of this option can be best understood when contrasted with the attributes and limitations of others, as the reader will see in the discussion of subsequent options.

A second option is to use dialectal readers. Again, in a transitional program, children would learn initial reading in Spanish. Chicano Spanish readers, as the main or supplementary series, would constitute all or part of the option.

Educators have often posed the question: If it is better to begin reading instruction in the native language, for Chicanos, shouldn't initial reading begin in Chicano Spanish rather that standard Spanish? In many of the Southwest's bilingual education programs this logic would apply.

This approach is the most controversial. While the Chicano movement has resulted in increased awareness and acceptance of Chicano language and culture, it has not overcome the strong opposition by various publics to the use of Chicano Spanish as an official vehicle of instruction. Parents and teachers are among the most vocal groups that oppose such a role for Chicano Spanish, paticularly if its use for initial and developmental reading will supplant in some manner the reading texts in standard Spanish or English.

Commercial publishing companies will not attempt to develop and market dialectal reading materials in Spanish or English. Fishben (1973) best represents the publisher's position: "because attitudes and concerns are divided and in transition--the publishing opportunities are not very attractive." It simply is not cost effective to produce reading series for each of the many varieties of Spanish and English (Ching, 1976).

At one time, the Spanish Curriculum Development Program in Miami, a federally funded program, went so far as to produce regional Spanish reading series: a Southeastern edition for Cubans, a Southwestern edition for Chicanos, a Northeastern edition for Puerto Ricans, and a combined Midwestern edition for all three Hispanic groups. That effort represented the only large-scale production of reading materials varied by language region. Such language variation was possible, because it was primarily lexical. The reading series and materials were not geared to address dialectal variations to any significant extent.

Some school districts have developed their own reading series, mostly as an alternative to materials from South America, the Caribbean, or México. Many educators felt the context and some of the vocabulary was not relevant to the background of Chicanos. The Cristal City and the Edgewood School Districts in Texas, to cite two examples, used federal funds to develop reading series and materials with themes that revolved around the culture and settings of their areas. Again, dialectal variations were not really addressed, only regional ones at the lexical level within the range of standard Spanish. Furthermore, without federal subsidies, those and most school districts could not afford to develop such materials.

While dialectal readers are potentially effective tools to acquire basic literacy skills, one must ask, are they absolutely essential? Are the differences so great and overwhelming between standard Spanish and the forms of Chicano Spanish that decoding and comprehension are significantly affected? Coballes-Vega (1985) reports that the differences are mostly lexical and are not considered an impediment to learning to read. The differences extend beyond the lexicon, but are quite surmountable when the teacher accepts the nonstandard features of the student's language and adds the standard as an alternative option for communication.

The standard Spanish reading series, with the caveats previously mentioned, remains the most viable option for initial reading instruction. Rather than discard this approach, school districts can supplement the reading series with approaches in which Chicano Spanish plays a powerful role. Standard Spanish reading materials can also be modified or supplemented in other ways, as discussed in the options that follow.

The third option is to neutralize the negative effects of the standard variety reading materials on the speakers of Chicano Spanish. This strategy has been proposed before under the banner of dialect free reading series and materials. Many scholars have written for some time about the difficulties surrounding the neutralization of the standard variety. Total neutralization, suggests Somervill (1975), may result in lengthy and cumbersome reading material. Instead, Wolfram, and Christian (1978) and Seymour (1973) suggest a more limited neutralization. Neutralization of selected features (those that have deterred effective reading in the classroom) is the most pragmatic route available under this option. Educators should restrict the neutralization process to aspects of standard Spanish that cannot be mastered without appreciable difficulty. This approach should be at best a tool used sparingly in cases of demonstrable need in reading standard Spanish.

At the developmental stage, as a variation of the preceding option, teachers can insure that students can decode, in isolation and in context, words that are problematic because of dialect differences. That is, teachers can address dialect-based difficulties as part of the reading preparatory work and post-reading activities normally performed by teachers. They can combine the aforementioned routes at their discretion.

The fourth option is to allow students to read standard readers in dialect form, a strategy originally proposed by Goodman (1969). As noted earlier, speakers of Chicano Spanish and English may give a dialectal rendition of the printed matter, particularly as they acquire fluency. At this and later stages of development the reader is more concerned with comprehension. He/she is sampling different clues in order to apprehend the significance of the printed matter. It is at this stage that "errors" caused by psycholinguistic guessing are likely to occur, but as Goodman (1971) indicates, they do not interfere with comprehension. The teacher's perception of such "errors" and the latitude given the student in oral reading are crucial variables in the success of this option. If the student is constantly interrupted and corrected, he/she cannot help to feel rejected. On the other hand, if a student is allowed to develop fluency, for example about 60 words per minute in initial reading in Spanish, he/she can continue to improve by not being afraid of making what, in many cases, are not errors.

The language experience method is the fifth option. Van Allen (1976) proposed this approach as a broad comunication development strategy that accepts and uses the child's culture and socioeconomic background through his/her language. In reading, students dictate stories or paragraphs that become the material to be read later, and which they are bound to understand since they dictated the content (Adler, 1979).

This approach has growth limitations, because the reading material is restricted to the child's language and experiences. The expansion of vocabulary and concepts beyond initial literacy has to occur mostly through commercial materials. Mace-Matluck (1982) indicates that the effective acquisition of literacy transcends the use of language for interpersonal communication, which is primarily context-supported. She suggests language development must include the use of language in context-reduced, relatively more abstract situations, if commmunicative competence through printed matter is to be achieved. Horowitz (1984) indicates that the more advanced the level of reading, the more removed the reading skills are from oral language development skills. Therefore, the language experience method should not be used as the sole means to teach initial reading. Rather, its use in tandem with a basic initial reading method allows additional development of reading skills. The use of language experience materials containing dialectal features and standard Spanish readers is but one of several possible combinations.

It is important to note that in this approach teachers should not modify the content dictated by the student. The implied rejection of their language by omitting dialectal features is not lost on students. They may become less productive with the language experience approach if they fear censoring or excessive correction.

Conclusions

There are five instructional options for the acquisition of initial literacy available to bilingual education teachers. They are not mutually exclusive; they can be combined in an eclectic manner to address the individual needs of students. All the options have the common element of accepting or at the very least respecting the home language. When the first option (standard Spanish readers) is combined with some of the other options and used with latitude (not in a prescriptive manner), it can be a most effective tool for teaching initial reading in bilingual education. The problems and limitations of other approaches makes this eclectic approach the most viable strategy.

To the extent that literacy in standard Spanish and English is the implicit goal of transitional bilingual education, teachers would at best relegate Chicano Spanish to a transitional role under any of the five options. If bilingual education programs intend to accept fully the regional and nonstandard varieties of Spanish and English, developmental materials must be designed to include themes best expressed by features of the dialects into the standard language curriculum. At the end of this stage of development, students should begin to demonstrate some competence in handling dialect variations as alternative forms of communication.

The bilingual education teacher should first concentrate on children's learning how to read, not on the social status of the reader's speech. Accepting and using the nonstandard language of children with flexibility and sensitivity will contribute to the creation of a positive literacy acquisition environment. Students can later make communicative choices, but first they should demonstrate the **capacity** to choose. Teachers can best develop this capacity by building a communication repertoire based on the linguistic foundation the child brings to school. The optimal approach in initial literacy, then, is one that includes the standard of Spanish and English but does not preclude dialectal variations.

Students of bilingual education need research which determines how the oral and written use of Chicano Spanish affects the acquisition of literacy skills. It is important to identify under what circumstances and to what extent Chicano Spanish can aid or hinder the attainment of literacy.

References

Adler, S. *Poverty children and their language: Implications for teaching and treating.* New York: Grune & Stratton, Inc., 1979.

Cárdenas, J. The role of native language instruction in bilingual education. *The NABE Journal*, 1984, *VII* (3), 1-10.

Ching, D.C. *Reading and the bilingual child.* Newark, Delaware: International Reading Assocation, 1976.

Coballes-Vega, C. La enseñanza de la lectura en español en la escuela primaria. In George M. Blanco, María I. Duke dos Santos and José A. Vásquez-Faría (Eds.), *Ensayos sobre la educación bilingüe.* Dallas: Evaluation, Dissemination, and Assessment Center, Dallas Independent School District, 1985.

Edwards, V. Language issues in school. In Maurice Craft (Ed.), *Education and cultural pluralism.* Philadelphia: The Falmer Press, 1984.

Fishben, J.M. A non-standard publisher's problem. In James L. Laffey and Roger Shuy (Eds.), *Language differences: Do they interfere?* Newark, Delaware: International Reading Association, 1973.

Goodman, K.S. Psycholinguistic universals in the reading process. In P. Pimsleur and T. Quinn (Eds.), *The psychology of second language learning.* London: Cambridge University Press, 1971.

Goodman, K.S. *Miscue analysis: Applications to reading instruction.* Urbana, Ill.: ERIC Clearinghouse on Reading and Communication Skills and the National Council of Teachers of English, 1973.

Goodman, K.S. El proceso de la lectura: consideraciones a través de las lenguas y del desarrollo. In Emilia Ferreiro and Margarita Gómez Palacio (Eds.), *Nuevas perspectivas sobre los procesos de lectura y escritura.* México, D.F.: Siglo Veintiuno Editores, SA., 1982.

Goodman, K.S.; Goodman, Y.; & Flores, B. *Reading in the bilingual classroom: literacy and biliteracy.* Rosslyn, Virginia: National Clearinghouse for Bilingual Education, 1979.

Goodman, K.S. Dialect barriers to reading comprehension. In Joan C. Baratz and Roger W. Shuy (Eds.), *Teaching black children to read.* Arlington, Virginia: Center for Applied Linguistics, 1969.

Horowitz, R. Orality and literacy in bilingual/bicultural contexts. *The NABE Journal*, 1984, *VII* (3), 11-26.

Joag-deu, C. & Steffensen, M.S. *Studies of the bicultural reader: Implications for teachers and librarians.* Reading Education Report No. 12, Center for the Study of Reading, University of Illinois at Urbana Champaign, January, 1980.

Kress, G. *Learning to write.* London: Routledge and Kegan Paul, 1982.

Mace-Matluck, B.J. *Literacy instruction in bilingual settings: A synthesis of current research.* Los Alamitos, Cal.: National Center for Bilingual Research, 1982.

Seymour, D.Z. Neutralizing the effects of the nonstandard dialect. In James L. Laffey and Roger Shuy (Eds.), *Language differences: Do they interfere?* Newark, Delaware: International Reading Association 1973.

Somervill, M.A. Dialect and reading: A review of alternative solutions. *Review of Educational Research,* 1975, *45* (2), 247-262.

Troike, R. *Research evidence for the effectiveness of bilingual education.* Rosslyn, Virginia: National Clearinghouse for Bilingual Education, 1978.

Van Allen, R. *Language experiences in communication.* Boston: Hougton Mifflin Company, 1976.

Wolfram, W. & Christian, D. Educational implications of dialect diversity. In M.A. Lourie and N.F. Conklin (Eds.), *A pluralistic nation: The language issue in the United States.* Rowley, Mass.: Newbury House Publishers, Inc., 1978.

Wolfram, W.; Potter, L.; Yanofsky, N.M.; & Shuy, R. *Reading and dialect differences.* Arlington, Virginia: Center for Applied Linguistics, 1979.

Zappert, L.T. & Cruz, R.B. *Bilingual education: an appraisal of empirical research.* Berkeley, Calif.: Bay Area Bilingual Education League/Lau Center, Berkeley Unified School District, 1977.

Discourse Analysis:
Key to Teacher Style in Spanish Reading Classes
by Mary McGroarty

Introduction

In order to conduct their own classroom research, bilingual education teachers need techniques that are valid in terms of their experience, useful in yielding insights about teaching, and feasible for use in everyday classroom situations. The growing field of discourse analysis offers many such techniques. In this chapter I will show how linguistic analysis based on the discourse recorded during two Spanish reading classes provides helpful clues for understanding the instructional styles of the teachers involved and their possible effects on student learning. The two teachers described here have very different classroom styles, and one application of discourse analysis, that based on categorization of teacher questions, furnishes one key to their contrasting approaches to reading instruction in Spanish. The use of similar techniques will help all teachers wishing to step back for a moment from their active roles in busy classrooms to see what they do more clearly.

The two classes discussed here present just one application of one technique included under the general rubric of discourse analysis. As Stubbs (1983) has noted, the term itself is ambiguous and may refer either to the study of language above the sentence level or to the study of naturally occurring language as against the study of artificial language or hypothetical examples. Following Stubb's use, I employ discourse analysis here to mean "the linguistic analysis of naturally occurring connected spoken discourse" (1983:1). Hatch and Long also drew attention to "the wide variety of work, all of which at some point has been called 'discourse analysis'"(1980:1) in their comprehensive survey of the area; the additional articles in that volume provide numerous illustrations of the ways discourse analysis can assist those interested in second language learning. Coulthard (1977) too offers a good introduction to the field. Readers interested in the full range of techniques used in discourse analysis should consult these volumes for more information.

The analysis employed here concentrates on one aspect of teacher discourse, the frequency and type of the questions teachers use in conducting reading lessons in Spanish. Teacher questioning behavior was chosen because of its theoretical and practical importance. Cook-Gumperz and Gumperz (1982) and Ervin-Tripp (1982) have emphasized the need for improved theoretical understanding of teachers' linguistic behavior. Given the unequal status of teacher and students and the teacher's responsibility to promote student learning, we need to know more about what teachers do in order to construct a model of effective teaching. Practically, it has been observed for some time that teachers not only use frequent questions (see Hargie, 1978), they often use certain types of questions, usually called display questions because they require pupils to display knowledge already known by the teacher, characteristically restricted to school settings. In normal conversation, we do not ask what is already known, but teachers often do so in order to monitor student learning. Indeed, as Stubbs observes, "Teachers constantly check up to see if they are on the same wavelength as their pupils, if at least most of their pupils are following what they are saying, in addition to actively monitoring, editing and correcting the actual language which pupils use" (1983:50). Questions are one of the principal means available to teachers who must keep in constant touch with student progress in a lesson.

In selecting teacher questions as the focus of this analysis, we are hence limiting our examination to one aspect, albeit an important one, of language use in classrooms. The selection of questions is well motivated, as shown above, but it is also incomplete. More exhaustive treatments of classroom language use can be found in Sinclair and Coulthard (1975), who present a comprehensive system for analysis of classroom discourse, and in Mehan (1979), who provides an ethnographic account of the language of an elementary classroom. Those interested in using discourse analysis to define a comprehensive approach to teacher language in second language classrooms will find Hernández' (1981) work valuable; using a variety of analytic systems, she was able to describe differences in the language use of two groups of four teachers of English as a second language. One group had been determined to be effective teachers because of the gains their students made in mastery of English; the other group was less effective, and discourse patterns revealed contrasts in the type and frequency of language behaviors used by these two groups.

Peñaloza-Stromquist (1980) and Ramírez (1979) have presented similar work that deals specifically with the teaching of reading in Spanish. In that study, 18 teachers were observed four times, their students pre and post-tested, and teacher behaviors related to gains in student improvement in Spanish reading. That study yields important information regarding the types of teacher language behaviors that promote student learning. Some types of questions had positive effects on student learning, others had a negative impact; while findings from that large-scale study are not directly comparable to the relatively simple analyses used here, they also suggest that teacher questions influence student learning in various critical ways.

That is, in fact, a major assumption underlying this analysis. It is defensible because of research like that summarized by Peñaloza-Stromquist and Ramírez, which links teacher behavior to student learning. The work presented here is preliminary, though, and does not include any measures of student outcomes. Nevertheless, it is still reasonable to assume that student learning is related to student participation, which in turn is related to the way the teacher solicits and develops student remarks in the course of a lesson. Hence this exploration of teacher style in the Spanish reading classroom will emphasize the teacher's role in guiding student activity during the reading period.

The work here is different from that typically conducted in bilingual classrooms. Many earlier descriptions of language use in bilingual education programs have dealt mainly with the language choice and code-switching patterns of teachers and students (see, for example, Milk 1984; Zentella, 1978b; Bruck and Schultz, 1977; Legarreta 1977; Townsend, 1976; Townsend and Zamora, 1975) or with the oral reading errors observed (e.g. Silva 1983). These studies, valuable in understanding how and why various amounts of Spanish and English came to be used and what kinds of errors occur, tell us little regarding the type of interaction found in classes where the language of instruction is exclusively a 'marked' language in relation to the school environment, in this case Spanish, in a mainly English-speaking school. Thus it is important to look at classes conducted entirely in Spanish to see just how lessons are carried out.

Additionally, and also relevant to the themes treated in this volume issues of dialect differences between various types of Spanish used in the classroom and found in instructional materials must be identified and addressed if reading instruction is to build on and develop students' literacy skills in the first language. Teachers and teacher trainers wishing to study the interaction patterns created in reading classes will find many techniques for doing so in the handbook of Acheson and Gall (1980). This information, along with inferences based on Spanish reading research such as that reported in the Ramírez article, can then assist teachers in identifying and employing more effective instructional language in Spanish reading classes.

Setting

The two classes analysed here took place in schools serving lower- and lower-middle-class areas in a large city in the San Francisco Bay area. Both were taught by male teachers who were native speakers of Spanish, bilingual in Spanish and English, and favorably disposed towards the use of Spanish in the classroom. Both classes occurred as part of the normal pattern of instruction in these bilingual classrooms; while each classroom had other reading groups in English, these two groups were those in which Spanish had been developed as the language of literacy because of the children's greater proficiency in that language. All involved, both teachers and students, expected the students to learn to read in English within the next school year (or two, depending on the child's proficiency and home language use). These classes, then, were aimed at strengthening the Spanish decoding, grammatical recognition, and comprehension skills that would be a part of reading in any language. The children in these classes were in the third and fourth grades and were between 8 and 10 years of age. Classes were small; Teacher X had seven children, six girls and one boy, in the Spanish reading class; Teacher Y had three children, two girls and one boy, in his class.

Data was collected by means of audiotapes which were then transcribed. The tape of Teacher X's class was made from a videotape observation carried out as part of a larger research project.1 The tape of Teacher Y's class was made during the usual reading period; an observer was present during the lessons and took notes but did not participate in the instruction. For both classes the text of the lesson observed was the story "Viajes y aventuras de Lolita," the last story in the Santillana series reader *La Ciudad*.

The Analysis

Discourse analysis can help to answer the question of what makes one classroom different from another. These two classes, similar on the basis of age and skill levels of students, ethnicity and language background of students and teacher, and type of lesson being taught, are yet dramatically different in the verbal processes used in lesson development. Looking at these differences of style gives us some sense of the probable differences in the educational experience of those involved. By using analysis of discourse to answer the descriptive question 'How is a Spanish reading lesson taught?' we can better understand the possibilities and limitations of this technique.

Before proceeding to the analysis, a caveat; while discourse analysis, the consideration of the sequence of speech events occurring in any situation, provides a more complete linguistic record of activities than does a categorical observation system, such analysis does not provide the depth or completeness of ethnographic studies such as those conducted on a classroom level by Moll and Díaz (forthcoming) and Mehan (1978, 1979) or on a community level by Heath (1983). Valuable because it extends linguistic research beyond the boundaries of single utterances, discourse analysis does not encompass the detailed nonverbal description or the comprehensive background knowledge required by ethnography. Thus it is an intermediate form of analysis, a bridge between discrete units of speech and the larger patterns of community interaction.

Discourse analysis can be put to various uses within classrooms. Here I take one approach, that of analysis of naturally occurring language and categorization of the types of questions used by two teachers. This approach could be used by any teacher who wanted a system of self-evaluation that would provide information relevant to reading instruction. Of major importance is the selection of the aspects of discourse to be examined; in making the choice, teachers can be guided by theoretical formulations and empirical work related to reading. In this chapter, teacher questions have been selected because of their frequency and importance. Other language behavior observed in classrooms--teacher feedback, for example, or student responses--also merits close examination through the analytic techniques described. Because my major interest is the way Spanish reading lessons are developed, I have analyzed teacher questions in terms of the behaviors they elicited from students. Analysis of teachers' questioning strategies suggests very different lesson development in these two classes.

A construct that helps to illuminate the differences between the two classes observed is that of teacher-centered versus student-centered instruction. While earlier investigators have found identification and validation of these instructional approaches to be problematic (Costin, 1971), their work has been based most often on student (frequently college student) reports of teacher or classroom characteristics. By examining classroom data directly through analysis of speech, rather than indirectly through student report, we obtain a much more vivid picture of the emphasis of classroom activity.

The two teachers set up the reading lesson in very different ways, and their methods of introducing the lesson are characteristic of their approaches. Teacher X gives an extensive preamble during which he comments on past work, sets forth the goal of the day's lesson, and specifies the group study of vocabulary words as a necessary preliminary to the activity. The discourse shows that he reserves the most active role, that of reader, for himself; indeed, the children do not even have books, for he wants to present the lesson as aural memory training. The reading lesson functions almost as a storytelling activity (see Donaldson, 1984) where the teacher, not the text, tells the story. Here is the introduction:

Example X-1

Teacher X: Voy ahora intoducir un vocabulario para una nueva historia. Esta nueva historia está en el libro que ustedes están leyendo *La Ciudad* . . . . Yo la voy a leer, para así conservar más tiempo, y luego van a haber preguntas . . . . El propósito de ésta historia es para ver *que tan bien . . . oyen*. OK? Ahora vamos a . . .a, a, a, investigar el asunto del OIR, a ver que tan bien oyen. Pero antes de empezar, yo quisiera nomás introducir unas palabras pronto que están en el pizarrón, y si alguien me las puede leer, y si, si, si sabe el significado de ellas.

The reading lesson will in fact be a listening lesson; the students will depend on memory to get them through. Before beginning to read the story, the teacher directs the class to read the vocabulary words on the board:

Example X-2

Vamos primero a leerlas. Este. . . . usted . . . Amelia . . . va a leer éstas; Celia, nos lees éstas; la siguiente, Oralia; y luego, las otras, este, Marta, ¿OK? So, vamos contigo, Amelia.

Of interest here is the strategy of dividing up the vocabulary list from the start; each student will have to read only a section of the list, and the teacher retains the right to decide when to move from one group of words to the next. This represents vocabualry development of a "decontextualized, dictionary variety" (Barrera 1982; 180), which is not optimal for developing student skill in dealing with connected texts. As Cazden (1976) and Ervin-Tripp (1982) also point out, teacher talk is a means of retaining power, and this teacher's allocation of turns for vocabulary reading is a clear demonstration of control over student talk with consequent limitations on student ability to comment on the words.

Teacher X's control over student talk is also apparent in this approach to the definition of vocabulary words. Although he has assigned students to read four- or five-word lists so that the class can discuss their meaning, he does not allow any student to give more than a word or a brief phrase as definition before stepping in to supply the meaning himself. The following pattern is typical of this approach to vocabualry:

Example X-3

Amelia: (reads from blackboard): Viajes, aventuras, mercado, flores, pétalos.
Teacher X: OK, ¿sabes tú qúe son viajes?
Amelia: ¿Trajos?
Teacher X: Mm-Hm. ¿Aventuras?
(Amelia and others are silent for a moment.)
Teacher X: ¿Entiende lo qué es una aventura? Como cuando . . . sucede algo . . . o cuando va uno de viaje y . . . y, y que . . . em . . . pasa algo, ya eso es una aventura.

The teacher then proceeds to illustrate the meaning of 'aventura' with a funny story about having a flat tire when out for a drive. After telling the story, he does not ask for further proof of comprehension, but moves on to the next item. In fact, by the end of the vocabulary section, the teacher does not wait for children to offer any defintions of the vocabulary items but simply supplies them himself. The closing exchange in the vocabulary study which forms the introduction to the day's lesson is illuminating:

Example X-4

Martha (reading from board): . . . gallinitas ciegas . . .
Teacher X: ¿Qué son las gallinitas ciegas?
Martha: Esas que . . . juegan y se tapan los ojos y . . .
Teacher X: Aaaah, sí. Nosotros en inglés le llamamos 'hide and go seek.' Lo podemos así contar hasta diez o veinte y luego varios se esconden y tenemos que ir a buscarlos, la gallinita ciega . . . 'Parque.' ¿Sabes qué es un parque, verdad? Eso . . . donde la gente va el domingo por la tarde . . . y se divierten así. Al parque. 'Chocolate.' Ay, en la mañana, especialmente chocolate con canela. Y una 'montaña,' ustedes saben que es eso. Bueno. ¡Pongan atención! No tienen nada pa' preguntar, parte del vocabulario . . . O.K.

In his extended turn, this teacher has defined not only the game hide-and-go-seek, a game which the student who read the Spanish name had already been explaining, but also the items 'parque,' 'chocolate,' and 'montaña,' all words which a student at this level could be expected to know. Indeed, the teacher observes aloud that they know at least 'montaña,' and then states, with the falling intonation usual for factual reports, that the students have no questions about the vocabulary. The vocabulary study completed, he begins to read the story. The teacher has dominated the discourse here, allowing only minimal student response.

Teacher Y's method of setting up a reading lesson is quite different from Teacher X's. In Teacher Y's reading group, the introductory activity is decoding and discussion of the title of the story, including attention to the grammatical forms of the words involved:

Example Y-1

Teacher Y: OK, todos ustedes por favor, saquen el libro de leer . . . quisiera acabar el libro de actividades . . . (in a lower voice as children put materials from previous lesson away and take out their reader) por favor por favor . . . Rosa, ¿puedes leer el título en la página ciento treinta y tres? . . .¿qué dice?

Rosa (reads): Viajes y aventuras de Lolita.

Teacher Y (couldn't hear): ¿Qué?

Rosa: Viajes y aventuras de Lolita.

Teacher Y: OK, Viajes y aventuras de Lolita. OK. So, ¿de qué trata éste cuento? ¿Ah? ¿Fabiola?

Fabiola: De un viaje

Teacher Y: ¿De un viaje? ¿Sólo uno?

Fabiola: (silent, looks puzzled)

Teacher Y: ¿Sólo uno? ¿Es de uno o más de uno? . . . ¿Gerardo?

Gerardo: Más.

Teacher Y: Más. ¿Por que dice más'?

Gerardo: Porque son, son . . . más aventuras.

Teacher Y: Son más aventuras. Está bien. ¿Y cómo se dice, Gerardo, que hay más que uno? ¿Cómo sabes por? ¿Ah?

Rosa: Porque tenemos la 's'.

After establishing that the students will be reading about more than one 'viaje,' the teacher tells them to read the first half of the story silently. He also has established a group goal, to finish the workbook, but suspends mention of that as the students work through the meaning of the title and go on to read the first part of the story. In contrast to Teacher X's long statements, this teacher uses several short questions to direct the discourse throughout the lesson.

The differences in these two teachers' methods of setting up the lesson carry through in the rest of the activity. Teacher X reads the story to the children, interpolates his own comments and anecdotes, has the children memorize the "magic words" that appear in the story and recite them on cue, and asks them occasional questions about their experiences or opinions. Teacher Y, on the other hand, asks numerous questions about the plot and meaning of the story, corrects the children frequently, and draws as much information as possible out of the students. Teacher X is deductive, Teacher Y is inductive, and their patterns of verbal interaction with the students bear out this difference in style.

To get a better sense of the overall conduct of the lessons it is helpful to combine these analysis of short segments of discourse with a catergorical system which provides a notion of the frequency of various kinds of teacher and student talk. Because I am concerned chiefly with teacher talk, I have devised a classification system for the types of verbal behavior--specifically, the types of questions--the teachers use. These categories were selected after study of the two transcripts involved. After summarizing the results of this more quantitative system, I will present examples of each teacher's most frequent type of questioning behavior. This combination of a categorical system based on the data at hand and the close analysis of the most typical kinds of verbal interaction already offered a concise yet well differentiated sketch of classroom activity.

The types and numbers of questions used by the two teachers are displayed in Table 1. Each question represents an utterance; a turn may be comprised of one or more utterances. For the sake of simplicity, these categories have been employed as if they were mutually exclusive although a question may serve multiple functions such as management of social behavior and correction of decoding error at the same time, low-inference category systems like this are ill-equiped to handle multivalent speech acts. (See Stubbs 1983, pp. 40-66 for a more complete account of the many functions of teacher talk in classroom discourse.) These tallies are useful preliminary guides to each teacher's characteristic style, a style further reflected in the close analysis of the question types favored by each teacher.

Table 1
Frequency of Questions Used

Question Types (see Appendix examples)		Teacher X n	(rank)	Teacher Y n	(rank)
Text-related	Vocabulary	15	(1)	16	
	Grammar	0		5	
	Plot	1		38	(1)
	Inference	4		35	(2)
	Correction	3		33	(3)
	Decoding	0		6	
Not text-related	Repetition	0		7	
	Rhetorical	2		0	
	Opinion	13	(2)	7	
	Experience, General Knowledge	12	(3)	7	
	Management	0		2	
	n =	50		156	

From these figures, it is clear that Teacher Y asks three times as many questions as Teacher X. The types of questions each teacher asks most often also differ greatly. Teacher X favors questions about vocabulary words, student opinion, and general knowledge of the world, while Teacher Y asks more questions about the plot of the story being read, inferences from the story, and errors of decoding or interpretation made by the students.

A close analysis of the discourse shows that Teacher X's method of questioning students about vocabulary consists of asking for a word or, at most, a phrase. Often his question is longer than the answer sought, as in these examples:

Example X-5

Teacher X: ...Y...¿colores? Ya sabes cuáles son, ¿verdad? ¿Puedes nombrarme algunos colores? ¿Qué colores tiene aquí el chaqueta?
Celia: Café.
Teacher X: Eso, es un color.

Example X-6

Teacher X: ...'Amarillo' es un color, ¿verdad? ¿Miras alguna cosa amarilla en el cuar-to, Oralia? Nómbrame. ¿Qué ves tú amarillo?
Oralia: El sol.
Teacher X: Ah, eso es.

In both of these examples, the teacher uses at least three questions within one turn to elicit a one word answer from the student. The successive questions narrow the field of the student's possible answer. The teacher asks about the general concept of 'color' or 'yellow', asks the student to give an example, and in the first example even tells the student the desired answer by choosing a brown jacket as the topic for the last question. The vocabulary item is not related to the story, a technique that the research reported in the Ramírez (1979) article found nonproductive. Here there is no room to deviate, no way to give an unexpected answer, for Teacher X is asking students to say the obvious; the response is almost automatic.

The other two question types favored by Teacher X, questions of opinion and questions of experience or general knowledge, also demand almost-automatic responses. Although they are phrased as questions, the expected answer is most often simply 'yes' or 'no,' and usually the only acceptable answer is apparent in the form of the teacher's question, as in this instance:

Example X-7

Teacher X (reading story): 'Lolita empezó a llorar.' ¿Qué...hubieran hecho ustedes? Lo mismo, ¿no?
Students (together): Sí.

When the question is phrased in a tag form ('the same thing, right?') that signifies rhetorical agreement, it is virtually impossible to answer 'no' without transgressing social as well as grammatical rules. Thus the students have no choice; they must answer 'sí' whether or not they would actually do the same thing as Lolita in the story. Although there is a question form used, the answer is plain.

In fact, the pattern of the 'question that is not a question' is so pervasive in this classroom that the students do not seem to know what to do when the answer to the teacher's question is not obvious. Like all teachers, Teacher X is used to answering his own question. In order to maintain the convention of student participation in lessons, he often tries to ask another, more transparent question if the first one fails to get any response at all. This next segment of the transcript shows Teacher X shaping his opinion questions in order to get an answer.

Example X-8:

Teacher X (discussing the earth and the moon): ...si brinca uno seis pies en la luna, como el aire es tan liviano, puede brincar uno alla treinta y seis pies--seis veces más que lo que brinca uno aquí. ¿Les gustaría estar en la luna?

Students: (Silence)

Teacher X: Oí que alguien va a brincar ahora. Bueno, los mismo si usted pesa cien libras aquí, en la luna no pesa más que algunas treinta, cuarenta libras. Pesa menos. Yo sí quisiera estar en la luna cuando fuera pesarme con el doctor, en ese ratito estar en la luna pa' no pese tanto, porque me, me regaña ...porque ya estoy *muy gordo* (Note: Teacher X is portly)...comí mucho los frijoles. ¿A ustedes les gustan los frijoles?

Students: Sí.

Teacher X: Sí. Son muy sabrosos, ¿verdad? Pero con chilito y queso. Bueno. (Teacher returns to story and goes on reading.)

Although the students' initial reluctance to answer the question about wanting to be on the moon may be partly due to the influence of the Spanish idiom 'estar en la luna,' (to be "out of it," to lack understanding), their hesitation is more likely due to the fact that they cannot tell if the teacher expects them to say 'yes' or 'no'. Not knowing this, and knowing that the progress of the lesson depends on their giving an answer the teacher approves, they wait for him to hint at the answer or restate the question in a more comprehensible form. Feeling it wiser not to press for answers about being on the moon, the teacher proceeds to tell a funny story about himself and ends it with a question he knows the students can answer easily: whether or not they like beans. Unrelated to the original topic, this question gives the students a chance to answer in chorus to maintain their collective role as corporate rather than individual participants in the lesson. Teacher X asks experience questions that also elicit very short answers which the teacher uses to punctuate his reading of the story. In the following segment this is plain:

Example X-9

Teacher X: ¿Cuándo es que sale el arco iris?

Students: Cuando llueve.

Teacher X: ¿Cuándo llueve o después de que llueve?

Students: Después....

Teacher X: Después de que llueve. OK.

Like the opinion questions, the experience questions serve to maintain a momentum based on general world knowledge rather that knowledge of the specific text itself. They permit the student participation to occur as a choral backdrop to the teacher's central role in reading the story.

None of the three types of questions that Teacher X uses most often--about vocabulary, student opinion, or student experience--demand that the student give a reason for the answer or relate it to events in the story. Because the teacher usually directs his questions at the whole group, there is little chance to compare one student's answer against another's. The students operate as a foil for the teacher, who defines the vocabulary words, reads the story, tells humorous anecdotes about himself, and sometimes solicits student agreement with his questions: the discourse patterns show the teacher X runs a teacher-centered class which limits the possiblities for student participation.

Teacher Y's lesson, in contrast, appears to be more task and student centered. The types of questions he uses most frequently are those that deal with the plot or inferences from the story or correction of student's mistakes or misunderstandings. The investigation reported by Ramírez (1979) suggests that these questions promote student reading skills. We will examine examples of the discourse connected with each of these types of questions.

Teacher Y asks numerous plot questions to be sure the students recall what they have read. He encourages the students to supply answers longer than one word and insists that their answers reflect the story accurately, as we see in this series of exchanges:

Example Y-2:

Teacher Y: Lolita, Lolita estaba allí sola y triste y estaba llorando...¿Qué le pasó?...Rosa.

Rosa: Llego una señora muy bella con los ojos brillantes...de colores, y...y le dice que, que no, que no llorara, que lo que, que le iba dar, este que le iba dar una flor, una flor...del arco iris.

Teacher Y: OK. Entonces..¿y esta flor? ¿Qué pasó con esta flor?

Rosa: ¡Yo sé! Le dio...

Gerardo: Yo sé.

Teacher Y: Fabiola.

Fabiola: La puso en una florera y le quebró.

Teacher Y: No, antes de eso; no, antes, antes de eso.

The teacher encourages students to summarize the story in their own words but requires them to adhere to the order of events in the book and corrects them when they do not. Also, he continually nominates the individual students so that they must offer individual answers to the questions posed. Furthermore, their answers must be appropriate, and Teacher Y uses his two additional preferred types of questioning behavior, inference and correction, to direct students to the right answer.

The following segment of the transcript shows both of these two question types as the teacher tries to elicit discussion and evidence of comprehension of the word 'medioambiente' from the students. They have been talking about the numer of things Lolita saw on her trip to the market.

Example Y-3:

Teacher Y: El medioambiente de éste cuarto es ¿qué...Gerardo?

Gerardo: La mitad.

Teacher Y: Nooo? (Rising intonation, asking for another answer.)

Gerardo: Media, media, media...mitad.

Teacher Y: ¿Qué es el medioambiente de éste cuarto?...escritorios...

Gerardo: Es muy poca gente.

Teacher Y: ...sillas, la pared...eh...¿Qué más?

Gerardo: Hay muy poca gente.

Teacher Y: ...techo, pizzarón...

Gerardo: ...vidrios...libros

Teacher Y: Ustedes...¿Qué quiere decir la palabra 'medioambiente'?

Rosa: Que está todo junto.

Teacher Y: ¿Todo junto al qué?
Students   (together): Alrededor.
Teacher Y: ¿De qué?
Students   (together): De la escuela.
Teacher Y: ¿Y cuál cosas?
Students: De la escuela.
Teacher Y: ¿De quién? ¿De quién?
Gerardo: De gente.
Teacher Y: De gente. ¿Cuál gente?
Gerardo: De...todos, alrededor de medioambiente.
Teacher Y: No, no, no. ¿Cuál gente?
Gerardo: Los niños.
Rosa: Nosotros.
Teacher Y: OK...¿Cáda uno?
Gerardo: Nosotros.
Teacher Y: Sí. Cada uno tiene un medioambiente en este mundo ¿ah? OK, pues.

In this series of exchanges, Teacher Y is constantly hinting at the correct meaning of 'medioambiente' without saying it. He uses short questions to signal students that the first answer ('mitad') was not correct, that they too have a 'medioambiente' in the classroom, that this 'medioambiente' has something to do with people ('¿De quién?'), and that everyone has a particular atmosphere. We can trace the effect of the teacher's questioning patterns in Gerardo's answers, which begin with an incorrect statement that reflects literal attention to the first morpheme of the word in question rather than comprehension of the word ('mitad', which the student sees as equivalent of 'medio-'), progress through a series of features of the proper definition ('vidrios,' 'libros'), and end with statement the teacher accepts as proof of understanding of the word ('nosotros'). Teacher Y's questions, used both to help students infer the answer and to correct their misunderstandings, keep the lesson on the track and keep the students responding. The frequency and the type of student response is much different from that observed in the first class. Teacher Y makes his utterances only as long as the students' and uses short, specific questions, often directed at individuals by name, to draw the students into the stream of talk in the reading class. He questions the students in a rapid-fire manner. Moreover, these questions demand thoughtful answers: students cannot just say 'sí' or 'no.' Although the potential answers may be short, they must match the question asked in content as well as form. Hence Teacher Y's discourse patterns show that he is continually forcing the students to remember the plot of the story, infer the meanings of words, correct their errors, decode new forms--in short, to read. The central features of this class are the reading task and the responses of the students performing the task, and the classroom discourse shows this emphasis. Teachers of Spanish reading who want to know more about their own instructional styles can compare their own classroom questioning techniques to those analyzed here.

Conclusion

This application of techniques based on discourse analysis to the question of teacher style in Spanish reading classrooms has shown such analysis to be a valuable tool.

Discourse analysis can show us not only what teachers say, but the way they say things in order to create opportunities for various types of student response. The question patterns of the two teachers studied here provide striking evidence for differences in instructional emphasis due in part to style of speech. One class is teacher-centered, the other student-centered, and the amount and type of talk by teachers and students shows the difference in emphasis. The approaches to introducing the reading lesson and teaching new vocabulary words realized in the classroom discourse recorded here reveal great contrasts in the two Spanish reading classes observed.

The results obtained here, of course, are particular to the two classrooms for several reasons: the number of teachers, students, and observations is relatively small, and the participants were not selected at random. Furthermore, both teachers were native speakers of Spanish. Teacher language proficiency in Spanish has been associated with students' academic achievement (see Merino, Politzer, and Ramírez 1979) and with reading achievement in Spanish (Peñaloza-Stromquist 1980). Hence the techniques used here show only what happens in two reading classes where teachers are relatively proficient in the language of reading instruction. Other discourse patterns might have been observed if the teachers were less proficient in Spanish.

Another issue related to teacher language skill deserves mention. Because the teachers here were native speakers and familiar with the communities where the children lived, the discourse reveals no misunderstandings based on dialectal differences in Spanish. However, the absence of such difficulties here does not mean they can be overlooked. In one classroom observed as part of another research project, a teacher who was a native speaker of a South American variety of Spanish misunderstood a student who spoke Mexican Spanish: the class was reading a story written for U.S. Spanish speakers about an empty lot, which the book called 'el lote' and the teacher asked for other ways to say 'el lote' expecting 'un terreno' or 'la yarda.' The student thought the teacher wanted another way to say 'elote,' corn, and offered 'maíz' insistently for ten minutes. Not realizing the source of the student's confusion, the teacher kept asking questions of the other students, leaving the student to puzzle out the apparent connection between corn and an empty lot for himself. This is only one, isolated example of confusion arising from dialectal differences. Morales' 1982 investigation of the role of vernacular Spanish, language arts instruction provides a complete treatment of related issues. Hence it should be remembered that teacher's proficiency in Spanish, and especially in the varieties of Spanish spoken by the students and used in reading materials, is a basic issue in Spanish language arts instruction. Dialect differences in Spanish happened not to emerge directly in the discourse patterns observed here, but they should figure in any comprehensive teacher training program for bilingual education.

As shown in this brief examination of two Spanish reading classes, techniques based on discourse analysis provide a good descriptive base for asking many questions related to language structure, to language in use, and to instructional procedures. These linguistic, pragmatic, and pedagogical questions could all be explored through discourse analysis based on theoretical frameworks from linguistics or education. These techniques can sharpen the focus on language in educational research and move it closer to actual classroom realities as Cazden (1976: 81) notes, "the best focus is probably not what existing research can say the most about," and an examination of classroom discourse, considered along with insights from other kinds of educational research, can be more enlightening than research reports alone. Analysis of classroom discourse is one way to improve understanding of the way education does and doesn't occur as teachers and students talk their way through a lesson.

Recommendations

Teachers and teacher trainers interested in using techniques of discourse analysis to analyze the teaching of reading may wish to undertake related research in their own classrooms. Some recommended areas for such work are:

--Identification of Predominant Question Type.

Reading classes can be taped, and teachers can identify the question types they favor in interaction with students. At issue here are matters of the varieties of questions used and the types of responses they elicit from students.

--Analysis of Dialect Variations

Teachers can list local dialectal or regional variations for vocabulary items (e.g. 'palomilla/mariposa', 'papalote/cometa') or grammatical structures ('fuístes/fuíste') that are used by students or found in reading materials. Knowledge of the range of variation could then improve teacher comprehension of student work and insure that teachers instruct students in the variant forms they may encounter.

--Developing Various Methods of Contextualizing Vocabulary

Once teachers know how they typically deal with vocabulary items that must by identified during reading instruction, they can develop additional ways of involving students as individuals and as members of a group in the active definition of new terms. Knowing several methods of eliciting student response, correcting errors, and probing student comprehension will allow teachers more options in directing students' vocabulary growth.

--Devising Methods to Check Comprehension

As in the area of vocabulary, teachers can compare the ways they typically assess student comprehension with the many alternatives suggested by discourse analysis to increase the strategies they use to guide student comprehension of text on the literal and inferential levels.

--Comparing Discourse Related Literacy at Home and at School

To see what kinds of expectations related to reading students bring to school, teachers need to know about the kind of verbal exchange that accompanies reading outside of school. Through extended observation in the community like that done by Heath (1983) or ethnographic observations such as those reported by Trueba (1984), teachers can find out whether home and school uses of literacy are similar, requiring the common patterns of interaction, or different, requiring teachers to pay special attention to discourse skills demanded in school.

156

Notes

[1]This observation was performed as part of the research on bilingual classrooms carried out by the Stanford Program on Teaching and Linguistic Pluralism, Stanford University, under the sponsorship of Robert L. Politzer, Director, and Arnulfo G. Ramírez, then Associate Director. I am grateful to them for permission to use these data.

References

Acheson, A., & Gall, M.G. *Techniques in the clinical supervision of teachers.* New York: Longman, 1980.

Barrera, R.B. Bilingual reading in the primary grades: Some questions about questionable views and practices. In T.H. Escobedo (Ed.), *Early childhood bilingual education.* New York: Teachers College Press. 1983

Bruck, M., & Shultz, J. An ethnographic analysis of the language use patterns of bilingually schooled children. *Working Papers on Bilingual/Travaux de Recherches sur le Bilinguisme,* 1977, 13, 59-91.

Cazden, C. How knowledge about language helps the classroom teacher--or does it: A personal account. *The Urban Review,* 1976, 9, 74-90.

Cook-Gumperz, J., & Gumperz, J. J. Communicative competence in educational perspective. In L. C. Wilkinson (Ed.), *Communicating in the classroom.* New York: Academic Press, 1982.

Costin, F. Empirical test of the 'teacher-centered' versus 'student-centered' dichotomy. *Journal of Educational Psychology,* 1971, *62,* 410-412.

Coulthard, M. *An introduction to discourse analysis.* London: Longman, 1977.

Donaldson, M. Speech and writing and modes of learning. In H. Goelman, A. A. Oberg, & F. Smith (Eds.), *Awakening to literacy.* Exeter and London: Heinemann Educational Books, 1984.

Ervin-Tripp, S. Structure of control. In L. C. Wilkinson, (Ed.), *Communicating in the classroom.* New York: Academic Press, 1982.

Hargie, O. D. W. The importance of teacher questions in the classroom. *Educational Research,* 1978, *20,* 99-102.

Hatch, E., & Long, M. H. Discourse analysis, what's that? in D. Larsen-Freemen (Ed.), *Discourse analysis in second language research.* Rowley, Ma.: Newbury House, 1980.

Heath, S. B. *Ways with words.* Cambridge and New York: Cambridge University Press, 1983.

Hernández, H. *English-as-a-second-language lessons in bilingual classrooms: A discourse analysis.* Unpublished doctoral dissertation, Stanford University, 1981.

Legarreta, D. Language choice in bilingual classrooms. *TESOL Quarterly,* 1973, *11* (1), 9-16.

Mehan, H. Structuring school structure. *Harvard Educational Review,* 1978, *48,* 32-64.

Merino, B. J., Politzer, R. L., & Ramírez, A. G. The relationship of teachers' Spanish proficiency to pupils' achievement. *NABE Journal,* 1979, *III*(2), 21-37.

Milk, R. D. A comparison of the functional distribution of language in bilingual classrooms following languages separation vs. concurrent instructional approaches. Paper presented at annual meeting of the American Educational Research Association, New Orleans, April 1984.

Moll, L., & Díaz E. Teaching writing as communication: The use of ethnographic findings in classroom practice. In D. Bloome (Ed.), *Language, literacy, and schooling.* Ablex Publishing (forthcoming).

Morales, M. F. *Vernacular Spanish and Chicano culture content in the language arts curriculum for bilingual education.* Unpublished doctoral dissertation, Stanford University, 1987.

Peñaloza-Stromquist, N. Teaching effectiveness and student achievement in reading in Spanish. *The Bilingual Review/La revista bilingüe,* 1980, *VII*(2), 95-104.

Ramírez, G. Teaching reading in Spanish: A study of teacher effectiveness. *Reading Improvement,* 1979, *16(4),* 304-313.

Silva, A. The Spanish reading process and Spanish-speaking Mexican American children. In T. H. Escobedo (Ed.), *Early childhood bilingual education.* New York: Teachers College Press, 1983.

Sinclair, J. Mc H., & Coulthard, R. M. *Towards an analysis of discourse.* London: Oxford University Press, 1975.

Stubbs, M. *Discourse analysis.* Chicago and Oxford: The University of Chicago Press, 1983.

Townsend, D. R. Bilingual interaction analysis: The development and status. In A. Simoés, Jr. (Ed.), *The bilingual child.* New York: Academic Press, 1976.

Townsend, D. R., & Zamora, G. L. Different interaction patterns in bilingual classrooms. *Contemporary Education,* 1975, *XLVI*(3), 196-202.

Trueba, H. The forms, functions, and values of literacy: Reading for survival in a barrio as a student. *NABE Journal,* 1984, *IX*(1), 21-39.

Zahorik, J. A. Classroom feedback behavior of teachers. *Journal of Educational Research,* 1968, *62,* 147-150.

Zahorik, J. A. Teacher verbal feedback and content development. *Journal of Educational Research,* 1970, *63,* 419-423.

Zentella, A. C. Code switching and interactions among Puerto Rican children. *Sociolinguistic Working Paper No. 50.* Austin, Tx: Southwest Educational Development Laboratory, 1978a.

Zentella, A. C. Ta bien, you could answer me in cualquier idioma: Puerto Rican code switching in bilingual classrooms. Presentation at ETS conference on Chicano and Latino Discourse, Behavior, Princeton, 1978b.

Multilingual Assessment*
John W. Oller, Jr.

Multilingualism is a pervasive modern reality. Ever since that cursed Tower was erected, the peoples of the world have had this problem. In the United States alone, there are millions of people in every major urban center whose home and neighborhood language is not one of the majority varieties of English. Spanish, Italian, German, Chinese and a host of other 'foreign' languages have actually become American languages. Furthermore, Navajo, Eskimo, Zuni, Apache, and many other native languages of this continent can hardly be called 'foreign' languages. The implications for education are manifold. How shall we deliver curricula to children whose language is not English? How shall we determine what their language skills are?

A. Need

Zirkel (1976) concludes an article entitled 'The why's and ways of testing bilinguality before teaching bilingually,' with the following paragraph:

> The movement toward an effective and efficient means of testing bilinguality before teaching bilingually is in progress. In its wake is the hope that in the near future 'equality of educational opportunity' will become more meaningful for linguistically different pupils in our nation's elementary schools (p. 328).

Earlier he observes, however, that a 'substantial number of bilingual programs do not take systematic steps to determine the language dominance of their pupils'(p.324).

Since the 1974 Supreme Court ruling in the case of Lau versus Nichols, the interest in multilingual testing in the schools of the United States has taken a sudden upswing. The now famous court case involved a contest between a Chinese family in San Francisco and the San Francisco school system. The following quotation from the Court's Syllabus explains the nature of the case:

> The failure of the San Franciso school system to provide English language instruction to approximately 1,800 students of Chinese ancestry who do not speak English denies them a meaningful opportunity to participate in the public educational program and thus violates -601 of the Civil Rights Act of 1964, which bans discrimination 'based on the ground of race, color or national origin,'(Lau vs. Nichols,1974,No.72d-6520).

In page 2 of an opinion by Mr. Justice Stewart concurred in by The Chief Justice and Mr. Justice Blackmun, it is suggested that no specific remedy is urged upon us. Teaching English to the students of Chinese ancestry who do not speak the language is one choice. Further, the Court argued:

> Basic English skills are at the very core of what these public schools teach. Imposition of a requirement that, before a child can *effectively* participate in the educational program, he must already have acquired those basic skills is to make

*Chapter 4 in *Language tests at school: A pragmatic approach*. London: Longman Group Ltd., 1979.

a mockery of public education. We know that those who do not understand English are certain to find their classroom experiences wholly incomprehensible and in no way meaningful (1974, No. 72-6520, p.3).

As a result of the interpretation rendered by the Court, the U.S. Office of Civil Rights convened a Task Force which recommended certain so-called 'Lau Remedies'. Among other things, the main document put together by the Task Force requires language assessment procedures to determine certain facts about language use and it requires the rating of bilingual proficiency on a rough five point scale (1. monolingual in a language other than English; 2. more proficient in another language than in English; 3. balanced bilingual in English and another language; 4. more proficient in English than in another language; 5. monolingual in English).

Multilingual testing seems to have come to stay for a while in U.S. schools, but as Zirkel and others have noted, it has come very late. It is late in the sense of antiquated and inhumane educational programs that placed children of language backgrounds other than English in classes for the 'mentally retarded' (Diana versus California State Education Department. 1970, No. C-7037), and it is late in terms of bilingual education programs that were started in the 1960s and even in the early 1970s on a hope and promise but without adequate assessment of pupil needs and capabilities (cf. John and Horner, 1971, and Shore, 1974, cited by Zirkel, 1976). In fact, as recently as 1976, Zirkel observes, 'a fatal flaw in many bilingual programs lies in the linguistic identification of pupils at the critical point of the planning and placement process'(p.324).

Moreover, as Teitelbaum (1976), Zirkel (1976), and others have often noted, typical methods of assessment such as surname surveys to identify Spanish speakers, for instance) or merely about language preferences (e.g., teacher or student questionnaires) are largely inadequate. The one who is most likely to be victimized by such inadequate methods is the child in the school. One second grader indicated that he spoke 'English-only' on a rating sheet. but when 'casually asked later whether his parents spoke Spanish, the child responded without hesitation: Sí, ellos hablan español--pero yo, no.' Perhaps someone had convinced him that he was not supposed to speak Spanish?

Surely, for the sake of the child, it is necessary to obtain reliable and valid information about what language(s) he speaks and understands (and how well) *before* decisions are reached about curriculum delivery and the language policy of the classroom. 'But,' some sincere administrator may say, 'we simply can't afford to do systematic testing on a wide scale. We don't have the people, the budget, or the time.' The answer to such an objection must be indignant if it is equally sincere and genuine. Can the schools afford to do this year what they did last year? Can they afford to continue to deliver instruction on a language that a substantial number of the children cannot understand? Can they afford to do other wide scale standardized testing programs whose results may be less valid?

It may be true that the educators cannot wait until the research results are in, but it is equally true that we cannot afford to play political games of holding out for more budget to make changes in ways the present budget is being spent, especially when those changes were needed years ago. This year's budget and next year's (if there is a next year) will be spent. People in the schools will be busy at many tasks, and all of the available time will get used up. Doing all of it the way it was done last year is proof only of the disappointing fact that a system that purports to teach doesn't necessarily learn. Indeed, it is merely another comment on the equally discouraging fact that many students in the schools (and universities no doubt) must learn in spite of the system which becomes an adversary instead of a servant to the needs of learners.

The problems are not unique to the United States. They are world-wide problems. Hofman (1974) in reference to the schools of Rhodesia says, 'It is important to get some idea, one that should have been reached ten years ago, of the state of English in the primary school'(p. 10). In the case of Rhodesia, and the argument can easily be extended to many of the world's nations, Hofman questions the blind and uninformed language policy imposed on teacher and children in the schools. In the case of Rhodesia, at least until the time his report was written, English was the required school language from 1st grade onward. Such policies have recently been challenged in many parts of the world (not just in the case of a super-imposed English) and reports of serious studies examining important variables are beginning to appear (see for instance, Bezanson and Hawkes, 1976, and Streiff, 1977). This is not to say that there may not be much to be gained by thorough knowledge of one of the languages of the world currently enjoying much power and prestige (such as English is at the present moment), but there are many questions concerning the price that must be paid for such knowledge. Such questions can scarcely be posed without serious multilingual testing on a much wider scale than has been common up till now.

B. Multilingualism versus multidialectalism

The problems of language testing in bilingual or multilingual contexts seem to be compounded to a new order of magnitude each time a new language is added to the system. In fact, it would seem that the problems are more than just doubled by the presence of more than one language because there must be social and psychological interactions between different language communities producing complexities not present in monolingual communities. However, there are some parallels between so-called monolingual communities and multilingual societies. The former display a rich diversity of language varieties in much the way that the latter exhibit a variety of languages. To the extent that differences in language varieties parallel differences in languages, there may be less contrast between the two sorts of settings than is commonly thought. In both cases there is the need to assess performance in relation to a plurality of group norms. In both cases there is the difficulty of determining what group norms are appropriate at different times and places within a given social order.

It has sometimes been argued that children in the schools should be compared only against themselves and never against group norms, but the argument implicity denies the nature of normal human communication. Evaluating the language ability of an individual by comparing him only against himself is a little like clapping with one hand. Something is missing. It only makes sense to say that a person knows a language in relation to the way that other persons who also know that language perform when they use it. Becoming a speaker of a particular language is a distinctively socializing process. It is a process of identifying with and to some degree functioning as a member of a social group.

In multilingual societies, where many mutually unintelligible languages are common fare in the market places and urban centers, the need for language proficiency testing as a basis for informing educational policy is perhaps more obvious than in so-called monolingual societies. However, the case of monolingual societies, which are typically multidialectal, is deceptive. Although different varieties of a language may be mutually intelligible in many situations, in others they are not. At least since 1969, it has been known that school children who speak different varieties of English perform about equally badly in tests that require the repetition of sentences in the other group's variety (Baratz, (1969). Unfortunately for children who speak a non-majority variety of English, all of the other testing in the schools is done in the majority variety (sometimes referred to as 'standard English'). An important question currently being researched is the extent to which educational tests in general may contain a built-in language variety bias and related to it is the more general question concerning how much of the variance in educational tests in general can be explained by variance in language proficiency tests (see Stump, 1977 & Gunnarsson, 1978).

The parallel between multilingualism and multidialectalism is still more fundamental. In fact, there is a serious question of principle concerning whether it is possible to distinguish languages and dialects. Part of the trouble lies in the fact that for any given language (however we define it), there is no sense at all in trying to distinguish it from its dialects or varieties. The language is its varieties. The only sense in which a particular variety of a language may be elevated to a status above other varieties is in the manner of Orwell's pigs - by being a little more equal or in this case, a little more English or French or Chinese or Navajo or Spanish or whatever. One of the important rungs on the status ladder for a language variety (and for a language in the general sense) is whether or not it is written and whether or not it can lay claim to a long literary tradition. Other factors are who happens to be holding the reins of political power (obviously the language variety they speak is in a privileged position), and who has the money and the goods that others must buy with their money. The status of a particular variety of English is subject to many of the same influences that the status of English (in the broader sense) is controlled by.

The question, where does language X (or variety X) leave off and language Y (or variety Y) begin is a little like the question, where does the river stop and the lake begin. The precision of the answer, or lack of it, is not so much a product of clarity or unclarity of thought as it is a product of the nature of the objects spoken of. New terms will not make the boundaries between languages, or dialects, or between languages and language varieties any clearer. Indeed, it can be argued that the distinction between languages as disparate as Mandarin and English (or Navajo and Spanish) is merely a matter of degree. For languages that are more closely related, such as German and Swedish, or Portuguese and Spanish, or Navajo and Apache, it is fairly obvious that their differences are a matter of degree. However, in relation to abstract grammatical systems that may be shared by all human beings as part of their genetic programming, it may be the case that all languages share much of the same universal grammatical system (Chomsky, 1965, 1972).

Typically, varieties of a language that are spoken by minorities are termed 'dialects' in what sometimes becomes an unintentional (or possibly intentional) pejorative sense. For example, Ferguson and Gumperz (1971) suggest that a dialect is a 'potential language' (p.34). This remark represents the tendency to institutionalize what may be appropriately termed the 'more equal syndrome'. No one would ever suggest that the language that a middle class white speaks is a potential language - of course not, it's a real language. But the language spoken by inner city blacks - that's another matter. A similar tendency is apparent in the remark by The Chief Justice in the Lau case where he refers to the population of Chinese speaking children in San Francisco (the 1,800 who were not being taught English) as 'linguistically deprived' children: (Lau versus

Nichols, 1974, No. 72-6520, p.3). Such remarks may reflect a modicum of truth, but deep within they seem to arise from ethno-centric prejudices that define the way I do it (or the way we do it) as intrinsically better than the way anyone else does it. It is not diffficult to extend such intimations to 'deficit theories' of social difference like those advocated by Bernstein (1960), Bereiter and Engleman (1967), Herrnstein (1971), and others.

Among the important questions that remain unanswered and that are crucial to the differentiation of multilingual and monolingual societies are the following: to what extent does normal educational testing contain a language variety bias? And further, to what extent is that bias lesser or greater than the language bias in educational testing for children who come from a non-English speaking background? Are the two kinds of bias really different in type or merely in degree?

C. Factive and emotive aspects of mulitilingualism

Difficulties in communication between social groups of different language backgrounds (dialects of language varieties included) are apt to arise in two ways; first, there may be a failure to communicate on the factive level: or second, there may be a failure to communicate on the emotive level as well as the factive level. If a child comes to a school from a cultural and linguistic background that is substantiallly different from the background of the majority of teachers and students in the school, he brings to the communication contexts of the school many sorts of expectations that will be inappropriate to many aspects of the exchanges that he might be expected to initiate or participate in. Similarly, the representatives of the majority culture and possibly other minority backgrounds will bring other sets of expectations to the communicative exchanges that must take place.

In such linguistically plural contexts, the likelihood of misinterpretations and breakdowns in communication is increased. On the factive level, the actual forms of the language(s) may present some difficulties. The surface forms of messages may sometimes be uninterpretable, or they may sometimes be misinterpreted. Such problems may make it difficult for the child, teacher, and others in the system to communicate the factive-level information that is usually the focus of classroom activities-- namely, transmitting the subject matter content of the curriculum. Therefore, such factive level communication problems may account for some portion of the variance in the school performance of children from ethnically and culturally different backgrounds, i.e., their generally lower scores on educational tests. As Baratz (1969) has shown, however, it is important to keep in mind the fact that if the tables were turned, if the majority were suddenly the minority, their scores on educational tests might be expected to plummet to the same levels as are typical of minorities in today's U.S. schools. Nevertheless, there is another important cluster of factors that probably affect variance in learning far more drastically than problems of factive level communication.

There is considerable evidence to suggest that the more elusive emotive or attitudinal level of communication may be a more important variable than the surface form of messages concerning subject matter. This emotive aspect of communication in the schools directly relates to the self-concept that a given child is developing, and also it relates to group loyalties and ethnic identity. Though such factors are difficult to measure, it seems reasonable to hypothesize that they may account for more of the variance in learning in the schools that can be accounted for by the selection of a particular teaching methodology for instilling certain subject matter (factive level communication).

As the research in the Canadian experiments has shown, if the socio-cultural (emotive level) factors are not in a turmoil and if the child is receiving adequate encouragement and support at home, etc., the child can apparently learn a whole new way of coding information factively (a new linguistic system) rather incidentally and can acquire the subject matter and skills taught in the schools without great difficulty (Lambert and Tucker, 1972, Tucker and Lambert, 1973, Swain, 1976b).

However, the very different experience of children in schools, say, in the Southwestern United States where many ethnic minorities do not experience such success requires a different interpretation. Perhaps the emotive messages that the child is bombarded with in the Southwest help explain the failure of the schools. Pertinent questions are: how does the child see his culture portrayed in the curriculum? How does the child see himself in relation to the other children who may be defined as successful by the system? How does the child's home experience match up with the experience in the school?

It is hypothesized that variance in rate of learning is probably more sensitive to the emotive level messages communicated in facial expressions, tones of voice, deferential treatment of some children in a classroom, biased representation of experiences in the school curriculum, and so on, than to differences in factive level methods of presenting subject matter. This may be more true for minority children than it is for children who are part of the majority. A similar view has been suggested by Labov (1972) and by Goodman and Buck (1973).

The hypothesis and its consequences can be visualized as shown in Figure 1 where the area enclosed by the larger circle represents the total amount of variance in learning to be accounted for (obviously the Figure is a metaphor, not an explanation or model). The area enclosed by the smaller concentric circle represents the hypothetical amount of variance that might be explained by emotive message factors. Among these are messages that the child perceives concerning his own worth, the value of his people and culture, the viability of his life experience. The area in the outer ring represents the hypothetical portion of variance in learning that may be accounted for by appeal to factive level aspects of communication in the schools, such as methods of teaching, subject matter taught, language of presentation of the material, IQ, initial achievement levels, etc.

Of all the ways struggles for ethnic identity manifest themselves, and of all the messages that can be communicated between different social groups in their mutual struggles to identify and define themselves, William James (as cited by Watzlawick, et al, 1967, p. 86) suggested that the most cruel possible message one human being can communicate to another (or one group to another) is simply to pretend that the other individual (or group) does not exist. Examples are too common for comfort in the history of education. Consider the statement that Columbus discovered America in 1492 (Banks, 1972). Then ask, who doesn't count? (Clue: Who was already here before Columbus ever got the wind in his sails?) James said, 'No more fiendish punishment could be devised, . . . than that one should be turned loose in a society and remain absolutely unnoticed by all the members thereof' (as cited by Watzlawick, et al, 1967, p.86).

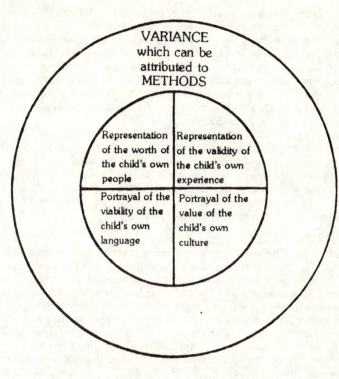

Figure 1. A hypothetical view of the amount of variance in learning to be accounted for by emotive versus factive sorts of information (methods of conveying subject matter are represented as explaining variance in the outer ring, while the bulk is explained by emotive factors).

The interpretation of low scores on tests, therefore, needs to take account of possible emotive conflicts. While a high score on a language test or any other educational test probably can be confidently interpreted as indicating a high degree of skill in communicating factive information as well as a good deal of harmony between the child and the school situation on the emotive level, a low score cannot be interpreted so easily. In this respect, low scores on tests are somewhat like low correlations between tests; they leave a greater number of options open. A low score may occur because the test was not reliable or valid, or because it was not suited to the child in difficulty level, or because it created emotive reactions that interfered with the cognitive task, or possibly because the child is really weak in the skill tested. The last interpretation, however, should be used with caution and only after the other reasonable alternatives have been ruled out by careful study. It is important to keep in mind the fact that an emotive-level conflict is more likely to call for changes in the educational system and the way that it affects children than for changes in the children.

In some cases it may be that simply providing the child with ample opportunity to learn the language or language variety of the educational system is the best solution; in others, it may be necessary to offer instruction in the child's native language, or in the majority language and the minority language; and no doubt other untried possibilities exist. If the emotive factors are in harmony between the school and the child's experience, there is some reason to believe that mere exposure to the unfamiliar language may generate the desired progress (Swain, 1976a, 1976b.).

In the Canadian experiments, English speaking children who are taught in French for the first several years of their school experience, learn the subject matter about as well as monolingual French speaking children, and they also incidentally acquire French. The term 'submersion' has recently been offered by Swain (1976b) to characterize the experience of minority children in the Southwestern United States who do not fare so well. The children are probably not all that different, but the social contexts of the two situations are replete with blatant contrasts (Fishman, 1976).

D. On test biases

A great deal has been written recently concerning cultural bias in tests (Briere, 1972,Condon,1973). No doubt much of what is being said is true. However, some well-meaning groups have gone so far as to suggest a 'moratorium on all testing of minority children.' Their argument goes something like this. Suppose a child has learned a language that is very different from the language used by the representatives of the majority language and culture in the schools. When the child goes to school, he is systematically discriminated against (whether intentionally or not is irrelevant to the argument). All of the achievement tests, all of the classes, all of the informal teacher and peer evalutions that influence the degree of success or failure of the child is in a language (or language variety) that he has not yet learned. The entire situation is culturally biased against the child. He is regularly treated in a prejudicial way by the school system as a whole. So, some urge that we should aim to get the cultural bias out of the school situation as much as possible and especially out of the tests. A smaller group urges that all testing should be stopped indefinitely pending investigation of other educational alternatives.

The arguments supporting such proposals are persuasive, but the suggested solutions do not solve the problems they so graphically point out. Consider the possibility of getting the cultural bias out of language proficiency tests. Granted that language tests though they may vary in the pungency of their cultural flavor all have cultural bias built into them. They have cultural bias because they present sequences of linguistic elements of a certain language (or language variety) in specific contexts. In fact, it is the purpose of such tests to discriminate between various levels of skill, often, to discriminate between native and non-native performance. A language test is therefore intentionally biased against those who do not speak the language or who do so at different levels of skill.

Hence, getting the bias out of language tests, if pushed to the logical limits, is to get language tests to stop functioning as language tests. On the surface, preventing the cultural bias and the discrimination between groups that such tests provide might seem like a good idea, but in the long run it will create more problems than it can solve. For one, it will do harm to the children in the schools who most need help in coping with the majority language system by pretending that crucial communication problems do not exist. At the same time it would also preclude the majority culture representatives in schools from being exposed to the challenging language system. If this latter event is to occur, it will be necessary to evalute developing learner proficiencies (of the majority types) in terms of the norms that exist for the minority language(s) and culture(s).

The more extreme alternative of halting testing in the schools is no real solution either. What is needed is more testing that is based on carefully constructed tests and with particular questions in mind followed by deliberate and careful analysis. Part of the difficulty is the lack of adequate data -not an overabundance of if. For instance, until recently (Oller and Perkins, 1978) there was no data on the relative importance of language variety bias, or just plain language bias in educational testing in general. There was always plenty of evidence that such a factor must be important to a vast array of educational tests, but how important? Opinions to the effect that it is not very important, or that it is of great importance merely accent the need for empirical research on the question. It is not a question that can be decided by vote -not even at the time honored 'grass roots level'- but that is where the studies need to be done.

There is another important way that some of the facts concerning test biases and their probable effects on the school performance of certain groups of children may have been over-zealously interpreted. These latter interpretations relate to the extension of a version of the strong contrastive analysis hypothesis familiar to applied linguistics. The reasoning is not unappealing. Since children who do poorly in tests in school, and on tasks such as learning to read, write, and do arithmetic, are typically (or at least often) children who do not use the majority variety of English at home, their failure may be attributed to differences in the language (or variety of English) that they speak at home and the language that is used in the schools. Goodman (1965) offered such an explanation for the lower performance of inner city black children on reading tests. Reed (1973) seemed to advocate the same view. They suggested that structural contrasts in sequences of linguistic elements common to the speech of such children accounted for their lower reading scores. Similar arguments have been popular for years as an explanation of the 'difficulties' of teaching or learning a language other than the native language of the learner group. There is much controverting evidence, however, for either application of the contrastive analysis hypothesis.

For instance, contrary to the prediction that would follow from the contrastive analysis hypothesis, in two recent studies, black children understood majority English about as well as white children, but the white children had greater difficulty with minority black English (Norton and Hodgson, 1973). While Baratz (1969) showed that white children tend to transform sentences presented in black English into their white English counterparts, and similarly, black children render sentences in white English into their own language variety, it would appear from her remarks that at least the black children had little difficulty understanding white English. This evidence does not conclusively eliminate the position once advocated by Goodman and Reed, but it does suggest the possibility of looking elsewhere for an explanation of reading problems and other difficulties of minority children in the schools. For example, is it not possible that sociocultural factors that are of an essentially non-linguistic sort might play an equal if not greater part in explaining school performance? One might ask whether black children in the communities where differences have been observed are subject to the kinds of reinforcement and punishment contingencies that are present in the experience of comparable groups of children in the majority culture. Do they see their parents reading books at home? Are they encouraged to read by parents and older siblings? These are tentative attempts at phrasing the right questions, but they hint at certain lines of research.

As to the contrastive explanation of the difficulties of language learners in acquiring a new linguistic system, a question should suffice. Why should Canadian French be so much easier for some middle class children in Montreal to acquire, than English is for many minority children in the Southwest? The answer probably does not lie in the contrasts between the language systems. Indeed, as the data continues to accumulate, it would appear than many of the children in bilingual programs in the United States (perhaps most of the children in most of the programs) are dominant in English when they come to school. The contrastive explanation is clearly inapplicable to those cases. For a review of the literature on second language studies and the contrastive analysis approaches, see Oller (1979). For a systematic study based on a Spanish-English bilingual program in Albuquerque, New Mexico, see Teitelbaum (1976).

If we reject the contrastive explanation, what then? Again it seems we are led to emotive aspects of the school situation in relation to the child's experience outside of the school. If the child's cultural background is neglected by the curriculum, if his people are not represented or are portrayed in an unfavorable light or are just simply misrepresented (e.g., the Plains Indian pictured in a canoe in a widely used elementary text, Joe Sando, personal communication), if his language is treated as unsuitable for educational pursuits (possibly referred to as the 'home language' but not the 'school language'), probably just about any teaching method will run into major difficulties.

It is in the area of cultural values and ways of expressing emotive level information in general (e.g., ethnic identity, approval, disapproval, etc.) where social groups may contrast more markedly and in ways that are apt to creat significant barriers to communication between groups. The barriers are not so much in the structural systems of the languages (not yet in the educational tests) as they are in the belief systems and ways of living of different cultures. Such differences may creat difficulties for the acceptance of culturally distinct groups and the people who represent them. The failure of the minority child in school (or the failure of the school) is more likely to be caused by a conflict between cultures and the personalities they sustain rather than a lack of cognitive skills or abilities (see Bloom, 1976).

In any event, none of the facts about test bias lessens the need for sound language proficiency testing. Those facts merely accent the demands on educators and others who are attempting to devise tests and interpret test results. And, alas, as Upshur (1969b) noted test is still a four letter word.

E. Translating tests or items

Although it is possible to translate tests with little apparent loss of information, and without drastically altering the task set the examinees under some conditions, the translation of items for standardized multiple choice tests is beset by fundamental problems of principle. First we consider problems of translating pragmatic tasks from one language to another. It may seem surprising at the outset to note that the former translation procedure is probably not feasible while the latter can be accomplished without great difficulty.

A doctoral dissertation completed in 1974 at the University of New Mexico investigated the feasibility of translating the *Boehm Test of Basic Concepts* from English into Navajo (Scoon, 1974). The test attempts to measure the ability of school children in the early grades to handle such notions as sequence in time (before versus after) and location in space (beside, in front of, behind, under, and so on). It was reasoned by the original test writer that children need to be able to understand such concepts in order to follow everyday classroom instructions, and to carry out simple educational tasks. Scoon hoped to be able to get data from translated tests which would help to define instructional strategies to aid the Navajo child in the acquisition and use of such concepts.

Even though skilled bilinguals in English and Navajo helped with the translation task, and though allowances were made from unsuccessful translations, dialect variations, and the like, the tendency for the translated items to produce results similar to the original items was surprisingly weak, It is questionable whether the two tests can be said to be similar in what they require of examinees. Some of the items that were among the easiest ones on the English test turned out to be very difficult on the Navajo version, and vice versa.

The researcher began to project hoping to be able to diagnose learning difficulties of Navajo children in their own language. The study evolved to an investigation of the feasibility of translating a standardized test in a multiple choice format from English into Navajo. Scoon concluded that translating standardized test is probably not a feasible approach to the diagnosis of educational aptitudes and skills.

All of this would lead us to wonder about the wisdom of translating standardized tests of 'intelligence' or achievement. Nevertheless, such translations exist. There are several reasons why translating a test, item by item, is apt to produce a very different test than the one the translators began with.

Translation of factive-level information is of course possible. However, much more is required. Translation of a multiple choice test item requires not only the maintenance of the factive information in the stem (or lead-in part) of the item but the maintenance of it in roughly the same relation to the paradigm of linguistic and extralinguistic contexts that it calls to mind. Moreover, the relationships between the distractors and the correct answer must remain approximately the same in terms of the linguistic and extralinguistic contexts that they call to mind and in terms of the relationships (similarities and differences) between all of those contexts. While it may sometimes be difficult to maintain the factive content of one linguistic form when translating it into another language, this may be possible. However, to maintain the paradigm of interrelationships between linguistic and extralinguistic contexts in a set of distractors is probably not just difficult - it may well be impossible.

Translating delicately composed test items is something like trying to translate a joke, a pun, a riddle, or a poem. As 'Robert Frost once remarked, when a poem is translated, the poetry is often lost' (Kolers, 1968, p. 4). With test items (a lesser art form) it is the meaning and the relationship between alternative choices which is apt to be lost. A translation of a joke or poem often has to undergo such changes that if it were literally translated back into the source language it would not be recognizable. With test items it is the meaning of the items in terms of their *effects* on examinees that is apt to be changed, possibly beyond recognition.

A very common statement about a very ordinary fact in English may be an extremely uncommon statement about a very extra-ordinary fact in Navajo. A way of speaking in English may be incomprehensible in Navajo; for instance, the fact that *you cut down a tree* before *you cut it up* which is very different from *cutting up in a class* or *cutting down your teacher*. Conversely, a commonplace saying in Navajo may be enigmatic if literally translated into English.

Successful translation of items requires maintaining roughly the same style level, the same frequency of usage of vocabulary and idiom, comparable phrasing and reference complexities, and the same relationships among alternative choices. In some cases this simply cannot be done. Just as a pun cannot be directly translated from one language into another precisely because of the peculiarities of the particular expectancy grammar that makes the pun possible, a test item cannot always be translated so as to achieve equal effect in the target language. This is due quite simply to the fact that the real grammars of natural languages are devices that relate to paradigms of extralinguistic contexts in necessarily unique ways.

The bare tip of the iceberg can be illustrated by data from word association experiments conducted by Paul Kolers and reported in *Scientific American* in March 1968. He was not concerned with the word associations suggested by test items, but his data illustrate the nature of the problem we are considering. The method consists of presenting a word to a subject such as *mesa* (or *table*) and asking him to say whatever other word comes to mind, such as *silla* (or *chair*). Kolers was interested in determining whether pairs of associated words were similar in both of the languages of a bilingual subject. In fact, he found that they were the same in only about one-fifth of the cases. Actually he complicated the task by asking the subject to respond in the same language as the stimulus word on two tests (one in each of the subject's two languages), and in the opposite language in two other tests (e.g., once in English to Spanish stimulus words, and once in Spanish to English stimulus words). The first two tests can be referred to as *intralingual* and the second pair as *interlingual*.

In view of such facts, it is apparent that it would be very difficult indeed to obtain similar associations between sets of alternative meeting of the School Board or some other organization will not suffice to justify the assumptions listed above, or to guarantee the success of the testing procedures, with or without adaptations to fit a particular local situation (Spolsky, 1974). What is required first is some careful logical investigation of possible outcomes from the procedures recommended by Spolsky, *et al*, and other procedures which can be devised for the purpose of crossvalidation. Second, empirical study is required as illustrated, for example, in the Appendix below.

Zirkel (1974) points out that it is not enough merely to place a child on a dominance scale. Simple logic will explain why. It is possible for two children to be balanced bilinguals in terms of such a scale but to differ radically in terms of their developmental levels. An extreme case would be children at different ages. A more pertinent case would be two children of the same age and grade level who are level in both languages. One child might be performing at an advanced level in both languages while the other child is performing at a much lower level in both languages. Measuring for dominance-only would not reveal such a difference.

No experimentation is required to show the inadequacy of any procedure that merely assesses dominance - even if it does the job accurately, and it is doubtful whether some of the procedures being recommended can do even the job of dominance assessment accurately. Besides, there are important considerations in addition to mere language dominance which can enter the picture only when valid proficiency data are available for both languages (or each of the several languages in a multilingual setting). Moreover, with care to insure test equivalence across the languages assessed, dominance scores can be derived directly from proficiency data - the reverse is not necessarily possible.

Hence, the question concerning how to acquire reliable information concerning language proficiency in multilingual contexts, including the important matter of determining language dominance, is essentially the same question we have been dealing with throughout this book. In order to determine language dominance accurately, it is necessary to impose the additional requirement of equating tests across languages. Preliminary results of McLeod (1975), Klare, Sinaiko, and Stolurow (1972), Oller, Bowen, Dien, and Mason (1972), and Bezanson and Hawkes (1976) suggest that careful translation may offer a solution to the equivalence problem, and no doubt there are other approaches that will prove equally effective.

There are pitfalls to be avoided, however. There is no doubt that it is possible to devise tests that do not accomplish what they were designed to accomplish - that are not valid. Assumptions of validity are justifiable only to the extent that assumptions of lack of validity have been disposed of by careful research. On that theme let us reconsider the four assumptions quoted earlier in this section. What is the evidence that bilingual dominance varies from domain to domain?

In 1969, Cooper reported that a word-naming task (the same sort of task used in the Spanish-English test of Spolsky, *et al*, 1972) which varied by domains such as 'home' versus 'school' or 'kitchen' versus 'classroom' produced different scores depending on the domain referred to in a particular portion of the test. The task set the examinee was to name all the things he could think of in the 'kitchen', for example. Examinees completed the task for each domain (five in all in Cooper's study) in both languages without appropriate counterbalancing to avoid an order effect. Since there were significant contrasts between relative abilities of subjects to do the task in Spanish and English across domains, it was concluded that their degree of dominance varied from one domain to another. This is a fairly broad leap of inference, however.

Consider the following question: does the fact that I can name more objects in Spanish that I see in my office than objects that I can see under the hood of my car mean that I am relatively more proficient in Spanish when sitting in my office than when looking under the hood of my car? What Cooper's results seem to show (and Teitelbaum, 1976, found similar results with a similar task) is that the number of things a person can name in reference to one physical setting may be smaller or greater than the number that the same person can name in reference to another physical setting. This is not evidence of a very direct sort about possible changes in language dominance when sitting in your living room, or when sitting in a classroom. Not even the contrast in 'word-naming' across languages is necessarily an indication of any difference whatsoever in language dominance in a broader sense. Suppose a person learned the names of chess pieces in a language other than his native language, and suppose further that he does not know the names of the pieces in his native language. Would this make him dominant in the foreign language when playing chess?

A more important question is not whether there are contrasts across domains, but whether the 'word-naming' task is a valid indication of language proficiency. Insufficient data are available. At face value such a task appears to have little relation to the sorts of things that people normally do with language, children especially. Such a task does not qualify as a pragmatic testing procedure because it does not require time-constrained sequential processing, and it is doubtful whether it requires mapping of utterances onto extralinguistic contexts in the normal ways that children might perform such mappings - naming objects is relatively simpler than even the speech of median-ranged three-and-a-half year old children (Hart, 1974, and Hart, Walker, and Gray, 1977).

Teitelbaum (1976) correlated scores on word-naming tasks (in Spanish) with teacher-ratings; and self-ratings differentiated by four domains ('kitchen, yard, block, school'). For a group of kindergarten through 4th grade children in a bilingual program in Albuquerque (nearly 100 in all), the correlations ranged from .15 to .45. Correlations by domain with scores on an interview task, however, ranged from .69 to .79. These figures hardly justify the differentiation of language dominance by domain. The near equivalence of the correlations across domains with a single interview task seems to show that the domain differentiation is pointless. Cohen (1973) has adapted the word-naming task lightly to convert it into a story-telling procedure by domains. His scoring is based on the number of different words used in each story-telling domain. Perhaps other scoring techniques should also be considered.

The second assumption quoted above was that a child's own report of his language use is apt to be 'quite accurate'. This may be more true for some children than for others. For the children in Teitelbaum's study neither the teacher's ratings nor the children's own ratings were very accurate. In no case did they account for more than 20% of the variance in more objective measures of language proficiency.

What about the child Zirkel (1976) referred to? What if some children are systematically indoctrinated concerning what language they are supposed to use at school and at home as some advocates of the 'home language/school language' dichotomy advocate? Some research with bilingual children seems to suggest that at an early age they may be able to discriminate appropriately between occasions when one language is called for and occasions when the other language is required (e.g., answering in French when spoken to in French, but it English when spoken in English, Kinzel, 1964), without being able to discuss this ability at a more abstract level (e.g., reporting when you are supposed to speak French rather than English). Teitelbaum's data reveal little correlation between questions about language use and scores on more objective language proficiency measures. Is it possible that a bilingual child is smart enough to be sensitive to what he thinks the interviewer expects him to say? Upshur (1971a) observes, 'it isn't fair to ask a man to cut his own throat, and even if we should ask, it isn't reasonable to expect him to do it. We don't ask a man to rate his proficiency when an honest answer might result in his failure to achieve some desired goal' (p.58). Is it fair to expect a child to respond independently of what he may think the interviewer wants to hear?

We have dealt earlier with the third assumption quoted above, so we come to the fourth. Suppose that we assume the interviewer should be a speaker of the minority language (rather than English) in order to counteract an English bias in the schools. There are several possibilities. Such a provision may have no effect, the desired effect (if indeed it is desired as it may distort the picture of the child's true capabilities along the lines of the preceding paragraph), or an effect that is opposite to the desired one. The only way to determine which result is the actual one is to devise some empirical measure of the relative magnitude of a possible interviewer effect.

G. Tentative suggestions

What methods then can be recommended for multilingual testing? There are many methods that can be expected to work well and deserve to be tried. Some of the ones that have been used with encouraging results include oral interview procedures of a wide range of types (but designed to elicit speech from the child and data of comprehension, not necessarily the child's own estimate of how well he speaks a certain language). Elicited imitation (a kind of oral dictation procedure) has been widely used. Versions

of the cloze procedure (particularly ones that may be administered orally) are promis-
ing and have been used with good results. Variation on composition tasks and story
telling or retelling have also been used. No doubt many other procedures can be devised.

In brief, what seems to be required is a class of testing procedures providing a basis
for equivalent tests in different languages that will yield proficiency data in both languages
and that will simultaneously provide dominance scores of an accurate and sensitive
sort. Figure 2 offers a rough conceptualization of the kinds of equivalent measures needed. If Scale A in the diagram represents a range of possible scores on a test in language
A, and if Scale B represents a range of possible scores on an equivalent test in language
B, the relative difference in scores on A and B can provide the basis for placement
on the dominance scale C (modelled after the 'Lau Remedies' or the Spolsky, et al,
1972, scales).

0%				100%
		Scale A		

0%				100%
		Scale B		

A	Ab	AB	Ba	B
		Scale C		

Figure 2. A dominance scale in relation to proficiency scales. (Scales A
and B represent equivalent proficiency tests in languages A and B, while
scale C represents a dominance scale, as required by the Lau Remedies.
It is claimed that the meaning of C can only be adequately defined in relation to scores on A and B.)

It would be desirable to calibrate both of the proficiency scales with reference to comparable groups of monolingual speakers of each language involved (Cowan and Zarmed,
1976, followed such a procedure) in order to be able to interpret scores in relation
to clear criteria of performance. The dominance scale can be calibrated by defining
distances on that scale in terms of units of difference in proficiency on Scales A and B.

This can be done as follows: first, subtract each subject's score on A from the score
B. (If the tests are calibrated properly, it is not likely that anyone will get a perfect score
on either test though there may be some zeroes.) Then rank order the results. They
should range from a series of positive values to a series of negative values. If the group
tested consists only of children who are dominant in one language, there will be only
positive or only negative values, but not both. The ends of the rank will define the
ends of the dominance scale (with reference to the population tested) - that is the A
and B points on Scale C in figure 2. The center point, AB on Scale C, is simply the
zero position in the rank. That is the point at which a subject's scores in both languages
are equal. The points between the ends and the center, namely, Ab and Ba, can be
defined by finding the mid point in the rank between that end (A or B) and the center
(AB).

The degree of accuracy with which a particular subject can be classed as A = monolingual in A, Ab = dominant in A, AB = equally bilingual in A and B, Ba = dominant in B, B = monolingual in B, can be judged quite accurately in terms of the standard error of differences on Scales A and B. The standard error of the differences can be computed by finding the variance of the differences (A minus B, for each subject) and then dividing it by the square root of the number of subjects tested. If the distribution of differences is approximately normal, chances are better than 99 in 100 that a subject's true degree of binguality will fall within the range of plus or minus three standard errors above or below his actual attained score on scale C. If measuring off ±3 standard errors from a subject's attained score still leaves him close to, say, Ab on the Scale, we can be confident in classifying him as 'dominant in A'.

Thus, if the average standard error of differences in scores on tests A and B is large, the accuracy of Scale C will be less than if the average standard error is small. A general guideline might be to require at least six standard errors between each of the five points on the dominance scale. It remains to be seen, however, what degree of accuracy will be possible.

KEY POINTS

1. There is a serious need for multilingual testing in the schools not just of the United States, but in many nations.
2. In the Lau versus Nichols case in 1974, the Supreme Court ruled that the San Francisco Schools were violating a section of the Civil Rights Code which 'bans discrimination based on the grounds of race, color, or national origin' (1974, No. 72-6520). It was ruled that the schools should either provide instruction in the native language of the 1,800 Chinese speaking children in question, or provide special instruction in the English language.
3. Even at the present, in academic year 1978-9, many bilingual programs and many schools that have children of multilingual backgrounds are not doing adequate language assessment.
4. There are important parallels between multilingual and multidialectal societies. In both cases there is a need for language assessment procedures referenced against group norms (a plurality of them).
5. In a strong logical sense, a language *is* its varieties or dialects, and the dialects or varieties are languages. A particular variety may be elevated to a higher status by virtue of the 'more equal syndrome', but this does not necessitate that other varieties must therefore be regarded as less than languages - mere 'potential languages'.
6. Prejudices can be institutionalized in theories of 'deficits' or 'deprivations'. The pertinent question is, from whose point of view? The institutionalization of such theories into discriminatory educational practices may well create real deficits.
7. It is hypothesized that, at least for the minority child, and perhaps for the majority child as well, variance in learning in the schools may be much more a function of the emotive aspects of interactions within and outside of schools than it is a function of methods of teaching and presentation of subject matter per se.
8. When emotive level struggles arise, factive level communication usually stops altogether.
9. Ignoring the existence of a child or social group is a cruel punishment. Who discovered America?

10. Getting the cultural bias out of language test would mean making them into something besides language tests. However, adapting them to particular cultural needs is another matter.
11. Contrastive analysis based explanations for the generally lower scores of minority children on educational tests run into major empirical difficulties. Other factors appear to be much more important than the surface forms of different languages or language varieties.
12. Translating discrete point test items is roughly comparable to translating jokes, or puns, or poems. It is difficult if not impossible.
13. Translating pragmatic tests or testing procedures on the other hand is more like translating prose or translating a novel. It can be done, not easily perhaps, but at least feasible.
14. 'Blind back translation' is one procedure for checking the accuracy of translation attempts.
15. Measures of multilingual proficiencies require valid proficiency tests. The validity of proposed procedures is an empirical question. Assumptions must be tested, or they remain a threat to every educational decision based on them.
16. Measuring dominance is not enough. To interpret the meaning of a score on a dominance scale, it is useful to know the proficiency scores which it derives from.
17. It is suggested that a dominance scale of the sort recommended in the Lau Remedies can be calibrated in terms of the average standard error of the differences in test scores against which the scale is referenced.
18. Similarly, it is recommended that scores on the separate proficiency test be referenced against (and calibrated in terms of) the scores of monolingual children who speak the language of the test. (It is realized that this may not be possible to attain in reference to some very small populations where the minority language is on the wane.)

References

Banks, J.A. Imperatives in ethnic minority education. *Phi Delta Kappan*, 1972, *53*, 266-69.

Baratz, J. A bidialectal task for determining language proficiency in economically disadvantaged Negro children. *Child development*, 1969, *40*, 889-901.

Bereiter, C., & Engelmann, S. *Teaching disadvantaged children in the preschool.* Engelwood Cliffs, N.J.: Prentice-Hall, 1967.

Bernstein, B. Language and social class. *British Journal of Sociology*, 1960, *11*, 271-276.

Bezanson, K. A., & Hawkes, N. Bilingual reading skills of primary school children in Ghana. *Working papers in Bilingualism*, 1976, *11*, 44-73.

Bloom, B. A. *Human characteristics and school learning.* New York: McGraw Hill, 1976.

Briere, E. Cross cultural biases in language testing. In J. A. Oller Jr., & J. C. Richards (Eds.), *Focus on the learner: Pragmatic perspectives for the language teacher.* Rowley, Mass.: Newbury House, 1973.

Chomsky, N. A. *Aspects of the theory of syntax.* Cambridge, Mass.: MIT Press, 1965.

Chomsky, N. A. *Language and mind.* New York: Harcourt, Brace, and Jovanovich, 1972.

Cohen, A. The sociolinguistic assessment of speaking skills in a bilingual education program. In L. Palmer, & B. Spolsky (Eds.), *Papers on language testing: 1967-1974.* Washington, D.C.: TESOL, 1975.

Condon, E. The cultural context of language testing. In L. Palmer, & B. Spolsky (Eds.), *Papers on language testing: 1967-1974.* Washington D.C.: TESOL, 1975.

Cooper, R. L. Two contextualized measures of degree of bilingualism. *Modern Language Journal*, 1969, *53*, 172-178.

Cowan, J. R., & Zahreh Zarmed. Reading performance of bilingual children according to type of school and home language. *Working Papers on Bilingualism*, 1976, *11*, 74-114.

Diana v. California State Education Department, CA No. c-7037, RFD (n.d. Cal., February 3, 1970).

Ferguson, C. A., & Gumperz, J. In A. Dil (Ed.), *Language structure and language use: Essays by Charles A. Ferguson.* Palo Alto, Calif.: Stanford University Press, 1971.

Fishman, J. A. *A series of lectures on bilingualism and bilingual education.* Albuquerque: University of New Mexico, 1976.

Goodman, K. S. Dialect barriers to reading comprehension. *Elementary English,* 1965, *42,* 8.

Goodman, K. S., & Buck, C. Dialect barriers to reading comprehension revisited. *The Reading Teacher,* 1973, *27,* 6-12.

Gunnarsson, B. A look at the content similarities between intelligence, achievement, personality, and language tests. In J. W. Oller Jr., & Kyle Perkins (Eds.), *Language in education: Testing the tests.* Rowley, Mass.: Newbury House, 1978.

Hart, N. W. M. Language of young children. *Education News,* December 1974, pp. 29-31.

Hart, N. W. M., Walker, R. F., & Gray, B. N. *The language of children: A key to literacy.* Reading, Mass.: Addison-Wesley, 1977.

Hermstein, R. IQ. *Atlantic Monthly,* September 1971, pp. 43-64.

Hofman, J. E. *Assessment of English proficiency in the African primary school.* Series in Education, University of Rhodesia, Occasional Paper No. 3, 1974.

John, V., & Horner, V. J. *Early childhood bilingual education.* New York: Modern Language Association, 1971.

Kinzel, P. *Lexical and grammatical interference in the speech of a bilingual child.* Seattle: University of Washington Press, 1964.

Klare, G. R., Sinaiko, H. W., & Stolurow, L. M. The cloze procedure: A convenient readability test for training materials and translations. *International Review of Applied Psychology,* 1972, *21,* 77-106.

Kolers, P. A. Bilingualism and information processing. *Scientific American,* 1968, *218,* 78; 84.

Labov, W. *Language in the inner city: Studies in the black English vernacular.* Philadelphia: University of Pennsylvania Press, 1972.

Lambert, W. E., & Tucker, G. R. *Bilingual education of the children: The St. Lambert experiment.* Rowley, Mass.: Newbury House, 1972.

Lau v. Nichols, 414 U.S. 563 (1974).

McLeod, J. Uncertainty reduction in different languages through reading comprehension. *Journal of Psycholinguistic Research,* 1975, *4,* 343-355.

Norton, D. E., & Hodgson, W. R. Intelligibility of black and white speakers for black and white listeners. *Language and Speech*, 1973, *16*, 207-210.

OCR sets guidelines for fulfilling Lau decision. *The Linguistic Reporter*, 1975, *18*, (1); 5-7

Oller, J. W. Jr. The psychology of language and contrastive linguistics: The research and the debate. *Foreign Language Annals*, in press.

Oller, J. W. Jr., Bowen, J. D., Dien, T. T., & Mason, V. Cloze tests in English, Thai, and Vietnamese: Native and non-native performance. *Language Learning*, 1972, *22*, 1-15.

Oller, J. W. Jr., & Perkins, K. (Eds.). *Language in education: Testing the tests.* Rowley, Mass.: Newbury House, 1978.

Reed, C. Adapting TESL approaches to the teaching of written standard English as a second dialect to speakers of American black English vernacular. *TESOL Quarterly*, 1973, *7*, 289-308.

Scoon, A. *The feasibility of test translation--English to Navajo.* Unpublished doctoral dissertation, University of New Mexico, 1974.

Shore, M. *Final report of project BEST: The content analysis of 125 Title VII bilingual programs funded in 1969 and 1970.* New York: Bilingual Education Application Research Unit, Hunter College, 1974. Mimeo.

Spolsky, B. Speech communities and schools. *TESOL Quarterly*, 1974, *8*, 17-26.

Spolsky, B., Murphy P., Holm, W., & Ferrel, A. Three functional tests of oral proficiency. In Palmer, L., & Spolsky, B. (Eds.), *Papers on language testing: 1967-1974.* Washington, D.C.: TESOL, 1975.

Stevens, J. H., Ruder, K. F., & Jew, R. Speech discrimination in black and white children. *Language and Speech*, 1973, *16*, 123-129.

Streiff, V. *Reading comprehension and language proficiency among Eskimo children: Psychological, linguistic, and educational considerations.* (Doctoral dissertation, Ohio University, 1977) New York: Arno Press, in press.

Stump, T. Cloze and dictation tasks as predictors of intelligence and achievement scores. In Oller, J. W. Jr., & Perkins, K. (Eds.), *Language in education: Testing the tests.* Rowley, Mass.: Newbury House, 1978.

Swain, M. Bibliography: Research on immersion education for the majority child. *The Canadian Modern Language Review,* 1976(a), *32*, 592-596.

Swain, M. *Lecture on the bilingual experiments in Canada.* Albuquerque: University of New Mexico, 1976(b).

Teitelbaum, H. Testing bilinguality in elementary school children. Unpublished doctoral dissertation, University of New Mexico, 1976.

Tucker, G. R., & Lambert, W. E. Sociocultural aspects of language study. In J. W. Oller Jr., & J. C. Richards (Eds.), *Focus on the learner: Pragmatic perspectives for the language teacher*. Rowley, Mass.: Newbury House, 1973.

Upshur, J. A. *TEST is a four letter word*. Paper presented at the EPDA Institute, University of Illinois, 1969.

Upshur, J. A. Objective evaluation of oral proficiency in the ESOL classroom. In Palmer, L., & Spolsky, B. (Eds.), *Papers on language testing: 1967-1974*. Washington, D.C.: TESOL, 1975.

Watzlawick, P., Beavin, J., & Jackson, K. *Pragmatics of human communication: A study of interactional patterns, pathologies and paradoxes*. New York: Norton, 1967.

Zirkel, P. A. A method for determining and depicting language dominance. *TESOL Quarterly*, 1974, *8*, 7-16.

Zirkel, P. A. The why's and ways of testing bilinguality before teaching bilingually. *The Elementary School Journal*, March 1976, 323-330.

Suggested Readings

Aquirre, A. Jr., Issue Ed. Language in the Chicano speech community. *International Journal of the Sociology of Language. V. 53*, 1985.

Amastae, J. & Elías-Olivares, L., Eds. *Spanish in the U.S.: Sociolinguistic aspects.* New York: Cambrige University Press, 1982.

Aukerman, R.C. *Approaches to beginning reading* (2nd ed.) New York: John Wiley and Sons, 1984.

Baca, L. M. & Cervantes, H.T. *The bilingual special education interface.* St. Louis: Times Mirror/Mosby, 1984.

Blanco, G.M., Duke dos Santos, M., & Vásquez-Faría, J.A., Eds. *Ensayos sobre la educación bilingüe.* Dallas, Texas: Evaluation, Dissemination and Assessment Center, Dallas Independent School District, 1985.

Christian, D. *Language arts and dialect differences.* Washington, D.C.: Center for Applied Linguistics, 1979.

Christian, D. & Wolfram, C. *Exploring dialects.* Washington, D.C.: Center for Applied Linguistics, 1979.

Elías-Olivares, L. *Spanish in the U.S. setting.* Rosslyn, Va.: National Clearinghouse for Bilingual Education, 1983.

Elías-Olivares, L., Leone, E.A., Cisneros, R. & Gutiérrez, J., Eds. *Spanish language use and public life in the USA.* New York: Mouton Publishers, 1985.

Escobedo, T. *Early childhood bilingual education.* New York: Teachers College Press, 1983.

Ferguson, C.A. & Heath, S.B., Eds. *Language in the USA.* Cambridge, Mass.: Cambridge University Press, 1981.

Ferreiro, E. & Gómez, M., Eds. *Nuevas perspectivas sobre los procesos de lectura y escritura.* México, D.F.: Siglo Veintiuno Editores, S.A., 1982.

Fishman, J.A. & Keller, G., Eds. *Bilingual education for Hispanic students in the United States.* New York: Teachers College Press, 1982.

García, E. *Early childhood bilingualism: With special reference to the Mexican American child*. Albuquerque. New Mexico: University of New Mexico Press, 1983.

García G. & Padilla, R., Eds. *Advances in bilingual education research*. Tucson, Ariz.: University of Arizona Press, 1985.

Green, G.K. & Ornstein-Galicia, J.L., Eds. *Mexican-American Language: Usage, attitudes, maintenance, instruction, and policy*. Rio Grande Series in Language and Linguistics No. 1. Brownsville, TX.: Pan American University at Brownsville, 1986.

Hernández-Chávez, E. Cohen, A. & Beltramo, A.F., Eds. *El lenguaje de los chicanos*. Arlington, Va.: Center for Applied Linguistics, 1975.

Joag-deu, R. C. & Steffensen, M.S. *Studies of the bicultural reader: Implications for teachers and librarians*. Reading Education Report No. 12, Center for the Study of Reading, University of Illinois at Urbana Champaign, January, 1980.

Keller, G., Teschner, R. & Viera, S., Eds. *Bilingualism in the bicentennial and beyond*. Jamaica, N.Y.: Bilingual Press/Editorial bilingüe, 1976.

Lourie, M.A. & Conklin, N.F., Eds. *A pluralistic nation: The language issue in the United States*. Rowley, Mass.: Newbury House Publishers, Inc., 1978.

Penfield, J. & Ornstein-Galicia, J. *Chicano English: An ethnic content dialect*. Amsterdam and Philadelphia: Benjamins Publishing, 1984.

Peñalosa, F. *Chicano sociolinguistics: A brief introduction*. Rowley, Mass.: Newbury House Publishers, Inc., 1981.

Ramírez, A. *Attitudes toward speech variation and Spanish/English bilingual pupils: Some implications for the teacher and the learner*. Los Angeles, Calif.: National Dissemination and Assessment Center, 1979.

Ramírez, A. *Bilingualism through schooling: Cross cultural education for minority and majority students*. Albany, New York: State University of New York Press, 1985.

Teschner, R.V. *Español escrito: Curso para hispanohablantes bilingües*. New York: Charles Schribner's Sons, 1984.

Teschner, R.V. *Spanish orthography, morphology and syntax for bilingual educators.* Lanham, Maryland: University Press of America, 1985.

Trueba, H.T. & Barnett-Mizrahi, C., Eds. *Bilingual multicultural education and the professional: From theory to practice.* Rowley, Mass.: Newbury House Publishers, 1979.

Valdés, G., Lozano, A.G., & García-Moya, R., Eds. *Teaching Spanish to the Hispanic bilingual: Issues, aims, and methods. New York: Teachers College Press, 1981.*

Ion T. Agheana

THE PROSE OF JORGE LUIS BORGES
Existentialism and the Dynamics of Surprise

American University Studies: Series II (Romance Languages and Literature). Vol. 13
ISBN 0-8204-0130-7   333 pages   paperback US $ 31.85*

*Recommended price – alterations reserved

Like the Kafka of one of his essays, Jorge Luis Borges imposes himself at first as a man of iconoclastic singularity, as a writer who, having considered and discarded seemingly all the «isms» of literature and philosophy, creates a world *ex nihilo*. Yet minutely studied, Borges, like Kafka, who under close scrutiny reveals subtle affinities with other literatures, exhibits an unmistakable existential strain. The analysis of Borges' existentialism, identifiable in his prose works not as an unitary system but as a philosophical premise, together with the dynamics of surprise, constitute the object of the present study.

Contents: Jorge Luis Borges and Existentialism – The Misleading Symmetry – The Dynamics of Surprise.

PETER LANG PUBLISHING, INC.
62 West 45th Street
USA – New York, NY 10036